ECLIPSE OF THE SUN

ECLIPSE OF THE SUN

An investigation
into
Sun and Moon myths

JANET McCRICKARD

GOTHIC IMAGE
PUBLICATIONS

First published in 1990 by
GOTHIC IMAGE PUBLICATIONS
7, High Street, Glastonbury, Somerset BA6 9DP

Cover picture and illustrations by Janet McCrickard

Designed and set in 11/12pt. Kennerley
by Creative Technology Associates, Somerton, Somerset
Imagesetting by LP&TS, Aller, Somerset
Printed by Castle Cary Press, Somerset

British Library Cataloguing in Publication Data
McCrickard, Janet
    Eclipse of the Sun
    1. Myths. Symbolism
    I. Title
    291.13
    ISBN 0-906362-13-X

To Frances

Contents

ACKNOWLEDGEMENTS   XV

INTRODUCTION   xvii

CHAPTER 1   1

The Woman Who Stands On the Moon

Why we speak of the Sun as 'he'—Christian objection to the feminine Sun—the Hebrew background—Greek influences—the Graeco-Roman Sun cult—Syrian influence—Constantine and the Christian Sun-cult—how the feminine element was excluded—Mary the Moon and the Woman Clothed with the Sun—rejection of the Moon-god—the invisible Sun—the Renaissance revival of magic—the Western tradition of Sun and Moon.

CHAPTER 2   9

Not a Job for a Woman

Early modern study of myth—Universal Mythic Language and Fraser's Golden Bough—Mueller and the Solar School—Briffault and the Lunar School—the rejection of astral mythology—modern study of myth more secular and plural—Sun-goddesses still rejected as rare, spurious, not real Sun deities—common ways of eclipsing the feminine Sun—scholarly contempt—dishonest methods of argument—Sun-goddess is a woman doing a man's job—many Moon goddesses interpreted into existence—keeping Sun male and Moon female is paramount—higher wisdom or cultural imperialism?

CHAPTER 3   21

The True Feminine

Astral myth important to Jungians—Jung, archetypes, anima and animus, *logos* and *eros*—Masculine principle always solar, feminine always lunar—the inescapable Moon-goddess—the rule of the solar male and the inevitability of patriarchy—the true lunar woman—the essential dignity of woman—Victorian concepts of the true feminine—Eliza Farnham and the Truth of Woman—Myth, Religion and Mother-Right—the development of spiritual feminism—lunar commitment of the Goddess Movement—the results of Moon-consciousness—do we need the True Feminine?

CHAPTER 4   33

The Paths of the Moon and the Sun

Creating myth—ancient questions—the Sun's cycle and the seasons—changes in Sun and Moon—solstices and disappearing deities—the night journey of the Sun—the phases of the Moon—lunar and solar calendars—lunar and solar trinities—the sky and nomads—temples of Sun and Moon—New Grange and cosmic sex—closing the question.

CHAPTER 5   41

Holy Blood, Holy Moon

The Moon and menstruation—the Transylvania effect—lunar influences; claims and tests—
lunar beliefs—Moonlight and light-bulbs—day-length and hormones—the lunar emanation—
lunar gravity and tides—homeostasis—does the Moon influence menstruation?—myth and
menstruation—having one's Moon-cheese and eating it.

CHAPTER 6   51

The Sun, the Moon and Mother Earth

Celestial influences and the world of Nature—lunar energies—sympathetic magic—solar energy and plants—respiration and the natural balance—the fire of the Sun—the Sun as life-giver
and killer—the Sun and sap—herbs and the Moon—the role of darkness—germination—
Mother Nature's way.

CHAPTER 7   61

Great Female Possessor of Noon
Japan

The Sun-goddess Amaterasu—Shaman-queens and the matriarchate—the Kojiki and Nihongi—
the advent of Buddhism—folk Shinto—the character of Shinto—contemplative reverence and
the Sun-goddess—the mirror of the Sun—the Moon-god—the storm-god—the trials of
Amaterasu—the withdrawal of the Sun-goddess—the luring of the Sun-goddess—the great
shrine of Ise—the Ise pilgrimage—the Sun-vigil—Western misconceptions.

CHAPTER 8   73

Dearest Goddess, Mother Sun
Baltic Lands

The ancient Baltic religion and language—song and the Sun-tradition—the Sun-goddess Saule,
her central importance—her roles—her colours and costume—Sun-symbols—the Sun's horses—
the sky-god—the island of the West—the drowned Sun—the Sun's daughters—the wedding
and divorce of Sun and Moon—the Moon-god—the storm-god—the Midsummer feast—the
Sun's dance—the winter imprisonment of the Sun—the fire cult—academic disappointment.

CHAPTER 9   85

Fair Maiden Bright Sun
Russia and the Slavonic Lands

The official Slav religion—the feminine Sun tradition—the Sun-goddess Solnitse—the Moon-
god Myesyats—the cult of the dead—the Western island and the goddess Zorya—the Sun-
palace—Sun's daughters—Perperuna—the Moon-god—the swans of the Sun—firebirds and
Sun-eggs—the Sun and Moon mirrors—the Sun's dance—Winter Solstice and Holy Kolyada—
ritual baths—the storm-god.

CHAPTER 10   95

Sun-Woman of Ireland
The British Isles

Celtic religion, Romans and Druids—Sun and Moon among the Gaels—the Sun-goddess Grian—
the Sun and fire—the May feast—the Sun's dance—Sun-wells and Sun-stones—the waters of
Sulis—the abode of women—Sun-women of legend—Celtic sun-mares—the feminine Sun in
England—Wading of the Sun.

CHAPTER 11   105

Grandmother Sun, Good Lady
The Basque Country

The Sun-goddess Eguski—the Moon-goddess Ilargi—Grandmother Sun—Christianization of
the Sun-goddess—the mother of the Sun—the Sun-vigil—the Sun's dance—ritual baths—the
Midsummer fires—symbols of the Sun—Grandmother Moon—a multitude of deities.

CHAPTER 12   111

She Who Makes the Day Glad
Germany and Northern Europe

The Man in the Moon and the Woman in the Sun—the Eddas and the Sun-goddess Sol or
Sunna—the titles of the Sun-goddess—what the Prophetess says—the horses of the Sun—the
shield of the Sun—the fate of the Sun—the re-born Sun-goddess—the Sun's daughter—spinner
of sunbeams—the light-elves—the blazing wheel—the darkened Sun—Sun-set and Sun-rise—
prayers and charms—the marriage of Sun and Moon—the Sun-vigil—the Sun's dance—charioteers of Sun and Moon—Tolkien's Sun-goddess and Moon-god—Will the real Sun stand up?

CHAPTER 13   121

Mother of the Merciful Rays
Finno-Ugria and Siberia

Sun-mother of the Lapps—mother of animals—the Sun-ring—sacrifices and offerings—seasonal
celebrations—the Sun-cake—the solstices—Sun-goddesses of other tribes—the Sun-goddess in
Siberia—the mirrors of Sun and Moon—the shamanic tradition—the Mongol Sun and Moon-
goddesses—bold Sun-woman—Mother Sun of other tribes—the theft of the Sun and Moon
mirrors—the Moon-god.

CHAPTER 14   127

The Great Warmer
Alaska, Greenland and the Arctic

The Eskimo (Inuit) and their deities—the Sun-goddess of Greenland—the incest of Sun-sister
and Moon-brother—the solar eclipse—the house of Sun and Moon—the midnight Sun—cat's
cradle and cup-and-ball—the return of the Sun—the solstice feast—Sun-traditions of the Copper
Eskimo—Sun traditions in Alaska—the Moon-god.

CHAPTER 15   133

Great Sun, Six-Killer
North America

The Siberian influence—Sun-goddesses changing sex—the Sun-goddess of North-West tribes—
Coos Sun-woman—Chinook Sun-woman—the parhelion—Maidu Sun-woman—the frog who
swallows the Sun—Achomawi Sun-woman—Lake Miwok Sun-woman—Mewan Sun-
woman—Cherokee Sun-woman—the Sun-goddess's titles—the Sun decrees death—the bringing of the Sun—the great sky-arch—Sun-sister and Moon-brother—a fierce goddess—the Sun's
revenge—the death of Sun's daughter—Sun-goddess of the Yuchi—Son of the Sun—the solar
eclipse—the Sun goes backward.

CHAPTER 16   145

Tales of the Sky-Women
South America

Diversity of Sun and Moon traditions—Sun-sister and Moon-brother—the sky women—the
subjection of women—the Sun-goddess Akewa—the solar eclipse—the solar cycle—the universal mother—Christian attitudes—the Moon-god.

CHAPTER 17   149

Goddess of Life
Australia

Stories of the Dreamtime—Sun-goddess and Moon-god found throughout Australia—Yhi, the
Goddess of Life—Yhi, the Primal Creatrix—Bahloo the Moon-god—Wotjobaluk Sun-Woman—
Yulengor Sun-woman—the rays of the Sun—Worora Sun-woman and Sun's daughter—
Aranda Sun-woman—sun charms and rites—the Sun, sister of everyone—the fire of the Sun—
Wiimbaio Sun-woman—the fiery daughter—the dangerous Sun-goddess—the return of the
Sun—sacred tablets of the Sun—Aluridja Sun-woman and Moon-man—the Sun-goddess visits
the dead—the Moon-god.

CHAPTER 18   159

She Who Darts Forth Her Rays
Arabia

The feminine Sun, the masculine Moon and Morning Star—the Arabian trinity—Shamash
becomes a god—the dual nature of the Sun-goddess—her titles and epithets—shrines of the
Sun—rites and devotions—the baetyl—the Sun-goddess in Morocco—the leading of the Sun—
the Moroccan Moon-goddess—the Sun-goddess among the Bedouin—the vindictive Sun—the
kindly Moon-god—the solar eclipse—the coming of Islam—the masculine Moon and monotheism—Al-Lat, greatest of all—the Meccan trinity of goddesses—the sublime princesses—the Sun
in Islam—the Sun as a mixed blessing.

CHAPTER 19   169

Shakti Power of the Sun's Light
Tribal India

Aboriginals, Dravidians and Indo-Europeans—the village goddesses—the Sun-goddess Bisal-Mari—the eye-mirror—the sacred lamp—a spiteful goddess—smallpox and the Moon—other tribal Sun-goddess traditions—the Sun-goddess of Orissan tribes—Sun and Moon eat their children—the Sun-cow—the seven powers—the matriarchal Khasis of Assam—the creation story—Sun-sister and Moon-brother—the ancestral priestess.

CHAPTER 20   177

She Who Maintains the World
Hindu India

The Vedic Hindus—traces of the matriarchate—Vedic revival—the Vedic Sun and Moon gods—the feminine Sun—the Wedding of the Sun-maiden—Sun-maiden and the Asvin twins—the cult of the Sun-god Surya—Savitar and Savitri—the Dawn-goddess and Sun-mare—Tantric rites of Sun-goddess and Moon-god—the Hindu Moon-god, a typical masculine Moon—the Cow of Light, the imprisoned Sun.

CHAPTER 21   185

Fiery Needles
Armenia and Georgia

Many influences—the sky vault—Sun-goddess and Moon-god—a proud goddess—Sun-sister and Moon-brother—the separated lovers—Sun's mother—the cult of the feminine Sun in folklore—the Sun-goddess of Georgia—the Knight in the Panther's Skin—Sun-women in Georgian literature—the Scythian Diana—the Amazon tradition.

CHAPTER 22   191

She Who Dwells in the Spacious Disc
Egypt

Many local cults—Hathor of Dendera—a goddess of the Sun's power—house of the sky—goddess of joy and pleasure—the fierce eye of the Sun—the jealous eye—the absence and return of the Sun-eye—the mirror of Hathor—the rage of Hathor—Sekhmet the mighty—Bast, Lady of Flame—Akhenaton and the feminine Sun—Rat-taui—the Moon-god.

CHAPTER 23   199

Lady Sun, Light of the Gods
Canaan/Syria

Nomads and farmers—rule of the Moon-god—the destruction of Canaanite religion—the Ugarit tablets—Shapash, the Sun-goddess—Baal not a Sun-god—the poem of Aleyin Baal—the adventures of the Sun-goddess—hymn to the Sun—Poem of the Gracious Gods—the fertile heat of summer—the wedding of the Moon-god—the town of Lady Sun.

CHAPTER 24   205

Mistress of the Righteous Judgement
Anatolia

The lost city of the Sun-goddess—the tolerant religion of the Hittites—blessed mistress of judgement—goddess of battles—the Hittite queens and the Sun-goddess—the Sun who visits the dead—the Sun's daughters—eclipsing the Hittite Sun-goddess.

CHAPTER 25   213

Far-Seeing Mother of the Eyes
Rome and Greece

Juno Lucina—Etruscan Losna—Christianization of Lucina—folklore of Saint Lucy—the Swedish Lucia queen—Theia of Greece—Pindar's ode to the Sun-mother—the Heliades or Sun-maidens—the mysterious femininity of the Sun—the Greek Moon-god—Selene probably a Sun-goddess—Helen as Sun-maiden—the proto-Indo-European tradition—keeping the Sun masculine—taking a wider view.

CHAPTER 26   221

Releasing the Sun

The implications of the female Sun for our attitudes to myth—the holistic view of mythology.

NOTES ON THE TEXT   231

BIBLIOGRAPHY   257

INDEX   269

Illustrations

Cover Illustration:
Balto-Slavic mythology. The Moon-god abducts the Sun-goddess' daughter.

Chapter headings:
Author's original drawings based on the following:-
1   Angels and chi-ro from Byzantine ivory plaque.
2   King, God the Father represented as the Sun, and priest from English and French mediaeval manuscripts.
3   Wiccan (modern neopagan) conceptions of Moon-goddess and Sun-god. Taoist *yin/yang* figure. Author's original design.
4   Author's original design.
5   Author's original design.
6   Author's original design, and Palaeolithic Venus of Willendorf.
7   Japanese imperial chrysanthemum (a Sun-symbol).
8   Sun-wheels from Lithuanian distaffs.
9   Solarium patterns, running flame pattern and "Mary's tears" from Ukrainian *pysanky* eggs.
10 Ritual mirrors, suns, moons and eagles from Pictish Spey Eagle Stone and Rossie Priory Stone.
11 Monstrances, "shepherd's rose," Basque cross and tree of life from traditional door-lintels, Basque country.
12 Sun-discs, Bronze Age, from Trundholm chariot (Denmark) and Moordorf Sun-disc (Germany).
13 Sun-lozenge and embroidery border, traditional Lapp costume.
14 Smiling Sun-goddess, after stone-carving by Eskimo woman artist Kenojuak. Eyes and meanders from prehistoric bone harpoon-flights.
15 Traditional Cherokee drawings.
16 Woven "God's Eye" ornament, Sherente tribe.
17 Motifs from Djanggawul (Sun's Daughters) story, after bark painting by native Australian artist Malawan.
18 Sabaean stone-carving of mother-goddess. Sun from pre-Islamic clay token, Palmyra. Inscription from Saba honouring the Moon-god.
19 Arcading of village shrine. Lotuses, *neem* leaves, swastikas from traditional house and shrine decoration.
20 Chakras (Sun-wheels) from Surya-kind, Benares.
21 Scythian ornament with gryphons. Ornament from gold helmet found in Scythian prince's tomb.
22 Eye of Re. Lotuses growing in water. Ankh (symbol of life).
23 "Shamash star" (Sun-symbol), Babylonian relief. Moons, Canaanite baetyl. Borders, Ugaritic relief.
24 Lionesses, winged Sun, Yazilikaya relief. Winged Suns, Hittite royal seal. Eye-motifs, Yazilikaya.
25 "Medusa as the Sun-disc" (Frothingham p. 370). Entablature from Tholos, Epidaurus.
26 Author's original design.
Notes on the text: Author's original design.
Bibliography: Motifs from late Roman furniture and weapons.
Index beginning: Motifs from bone pendants, Mississippian culture, showing Sun and fire-cross.
Index end: Spider-woman bearing sacred fire, emblem of four directions.

Illustrations in the Text:

Ame-no-Uzume 68
Amulet from Ise 70
Latvian costume 75
Sun wheel, Baltic pendant, Bronze Age 76
Russian Head-dress 91
Rare Celtic coin showing female Sun-figure 99
Monstrance (Basque) 107
Basque Rosary-ring 108
Sun-sister and Moon-brother—Eskimo finger-masks 129
Traditional Cherokee representation of Sun-goddess 139
Mother-goddess, Venezuela 147
Mother-goddess, prehistoric Australian aboriginal painting 153
Sun and lion, from Islamic banner 163
Shrine and baetyls of Bisal-Mari 171
Scythian gold plaque with mirror-goddess and warrior 187
Mirror with handle in the form of papyrus-stem and Hathor-face 193
Sun-goddess of Arinna 209
Saint Lucy, Château Fort, Lourdes 215

Acknowledgments

My grateful thanks are due to the many individuals who helped, in ways both great and small, to make this book a reality. In particular I would like to thank Frances Howard Gordon for her constant, patient encouragement and for sharing in this vision. Also Patricia Monaghan, for many years of support and her enthusiasm for the Sun-goddess idea; while working on her own book she generously shared research and ideas.

I would also like to thank the staff of many libraries which I consulted: Darlington Public Library, for their patient, friendly and efficient help, also Glastonbury, Bristol, Bristol University Main Library, the Horniman Museum Library, the Folklore Society Library, the British Museum Department of Ethnography Library, and the public libraries at Newcastle-upon-Tyne, Oxford and Stratford-upon-Avon.

Chief Hugh Gibbs of the Etowah Cherokee Nation kindly made recommendations on the relevant section of this book, and I also thank him for permission to use the illustration of the Sun-goddess.

Among the many others to whom I owe thanks I would like to mention Eileen Goodchild, Wendy and Michael Newall, and M.V. Devine. Last but not least, I would like to acknowledge the help and kindest thoughtfulness of my family.

Janet E. McCrickard, July 1990.

Introduction

"When an old feminine myth became troublesome, it was
either ridiculed, or invented and given a male image... what
was good becomes evil, what was feminine becomes masculine, what was broad daylight fades into darkness, and
what was on the surface of the earth disappears under the
waters or down into subterranean depths...

"...What are regarded as the normal roles of men and
women have been reversed. The concept of active femininity never for one instant occurs to the men who believe
that they dominate the world and regulate the established
order. Yet it may well explain why, in those languages
which have retained traces of earlier epochs, the Germanic,
Celtic and Semitic to name but a few, the sun is feminine
and the moon masculine."

—Jean Markale, *Women of the Celts*

This book is a compendium of Sun and Moon mythology from countries around
the world—hardly an extraordinary subject, except that these are myths with
a difference. They are from cultures which see the Sun as *feminine* and the Moon
as *masculine*.

When I mentioned to friends or strangers that I was researching a book
about Sun-goddesses and Moon-gods, they invariably looked at me strangely for
a moment and then said, "Did you say Sun *goddesses* and Moon *gods*? Isn't that
the wrong way round?" or even, "Sun goddesses! There aren't any, are there?

Surely the Sun is a male god?"

Indeed, according to accepted and acceptable belief, that's just how it is. The sun is 'naturally' masculine, the Moon, 'naturally' feminine. Sun-goddesses, if they occur at all, must surely be very rare. Even quite young school-children know that the sun is *he*, and they too would put me right ("Oh, *Miss*, haven't you heard of *Ra*?"). Yet in my researches I had discovered that, far from it being natural and universal to see the Sun as masculine, many primitive and ancient peoples worldwide regarded the Sun as a goddess.[1] Likewise it was extremely common for the Moon to be a male god. I found Sun-goddesses everywhere — from Australia to the Baltic, from Siberia to Southern India, from Ireland to Japan, from Russia to Malaya, in every era and in every kind of culture, from aboriginal hunter-gatherers to settled farmers.

In many of these cases, I was alerted to the existence of the feminine Sun by the evasive wording in an ordinary book of mythology or folklore. The use of a neuter term such as *Sun-deity* or *Sun-parent*, rather than Sun-god or goddess, together with the careful avoidance of personal pronouns, or any other clue to the Sun's sex, were often used by authors to conceal the existence of a feminine Sun. Further research invariably revealed this unacceptable Sun-goddess. Many other techniques were commonly used by writers, both popular and scholarly, to deny or obfuscate the fact of a feminine Sun. Oddly, the masculine Moon, who is usually the Sun-goddess's partner, would often be accepted without demur at the same time as the Sun-goddess was rejected, or arbitrarily replaced by some other, invariably *male* god from the same pantheon. It was clearly important to many authors that knowledge of the feminine Sun should be withheld from readers. Others were happy to admit to the existence of a Sun-goddess, providing she could be made out to be totally unimportant. Here again, information was manipulated in less-than-honest ways, in order to belittle this goddess as far as possible.

My research soon became a personal quest for a hidden goddess. Like the women poets and artists in Patricia Monaghan's inspiring essay "She Want It All,"[2] I had since my late teens been using feminine solar imagery in my own artwork, in a spontaneous way which felt quite natural, and which had nothing to do with stereotypical 'solar' matters — men, virility, war, unfeeling logic. The Sun-woman as I saw her was a radiant, warm, majestic goddess of life, present in the world of Nature which she sustained by her vital force. When later I read extensively about Japanese religion and society, I was delighted to find that their Sun-goddess *Amaterasu-O-mikami* was a deity of just this kind. Yet I went on believing what I had always been told — that Sun-goddesses are too rare to be of any significance or value, that the Sun is *essentially* masculine.

Brought up as a Roman Catholic, I had been imbued with the notion that Christ himself was the mystic Sun, the *solar logos*; while the Virgin Mary and women generally were pale, delicate and emotional, personifications of the eternal Moon.

Along with many other feminists during the early 'seventies, I began actively to investigate the world of ancient and primitive religion, with its many powerful goddesses and heroines. Among these I was surprised to find Sun-goddesses in every age and land, feminine figures who in every conceivable way contradict the popular stereotypes of Sun and Moon. As I read, I also discovered that rejection of and contempt for the feminine Sun was quite usual—authors set out with the *a priori* judgement that a Sun-goddess could never be a genuine spiritual motif, even when evidence to the contrary was before their eyes.

To some extent I could understand that men might reject the Sun-goddess for the same kinds of reason that they still want to exclude women from being priests, judges or members of the Kennel Club. It's just not a proper job for the girls. But, personally speaking, it is much more difficult to understand why women, particularly those involved in the women's spirituality movement (the 'Goddess revival') should be hostile to the concept of the feminine Sun. During my twelve years in the Goddess movement I experienced negative reactions from many women when I spoke of my discoveries about the Sun-goddesses. While some women welcomed such goddesses as breaking old stereotypes of masculinity and femininity, others found the Sun-woman idea too disturbing and became angry, accusing me of all kinds of spiritual and political errors. What is it about this area of women's heritage that can provoke such a reaction? Clearly, there are important issues here about how we see ourselves as women or as men, issues about the mythological and the personal, as well as issues of religious truth.

The new, 'alternative' religious movements—feminist spirituality, 'green' neopaganism (or ecopaganism) and Wicca—all more or less claiming to be replicas of early prehistoric Nature religions, draw on ancient and tribal religions for their synthetic theology.[3] While there is both diversity and factionalism here, nevertheless there is a shared underlying orthodoxy about Sun and Moon. It goes something like this:

The Moon and the Earth are feminine.
All goddesses are Moon and/or Earth goddesses.
The Sun and the sky are masculine.
All gods are Sun and/or sky gods.

The earliest religions worshipped a supreme Moon-mother or Earth-mother. All societies were matriarchal.

These religions and societies were violently overthrown by men, who introduced sky and Sun gods together with patriarchal social organization.

There is a lunar principle (or *yin*[4]) expressing itself in humans as intuition, feeling, magic and paranormal abilities. The solar principle (or *yang*) expresses itself as logic, the rational faculty, scientific inquiry and technology.

The solar and lunar principles are objectively true, externally-existing and operate throughout all religion and the whole of the cosmo.

Our world suffers from an excess of the solar principle. The remedy for our problems (especially the ecological crisis) is to restore Earth and Moon Goddess religions of prehistory.

More follows on from these tenets, but they are very much a fixed creed in themselves, taken for granted by every writer on alternative religion and appearing more or less unchanged and unquestioned in every new book on Goddess-spirituality. Where Sun-goddesses receive a positive mention, or some credit for being valid spiritual expressions, writers still seem quite unable to make anything of them. 'Starhawk' (Miriam Simos) for example, says that "Sun goddesses and Moon gods have roles to play in the drama of birth, growth and death," but seems unwilling to try and tell us quite what those roles might be.[5] Margot Adler's 1979 review of alternative religion in North America claims that feminist Wiccans accept both Moon and Sun goddesses in a relativistic theology, "reject[ing] most of the polarizing concepts common to Western occult circles: male-female, active-passive, light-dark, and so forth." and seeing solar and lunar identifications as culturally determined.[6] Things may have changed in the decade since *Drawing Down the Moon* was written, but at any rate, the Goddess-literature and virtually every woman I consulted for this study stood firmly by the yin-yang paradigm. One woman, a PhD student, said to me, "Sun-goddesses don't *connect* with anything," by which she meant not only that she herself believed the Sun to have no role in Nature, but also that the feminine Sun—unlike the feminine Moon—is only an *arbitrary metaphor*, without the *dynamic relationships* which characterize other kinds of deities. Yet I found that the Sun-goddesses, and their partners the male Moon-gods, had a rich diversity and distinctive patterns of myth, rite and symbol. It became plain that a large part of women's rejection of the feminine Sun was due to a simple lack of information.

At this stage I began to piece together the scattered fragments. Odds and ends of scarce information, jotted down for my own interest, disclosed a mosaic of themes, and so this book was born. The motivation for this was three-fold. I found the Sun-goddesses beautiful and fascinating, and wanted to communicate this to anyone interested in religion and mythology. But, more importantly, I was disturbed by the inflexible dichotomy of lunar feminine versus solar masculine, and the way in which this paradigm is presented by modern people as eternal, changeless truth. I felt that these are stereotypes, not archetypes; dogmatic categories which distort our understanding of mythology and serve to disadvantage actual women and men. I wanted to make some contribution towards dispelling the popular (and scholarly) fallacy that the Sun is inherently masculine. And I wanted by this means to open up a wider, more inclusive perspective on mythology, a more humanistic view which sees all religious motifs as purely human expressions, rather than emanations from an eternal masculine or feminine 'principle.'

To accept that the female Sun is a valid theme in the diversity of human religious thought, instead of rejecting her as a mistake, heresy or irrelevance, has important consequences, many of which will become clear to the reader as he or she goes through this book. But, in simple terms, the Sun-goddess by her mere occurrence challenges the rigidity of our spiritual thinking, disrupting those safe old categories by which we set such store, demanding that we pay up on our claims to be plural and holistic. In facing up to her, we thus expand our conception of what it means to be female, or male—or human.

Chapter 1
The Woman Who Stands On the Moon

"The true Sun is Christ."
—*Confessio*, St. Patrick of Ireland

While it might perhaps be easy to think that some exotic tribe or peculiar religion calls the Sun 'she,' it is much more difficult to think of it being anything else but *he* in English tradition. Yet the *Oxford English Dictionary* tells us:

> "In conformity with the gender of Old English *sunne*, the feminine pronoun was used until the 16th century in referring to the sun; since then the masculine has been commonly used, without necessarily implying personification".[1]

This is really a warning that *he* and *she* used of the Sun are only a matter of grammatical gender, yet the idea of the Sun as a man is common and obvious, both in our sacred and secular art and literature. In earlier English tradition the idea of the Sun as a woman came with our Celtic and Nordic ancestors, who both saw the mythic Sun as a goddess, Scandinavian *Sol* (*or Sunna*) and Celtic *Grian*. The *OED* is not the only work to reveal this background:

> "The moon is masculine and the sun feminine among the Teutonic races. The moon was male among our own Anglo-Saxon ancestors; the name of the moon remained masculine up to the time when arbitrary genders disappeared from the language... Our habit of regarding the moon as a female is solely due to our training in the classical mythology of Greece and Rome."[2]

It is via the Saxons that we inherit our idea of 'The Man in the Moon,' although the folk-tale in which this pagan deity survives also tells of his wife, 'The Woman in the Sun'. If you have never heard of her, you might like to ask why? What has happened to this Sun-woman? Has she just faded away, or was she in some sense unacceptable?

Christian Rejection of the Feminine Sun

One might expect to find the Sun-goddess and Moon-god unacceptable to modern neopagans, whose view of Nature, history, religion and reality itself entirely depends on things being the other way round. They reject the Sun-goddess precisely because she threatens a whole cosmology. But those who are most contemptuous and dismissive of the feminine Sun are very often not pagans at all, but *Christians*. Initially this may seem odd. Why should members of a religion which until recent times has rejected all mythology as demonic deception, be at all bothered about such trifling details as the sex of a particular deity? Yet the issue is clearly important to them, and for a very good reason. Male solar imagery permeates Christianity. According to Christians themselves, this doesn't really mean anything, it's "just symbolic," by which they mean that descriptions of Christ as the *Sun of Righteousness*[3] or the *solar logos* are only poetic metaphors, and have nothing to do with the Sun of our solar system, nor the Sun-gods of paganism.

Such symbolism, however, does not arise in an arbitrary way. Religion always has its history and development; the meaning of symbols shifts and changes. At this point we need to go back and see how Sun-imagery got into Christianity in the first place.

The Light that Shines in the Darkness

In the Old Testament world of the sixth century B.C. when the first five books of the Bible were written[4], the Hebrews often used the symbolism of light when speaking of their god. Yet, because of the constant threat from polytheism, they were careful not to identify him with Sun or Moon, both important masculine gods in the Near East. Primitive Semitic religion (that of the Hebrews and Arabs) always regarded the Moon as a *male* deity, husband of the feminine Sun. While the Sun remained feminine in Canaan, Anatolia and Arabia, elsewhere she had been turned into a male god long before the Hebrews set down their sacred lore in writing. The Moon continued to be thought of as a divine man.[5] Some scholars believe that the Hebrew father-god was himself derived from the local Moon-god of *Ur*, Abraham's hometown, an important centre of Moon-god cult. The vagueness in the attribution of light to Yahweh, and the repeated assertions that he is "one" may be attempts to disguise his lunar origins.[6]

But influences from Greece affected Jewish philosophy, paving the way towards a conception of God as the Sun. Jewish theologians adopted the Greek idea of *logos*, the abstract, rational principle by which the world was created— the divine source of all Nature's ordered laws. It is interesting that the ancient Israelites enthusiastically personified *logos* as *Wisdom*, a quasi-divine *feminine* being, while the Greeks eventually personified it as the spiritual Sun, the god *Apollo*,(in contrast to *Helios*, the physical Sun). It is this Greek conception which passed into Christianity, while the Hebrew idea of the goddess-like Wisdom (which may have been an oblique reference to the old Semitic Sun-goddess) was suppressed by the misogyny and anti-Semitism of developing Christianity.[7] In the Fourth Gospel, an extremely Hellenistic creation, the Apollonian *logos* becomes Christ (the Word). This *logos* is "the light that shines in the darkness," Sun-imagery borrowed from paganism.[8]

The Graeco-Roman Sun-Cult

The first-century pagan world into which Christ was born was busily developing new theologies of male Sun-gods; religion itself was in a ferment of new and strange cults, imported from all parts of the Roman empire. There was constant religious tension between the Jews and their Roman overlords, but human religious processes being what they are, Graeco-Roman concepts seeped into developing Christianity even before it broke away from Judaism. By the mid-first century St. Paul was already quoting a rather solar-seeming Christian hymn:

> "Awake, arise from the dead
> And Christ will shine on you."[9]

The Romans adopted the Greek Apollo during a plague in 433B.C.—not as a Sun-god, but as a healer. For them he always retained this primitive character, only becoming formally worshipped as the Sun during the reign of Augustus (the same who reputedly commanded the census in the Christmas story). In any case, the Romans had their own Sun-god *Sol*, patron of charioteers. He had his own minor cult, but solar and lunar religion held little interest for the ancient Romans—they were much more concerned with the practical realities of family, field, home and farm, and making mutually beneficial contracts with the capricious spirits who might bring want or plenty.

Foreign influences gradually weaned the Romans onto the idea of a supreme Sun-god. When the emperor Septimus Severus (ruling from 193-211 A.D.)

married his empress Julia Domna, Sol's cult was established as the latest fashion in top people's religion. Nicknamed 'The Philosopher', the intellectual and ambitious Julia did much to combine Greek and Roman ideas with Sun-theology from her native Syria, and before long had persuaded her husband to have himself shown in art as the Sun-god. She was related to the mad and debauched Elegabalus, high priest of the Syrian Sun-god El-Gabal[10]. When he became emperor, Elegabalus instituted his god's cult at Rome with the greatest display and extravagance, generally misbehaving himself until assassins relieved him of his insanity in 222 A.D.

The emperor Aurelian (270-275 A.D.) was a different kind of Sun-devotee. He came from the East Danube region, an important area of Mithraic worship. By the time he came to the throne, the Sun-cult had taken over the whole pantheon, with Sol exalted over Jupiter, and all deities regarded as aspects of the Sun-father. When Aurelian sacked the rich city of Palmyra, putting down the rebellion of Queen Zenobia and her son, the spoils went to build Sol's temple back in Rome.[11] It was Aurelian who really instituted the heavily-subsidized state cult of *Sol Invictus*, with its college of priests interpreting the exotic blend of Persian, Syrian and Roman solar beliefs and rites. Every soldier in the Roman army was required to worship Sol, the virile god who gave victory.[12]

The Christian Sun-Cult

That the state Sun-cult influenced Christianity from an early stage is indisputable. In 200 A.D. Clement of Alexandria had described Christ as the Sun driving his chariot across the sky.[13] But the association of the Sun with the Christian god was not confirmed until the reign of Constantine, a devout worshipper of Sol Invictus. Shortly before the emperor met his rival Maxentius at the battle of the Milvian Bridge in 312, he received a visionary omen, a cross superimposed on the noon Sun, with the words "conquer by this." Upon winning the battle, the superstitious Constantine thought it expedient to become a Christian. All the evidence suggests that he identified the Christian god with his own beloved Sol Invictus.[14] Thus it was that, on the 25th December 336, Christmas was first celebrated as a Christian public festival—on the very day that had been Sol's birthday. But the involvement of the Church in the old solar theology went much deeper than this. Common ways of speaking about Apollo and Mithras were smoothly transferred to Christ, solar imagery was incorporated into the popular culture and official politico-religious art of the Holy Roman Empire, Christian altars were oriented towards the East (as in the pagan Sun-temples) and the liturgy blossomed with solar terminology. Even today the Constantinian legacy is evident in every Christian church-service—the Roman Catholic and Eastern Orthodox Easter liturgies in particular. Such constant reiteration of masculine solar metaphors impresses upon the faithful that Christ is the Sun, who rises, gives light, illuminates the world, dispels the darkness of night, and so forth. Even fundamentalist evangelicals, who in general try to purify their religion of all pagan elements, nevertheless use solar expressions for God and Christ. A recent T.V. programme showed the fundamentalist Easter gathering in Jerusalem, in which participants kept a Sun-vigil on a high place, facing the rising Sun and singing hymns towards it—a rite almost identical to the solar worship of the pagan Slavs, Celts, and others—but envisaging the Sun as Christ.[15]

To be a Christian is to take in the concept "Sun = divine masculinity" with one's every breath. Although some first century pagan nations known to the classical world still regarded the Sun as female, this strand of tradition was wholly unacceptable. The development of Christian solar theology, with its input from Apollonian and Mithraic traditions, the Roman imperial concept of masculine ruling power, and the misogyny of St. Paul and the early church fathers, all combined to exclude every trace of the feminine element from solar symbolism.[16]

Mary the Moon of the Church

Complementary to the symbolism of the Christ-Sun, and indeed a necessary part of it, is the traditional identification of Mary with the Moon, with its hints of mystic marriage. Again, much of this thinking comes straight from late pagan ideas, from mystery cults, such as Orphism, whose mystical and philosophical ideas so influenced early Christianity. The association of Mary with the Moon also rests on the famous passage from the Book of Revelations:

> "And there appeared a great wonder in heaven; a woman
> clothed with the sun, and the moon under her feet, and
> upon her head a crown of twelve stars...."[17]

The expression "under his (her) feet" occurs several times in the Bible, where it is always symbolic of *humiliation* or *defeat*. Far from the Moon being this woman's symbol, she is instead trampling it as a sign that she has overcome it, just as triumphant Israelite kings would publicly tread the crouching bodies of their defeated enemies. It is for this reason that Spanish pictures of the Blessed Virgin, painted as thank-offerings to celebrate the victory over the Muslims at Lepanto, showed her standing on the Moon to indicate the Christian victory over Islam.[18]

The Amorous Moon

Why should the visionary woman be overcoming the Moon, as if it were evil? To understand this it is necessary to look again at the pagan background. The Semitic Moon, always a masculine deity, was a typical, primitive Moon-god, the secret lover and patron of women, and divine begetter of children. His cult and that of his daughter, the "Queen of Heaven" or the planet Venus, involved ritual sex, in which resulting children were said to have been fathered by the Moon.[19] Herein may lie the real reason why the woman of Apocalypse tramples the Moon, for, at the time the book was written, belief in the possibility that a lunar god could impregnate a mortal woman was still very much alive in the Middle East and Mediterranean. The later Moon-goddesses of the Graeco-Roman world were also offered sexual worship, making the Moon the very emblem of demonism and lust, as far as the Christians were concerned. Whether the visionary woman represents the Blessed Virgin or, as evangelicals prefer, the Church, the "Bride of Christ," it would be especially necessary to show her renouncing these particular moons. It would hardly do for heathen converts to think of God the Father as the fecundating Moon-god, impregnating Mary. Nor would it be acceptable for them to confuse the mother of their god with the Moon-goddess, the very personification of sexual licence.

But a wide space of history lies between the Book of Revelations and the actual Christian theology of Mary. The apocalyptic vision was not identified with the Virgin until the fifth century,[20] while the Marian theology was not officially sanctioned until the sixth—a move to popularize Christianity at a time when its fortunes were flagging. By then the Roman empire was dead, its paganism technically so, allowing the Church to mop up the last of the resistance by Christianizing those persistent symbols which survived among the common people. By then the theologians, with their urge to control, define and standardize every area of belief and life into fixed dogma, were unable in any way to stand back from their own presuppositions about Sun and Moon symbolism. The Christ-Sun and Mary-Moon for them had no history, background or develop-ment; they were simply part of the nature of things. Paganism was seen in the lump, as it were, as Satanic. In so far as the Virgin Mary was the Moon, she was the new Moon of the redeemed creation, the holy opposite of the demonic goddesses of the past. The Moon was the ideal symbol of the Christian woman—passive, emotional, receptive, weeping—reflecting the glory of the solar male who ruled over her. In this sense her solar garment was seen as a divine reward for her submission—the soul which makes itself most passive best reflecting the divine glory. Like the submissive Moon, too, the Virgin was impregnated by the fiery, active solar *logos*, the creative "Word of God," Christ the Sun.

The Invisible Sun

Thus Mary became "The Moon of the Church," while the original meaning of the vision, and its old Semitic background, were forgotten[21] Modern inter-preters continue to see the apocalyptic woman as purely lunar in character. For all the notice that is taken of her solar garments, she might as well be stark naked. Christian writers traditionally interpret the crown of stars as the twelve apostles, the Moon as a maternal emblem poached from the pagans, and the Sun-robe as a vague metaphor of divine favour, the light of God the Sun/son 'clothing' the Moon.[22] Occult, neopagan and spiritual-feminist authors simply ignore the solar part of the vision:

> "[Mary] is depicted as 'clothed with the Sun and having the
> moon at her feet,' the crescent moon and crown of stars
> being her attributes."[23]

So what happened to the Sun? If a person is "standing" on one celestial body and "clothed" in another, why should one of these be totally meaningful and the other not worth mentioning? Even spiritual-feminist writers, who are usually so eager to take possession of important symbols for their cosmic, "holistic" goddess, ignore the Sun-dress as if it was meaningless or non-existent. This blind spot is quite remarkable. A visionary male figure who appeared wearing the Sun as a garment would instantly be identified as a Sun-god.

The Magical Tradition

While the Church inherited some late pagan symbols from the classical past, prolonging their life, it was chiefly the Arabs who rescued magical, gnostic and philosophical ideas from the wreck of the Graeco-Roman world. Astrological, alchemical and other esoteric Arab writings of the mediaeval period provided the principal sources for Renaissance occultists.[24] When these men (who were and who remained Christians) looked back to the classical roots of our civilization, they simply found confirmation of what everyone already knew about the masculinity of the Sun and femininity of the Moon. All the esoteric writings confirmed it. They saw this polarity as fixed by God himself, the eternal and changeless nature of the celestial bodies being part of the divinely-ordered universe. At this time in history they had no reason to suppose that things could ever be any different. The idea that there might be other cultures seeing things quite differently could not have occurred to them; the concept *feminine Sun* and *masculine Moon* would simply have been unintelligible.

Although the Church officially condemned emanationism, the Sun still tended to be thought of in the Neoplatonic way, as the visible expression of the supreme male godhead, the radiant Absolute from which all lesser existences emanated, like rays from the Sun. God, transcendence, fatherhood, rule, masculinity, fire, activity, were all one. *Woman by her very nature could never be solar.* God had seen fit to make her the uttermost opposite. Indeed, the Bible said so—*the male alone was an image of the divine glory*—woman was created expressly to reflect the glory of the male.[25] For her to try and do otherwise was like the Moon trying to usurp the Sun's place.

Mediaeval Arab and Renaissance occultisms were the ancestors of *all* later occult movements in the west—a fact which can be historically traced, but is also plainly evident in all esoteric writings, through 'Druidism', freemasonry, the so-called Western Mystery Tradition, modern astrology, Dianic witchcraft, green neopaganism and so forth. Their adherents prefer to believe that the similarities in all these traditions prove an underlying, eternal truth about the nature of things. They do not view the masculine Sun and feminine Moon in cultural and historical terms, but as pre-existing and eternal essences of "Sunness" and "Moon-ness," expressing themselves in the cosmos as the physical Sun and Moon, as male and female, mind and body, spirit and matter, light and darkness, hot and cold, heaven and earth—all the traditional polarities and dichotomies which are imagined to make up the universe. We take in this cosmology, as it were, from the drinking water, whether we see Sun and Moon in metaphysical terms or not; it permeates our culture, is reiterated in art and literature, and reinforces traditional ideas about masculinity and femininity every time we think of *Sun or Moon.*

Chapter 2
Not a Job for a Woman

"Solar passion, with its heroic and fierce character, clearly had to be assimilated to the masculine principle, and the pale and delicate nature of lunar light, with its connexion with the waters of the ocean, and the rhythm of woman, obviously had to be classified as feminine. These equations are not constant, but the exceptions do not invalidate the essential truth of this symbolism... the broadest and most authentic interpretation sees the sun as the cosmic *reductio* of the masculine force, and the moon of the feminine."

—J. Cirlot, *Dictionary of Symbols*[1]

In the mid-19th century, ethnologists first began to note and classify similarities between the myths of widely different peoples and places. These resemblances led them to assume a *universal mythic language*, of which the most typical and perfect example was to be sought in the Graeco-Roman world. Classical mythology, therefore, became a yardstick against which all other myths and legends were measured. Differences were assumed to be merely accidental, or due to mistakes and deficiencies in a culture's religious development.[2]

This way of thinking about myth, as we have already seen, was mediated in the very cultural lifeblood of the West. It was natural enough for scholars who had come to think in rather mechanistic terms—that human society might have fixed laws as immutable as the rules of engineering—to look for governing principles which would allow them to get a handhold on the teeming profusion of mythology. These laws were ready to hand. They were present in the assumptions about religious truth which permeated education and thought, and which had come in a long line of inheritance from the classical world. Had not the Greeks and Romans themselves set a precedent by identifying foreign deities with their own gods and goddesses?

The Golden Bough

It was inevitable that, in the attempt to make everything fit the Graeco-Roman paradigm, inconvenient protruding bits would have to be trimmed with shears, and deities who failed to fit the prescribed mould would have to have their corners knocked off. Thus began a process of distortion and misrepresentation which still continues today. The most famous product of this "universal mythic language" movement was Sir James Frazer's *The Golden Bough* of 1890 which traced the evolution of religion. Whatever else may be said of it, it has at least one major deficiency—a disregard for the social, cultural reality of myths. This has to be so, to preserve the theory intact. For if one is attempting to impose on many diverse cultures a single religious scheme, *context* and *differences* have necessarily to be sacrificed—they spoil the purity and disrupt the orderliness of supposedly universal truths.

Thus when Frazer came across the Eskimo Sun-goddess, he simply referred to her as "he." The connotations of *active femininity* implied in the idea "Sun-goddess" were especially unacceptable in Frazer's day, when Victorian patriarchy was beleaguered by the increasingly successful women's movement. Three years after the publication of *The Golden Bough*, the American suffragette Matilda Joslyn Gage, writing of the matriarchate, mentioned the Hindu Sun-goddess *Suryā* as an erstwhile example of feminine power—the first woman, as far as I could discover, to speak of the Sun-goddess and hint at the implications for women.[3] At the time, however, the Sun of myth and legend was enjoying its noontide of popularity.

Max Mueller and the Solar School

Another Victorian scholar who forced myth to fit classical and Christian assumptions was the German orientalist Max Mueller. He settled in England and founded the so-called *solar school* of mythology and folklore. Mueller and his associates believed the human religious impulse to be rooted in the response to the Sun, to its splendour, vigour and supposed virility. They therefore read all myths as pre-scientific attempts to explain solar phenomena. Every god was the Sun, every goddess the Dawn; every rite, every custom, popular superstition or legend, every folk-hero, gnome or sprite was traced to solar religion. The more mystical or religiously-devout among Mueller's fans believed his work to support the truth of Christianity. In the beginning of time, religion was a pure solar monotheism, the one, true, masculine godhead being manifest in the visible Sun, or at very least symbolized by it. Mueller's work seemed to prove that this Neoplatonic doctrine was not just a late idea, but went back to the Golden Age. Moreover he traced Indo-European themes back to the Vedic Hindus, the so-called *Indo-Aryans*, not just to the Greeks. Hence his work was eagerly welcomed by believers in the *Hyperborean tradition*, racists and occultists, who imagined this to be the primordial religion of the "pure Aryan race," supposedly Apollo-worshippers living in the far North.[4]

Nowadays it is customary to refer to the "*excesses* of the solar school." And indeed, the solar theory was excessive—it attempted to deny the diversity of religion in favour of a sweeping generalization. All deities and stories are not solar. But Mueller's work was happily accepted so long as it promoted the orthodox view—that the Sun is universally male—the mythological proof of masculine supremacy. When, in his later work, Mueller became more open and tolerant regarding the existence of Sun-goddesses, he was a marked man. His discovery that the Sun is not always male undoubtedly contributed to the intensely hostile reaction against his work. By 1915 no scholar would risk his reputation by talking about solar religion. Mueller's theories were ridiculed.

Although Mueller's basic claim for the solar origin of religion was discredited, the academic establishment, Christian theologians and the occult fraternity all found it expedient to retain one of his ideas—an erroneous idea, but still very much in vogue.[5] That is the identification of *all* male sky gods as the Sun (or "solar"), regardless of what they were actually god-of. In this way, the storm-god of a particular culture can be substituted for the Sun, in cases where the Sun inconveniently proves to be a goddess. Even today, lists of 'Sun-gods' in recently published diction-aries of mythology turn out to include storm or thunder-gods from mythologies where the Sun is female, and not infrequently there is not a single actual Sun-god on the list.[6]

Briffault and the Lunar School

It was inevitable that the violent reaction against Mueller's solar theory should lead to the formation of a *lunar school*. One of its major products, Robert Briffault's three-volume *The Mothers*, asserted that all religion was essentially lunar in origin and character. If a Sun-deity was important, then he was re-read as a Moon-god, often in the most arbitrary way. All Sun-symbols were really Moon-symbols, no matter what a particular culture said they were. Although many of Briffault's arguments were facile, *The Mothers* contains much valuable and interesting information, particularly about religions which perceived the

11

Moon as masculine. But here, Briffault blotted his copybook in the same way as Mueller had done, for the right ordering of spirituality and society meant that the Moon must be kept female. Yet he had discovered that the primitive Moon was almost invariably male, which meant that he could not help disclosing the Moon-god's other half—the feminine Sun. Thus *The Mothers* contains some important references to Sun-goddesses.

It is important to realise that Briffault's work was not a cool-headed, impartial survey of religion, but a passionate reaction against the solar theory. His heliophobia was extreme; it led him to a highly selective, biased and often unscrupulous manipulation of data, particularly in regard to the Sun-goddesses, whom he could only tolerate providing that they were (in his view at any rate) of no importance whatever. To this end he lied in his teeth about Sun-goddesses of the Eskimo, Latvians, Cherokee and others, shamelessly misleading the reader.[7]

Insofar as the Moon was extremely important, then it was fine for it to be a male god. But this involved Briffault in a contradiction, for the Moon is supposed to be the eternal feminine. He managed to have his Moon-cake and eat it by combining the two, claiming that the Moon was really bisexed, and that all goddesses were really Earth or Moon goddesses. These constructive interpretations were devoid of any real foundation in the facts of mythology, being based for example on the theological speculations of late classical writers, or the misidentification of women abducted by the male Moon as "the Moon-goddess." The real purpose of such ideas was to obfuscate the fact that *the Moon is not always female.*

The lunar school was as doomed as the solar school, for the same reasons— religion is no more exclusively lunar than it is exclusively solar, but more importantly, both schools of thought disclosed evidence which was far too disturbing. The most fundamental mythic paradigm of the Western world, by which the correct conceptions of male and female, and their separate roles, and the proper ordering of society, and the primacy of the male, and the acceptable nature of the female, and the correct spiritual cosmology, are all alike symbolized, was being subverted by contradictory evidence. Coming at the time it did, when women were pressing hard for emancipation and gaining too much ground for patriarchal comfort, the revelation that the Sun could be female was intensely threatening. Its implicit suggestion of female autonomy, intellect and sexuality was intolerable. Rather than allow the concept Sun-goddess free expression, the whole of astral mythology had to be suppressed, jeered off the academic stage.

And so it was. The net result for the serious study of mythology was to make scholars chary of *any* comparative study of astral deities, or astral interpretations of folklore survivals; both kinds of investigation necessarily end up exposing the solar male/lunar female fallacy. It is significant that, while Mueller's and Briffault's hypotheses have been discredited, the techniques they invented for dishonestly dismissing the female Sun are still in current use.

The Modern Study of Mythology

Modern mythologists—anthropologists and historians—approach myth in a more secular way, taking into account the many influences which shape it (ethnic, linguistic, geographical, social and so on) attempting to see myth and religion in a dynamic context and an organic way, like a living organism in its niche and ecosystem. While there are of course patterns to be detected in mythology (to say that it is plural is not to say that none of its parts can have any relationship) these are not attributed to any sort of underlying spiritual truth. There is no *yin* and *yang*, no universal masculine and feminine principles, no mystical, eternal verities shaping mythology and guiding us as to the orthodoxy (or otherwise) of gods and goddesses. In short, modern theories of mythology are naturalistic. They are explanations based in Nature, not in metaphysics. Mythic similarities and themes are attributed not to supernatural entities (whether "in" Nature or "outside" it) but to natural human processes and connections. Yes, mythology forms an interconnected whole, but it is a purely *human* whole.

From this perspective, deities, cults and symbols are allowed to be just what they are, without imposing the labels "solar" and "lunar" on them. These labels are themselves a cultural, historical product—to impose them on all religion is a kind of cultural (or should we say 'occultural'?) imperialism. Mythology is also recognized as having multiple causes. Every myth or deity or rite or symbol is the product of a complexity of events, stretching away like a web of threads in many directions through human history. The modern study of myth, seeing it in plural, relativistic and *functional* terms, rules out partisan religious interpretations.

Eclipse of the Sun

At least, that is the ideal. By and large most modern mythologists live up to it—until, that is, they are faced with the feminine Sun. Now, it seems not to matter that a particular culture actually sees the Sun as a female. For a culture to conceive of the Sun as female is not taken seriously—never accepted as a thread of religion's colourful tapestry, nor even as a creative, artistic variation on mythic themes. She is rejected, dismissed and explained away as if a Sun-goddess could never be a genuine spiritual motif. She is discussed as if it were already agreed by everyone that a Sun-goddess is merely an aberration or fallacy. More commonly, however, the inconveniently feminine Sun is just *erased*—left out of the literature.

What is it about the female Sun which causes scholars to abandon their scientific ideals in this way, and to represent this one kind of deity as somehow spurious? And if the Sun-goddess is "rare" or "unimportant," then why go to such lengths to cover up the fact of her occurrence? Evidently she is threatening, for *no other deity is treated like this*. Mistranslation (replacing "mother" with "father", etc.), false tricks of argument, equivocal language, double standards of interpretation, plain old fibs (some whoppers) and other sorts of technique are used to obfuscate the plain fact of the feminine Sun. They often follow immediately on a statement to the effect that the Sun is normally male and the Moon normally female, so clearly the Sun-goddess is seen (consciously or unconsciously) as spoiling *the purity of mythic truth*. It is not only misogynistic scholars who employ such techniques. The Sun-goddess is as likely to be dismissed in feminist works which claim to recover suppressed knowledge about women's religion, as she is in hoary old patriarchal tomes by Victorian clergymen. And the standard methods used to eclipse her seem not to change with time.

The Voice of Prejudice

The *language* used in speaking of the feminine Sun is prejudicial, and unless the reader is wide awake, and thinking clearly, these little words slip down unnoticed. Hastings' *Encyclopaedia* baldly states of Sun and Moon, "The gender... is sometimes reversed."[8] Reversed from what? Using *reversal* for *female Sun* gives us the subliminal message *female Sun* equals *wrong way round*. When Olcott in his collection of Sun-lore met with the feminine Sun he described this state-of-affairs as "confusion in the sex" and "no settled opinion regarding the sex."[9] From which we can derive the equation *male Sun* equals *clarity of thought or conception, female Sun* equals *confusion, muddled thinking*. And if male Sun equals *settled opinion*, i.e. *stability, ordered mind*, then of course female Sun will equal *unsettled opinion, chaos, disordered mind*.

Such language comes from an unconscious assumption that male Sun = *normal*, female Sun = *abnormal*, but in some contexts it can be conscious and deliberate. Another method of making the female Sun appear false is to put "sun goddess" thus, in inverted commas, or when talking about a Sun-goddess, to use *he* throughout, until the time comes when that Sun's femininity has to be revealed. Then one puts "she" in inverted commas—as if there were something jocular about it.[10] One scholar is unable to disguise his contempt for the idea of a feminine Sun, describing her as "Amaterasu, the so-called 'sun goddess'."[11] Other methods of denigration are more subtle:

> "Scholars believe that it was probably due to Hurrian influence that the Hittite sun goddess, consort of the Storm God, came to be regarded as his equal or even his superior."[12]

In the same way, Mircea Eliade routinely gave Sun God capitals and sun-goddess lower case, that is, when he admitted to the occurrence of Sun-goddesses at all. (He had personal religious objections to them.[13])

Readers lulled into a trance by the ritual repetition of "Sun... male, Moon...female" are fair game for the following technique:

> "The Sun (Saule) and Moon (Meness) are regarded as deities and are conceived as living like husband and wife."[14]

Wife and husband, actually—but why this carelessness? The article is supposed to give factual details of Baltic myth, which has a female Sun and male Moon, but this statement conveys quite the opposite of the facts.[15] Balys follows this up with straight mistranslation:

> "The morning star kindles the fire for the sun in the morning and the evening star spreads his bed."[16]

The source from which this motif is taken calls the Sun *Mother Sun*; it is a song about the Baltic Sun-*goddess* and her daughters.[17] Earlier editions of the Larousse Encyclopaedia also resort to falsification of the texts, this time the Icelandic *Eddas*, which tells us that the *Sun-goddess* Sunna will give birth to a *daughter*:

> "A new sun—the son of that which a wolf had once devoured—shone serenely in the sky."[18]

This method only works if you can rely on your readers not to check, and since the regular readers of coffee-table books and popular reference mythologies usually don't, then writers get away with it.

Merely Grammatical Gender

Mistranslation—*goddess* replaced by "god", daughter by "son," *she* by "he,"—is sometimes justified by claiming that the Sun's femininity is "merely grammatical gender." But the emptiness of this is shown by the fact that masculine gender counts perfectly well as evidence when it upholds a *male* Sun god. It is only when we come to the issue of female Suns and male Moons that *goddess* can be arbitrarily re-read as "god," *mother* as "father," and a woman's name as a man's— in other words, *the imperative need to keep the Sun male overrides all considerations of truth or intellectual honesty.*[19]

In the realm of mythology and personified natural forces, which is what we are talking about (not whether cups or saucers, trams or bootlaces are "feminine" or "masculine") names of gods appear in the masculine gender, names of goddesses in the feminine. The words goddess, mother, daughter, too, apply to female beings, and cannot be arbitrarily chosen to belong to male ones—except, that is, when a writer discovers a feminine Sun, and then he or she seems to have some peculiar difficulty. The gender then becomes unaccountably confused or uncertain. It has to be put right, made *clear, stable, ordered*; in other words, the plain sense of the text has to be ignored, and the Sun read as male. We can imagine how vital grammatical gender would immediately become, were someone to read all grammatically masculine Sun-names as referring to feminine deities!

Half-Measures

This neat technique allows a Sun-goddess myth to be described without disclosing the fact that the Sun in question is female. Edward Clodd, after assuring us that the Sun is naturally male and the Moon naturally female, paints himself into a corner by offering examples of myths where things are the other way round. Watch how cleverly he gets out of it:

> "In Slavonic myth the sun cleaves him [the moon] through for loving the morning star.

> "In Greenland the moon was in love with his sister, and stole in the dark to caress her."

...and so on, through the Salish, Khasi and Eddic myths of Sun-goddess and Moon-god, without once letting slip that the Sun of all these myths is *female.*[20]

Discussing the existence of the feminine Sun without actually openly mentioning her is a fine art:

> "The moon... was viewed as of the masculine gender in respect of the earth, whose husband he was supposed to be, but as a female in relation to the sun, as being his spouse... If modern science, discovering the moon's inferiority to the sun, call the former feminine, ancient nescience, supposing

the sun to be inferior to the moon, called the latter masculine."[21]

Making the reader giddy is certainly one way of distracting them from the simple fact of Sun-goddesses. Discussing Sun and Moon myths without exposing the masculine Sun/female Moon fallacy is a bit like trying to swim without getting wet. Once a writer has admitted to a feminine Sun, however, the next stage is to discredit and belittle her as far as possible.

Double Standards

The essence of this method is to disqualify *any* female Sun, on the grounds of characteristics which are not used to disqualify male Suns. Thus a Sun-goddess who goes into a cave or underground "must really be" an "Earth-goddess." Yet virtually every Sun-myth describes how the Sun goes down into (and then under) the earth at night, or lives in (or is born in, or withdraws into) a cave. Male Sun-gods such as Mithras, Helios, Phanes and Shamash are found in caves and underground, yet that is not taken to mean they are Earth-gods! If it is OK for a Sun-god to travel beneath the earth at night, why is a Sun-goddess who does the same disqualified from being the Sun?[22]

The motifs of male and female Sun-myths are routinely interpreted in this biased way to ensure that *no evidence is ever allowed to count towards a goddess being the Sun*. Now, this is a classic instance of dishonest argument. It would be possible to make a case for all swans being black, by refusing to count as a "real swan" any swan that wasn't black. In the same way a case is made for all Sun-deities being male, by refusing to count as the "real Sun" any deity that isn't male.[23] The definition of "Sun-deity" or "real Sun" presupposes maleness; it begs the question.

This is an extremely important point. When a writer on symbolism tells us:

> "All gods are sun and sky gods; all goddesses are moon and earth goddesses..."[24]

...and then goes on to say that any symbol is *solar* when found in connection with a male god, but that the same symbol becomes *lunar* when associated with a goddess[25] then the matter becomes as clear as day. There is really only *one* criterion by which a Sun deity is judged to be "real." It must be *male*. For a deity to be female is an automatic disqualification. Thus "All gods are sun and sky gods ... " actually tells us nothing but: "All male gods are male gods."

It is interesting to see how, in making masculinity the essential qualification for the post of Sun-god, the Sun-goddess then stands in relation to *the world of religious ideas* as woman has always stood in relation to *the world of men.* The Sun-goddess is nothing but a woman filling in because a man couldn't be found to do the job. She is no more a proper Sun than a woman medic was a proper doctor to the Victorians, or a woman priest is a proper priest in the eyes of conservative Anglicans. Strength, power, vigour, rule, reliability, *divinity* all belong properly to males, and as such find their ultimate symbol in the Sun. It must be kept male at all costs.

The Moon is Always Female

Feminists are evidently thinking in the same way when they depict the Sun-goddess as a sort of cosmic Mrs. Thatcher:

> "The Moon is always female, but the Sun is only female in lands where females are let into the Sun to rush and climb."[26]

In other words, the Sun-goddess is an honorary member of the old boys' club.

But none of this is true—Sun-goddesses, as I hope to show, are not like that, and the Moon is most certainly not always female. Like so many "Sun-gods," who on closer examination turn out to be impostors, the majority of "Moon-goddesses" are nothing of the kind. Anne Kent Rush's *Moon, Moon* is typical in listing any and every goddess as the Moon; dozens of goddesses in her lists have nothing whatever to do with the Moon. Such Moon goddesses have been interpreted into existence by this circular argument:

"All goddesses are Moon goddesses."

So what exactly *is* a Moon-goddess? A Moon-goddess is *any female deity.* Just for a deity to be female is enough to make her lunar. Femaleness = the Moon. So around we go: All female deities are Moon-goddesses because all Moon-goddesses are females. In other words, this tells us nothing but:

"All female deities are females."

Just as nothing is allowed to qualify a goddess to be the Sun, so nothing is allowed to disqualify a goddess from being the Moon. Such "evidence" as is commonly provided in support of a goddess being lunar is almost always the things which females, as women, naturally do anyway, such as menstruate; give birth; be of young, medium or old age (this covers all eventualities—how indeed could *anyone* not be young, medium or old? What other alternative could there be?), and have daughters or sons. In order not to be identified as a Moon-goddess, a goddess would have to do and be absolutely nothing. The moment she stirs hand or foot, she is identified as "lunar."

The male Moon-god is commonly obfuscated by replacing him with any convenient mother-goddess from that pantheon. Then she is dubbed "The

Great Moon Mother," and the Moon-god is explained away as being just her son or lover "and thus assigned her attributes."[27] This is constructive interpretation, allowing modern Westerners to read back their own beliefs into ancient religions, constructing feminine Moon-cults where none existed.[28]

A Higher Wisdom

Once the reader has been made (by these and many other techniques) to feel that a Sun-goddess is just a fake, or at best a second-class deity, he or she is bound to view any subsequent details of this goddess's cult as an account of a faulty religion, in which people didn't quite know what they were doing. Then the suggestion that some other, invariably male god was the "real" Sun gives that god an added glamour—it implies that way back in the past, before this people made their foolish mistake about the Sun and mistook him for a woman, there must have been a pristine, original, *true* cult of the Sun, and that this lost wisdom is preserved in the later cults of sky-gods. Thus the reader's attention is effectively distracted from the actual Sun, the Sun-goddess; and thus *we are prevented from learning anything different about the Sun*, from thinking about it in any but the acceptable sense of male sexual function and dominance.

Identifying all gods as the Sun and all goddesses as the Moon is supposed to be a more *spiritual* activity than looking at these deities from the point of view of actual, cultural beliefs. It is said to be a process of recognizing universal truths in mythology by *intuition*, i.e. something closely similar to the Christian idea of 'faith.'[29] Because it unifies, it is supposed to be a higher wisdom. In reality it is a grid of Western perceptions and Western values imposed upon myth. This may have been acceptable in Victorian times, when non-classical myth was a study restricted to academics, and cultural imperialism was a matter of national pride. But now the myths and religions of other cultures are, so to speak, out in the open, public, accessible and (through their current popularity) liable to influence people, it is time to try and get things right, to abandon our claims to a higher religious wisdom, and start looking at the facts.

Eclipse of the Sun

Chapter 3
The True Feminine

"Feminism, far from being able to confer on woman 'rights'
that are non-existent because contrary to the nature of
things, can only remove from her specific dignity; it is the
abolition of the eternal-feminine, of the glory that woman
derives from her celestial prototype... That femininity is a
necessary element in all spirituality, we would not think of
contesting, but one must know how to put each thing in its
place."

—Frithjof Schuon[1]

While astral mythology may be a dead issue as far as the modern comparative
mythologist is concerned, it is still important in at least one other field, that of
Jungian psychology. Two of the major works putting the case for the universally lunar nature of the female are by Jungian authors—Erich Neumann's *The
Great Mother, An Analysis of the Archetype*, and M. Esther Harding's
Woman's Mysteries. As well as these books, reprinted in response to the
growing interest in women's studies, numerous new works discussing the re-
emergence of the Goddess in terms of the Jungian hypothesis have appeared in
the last decade.[2]

Carl Gustav Jung (1875-1961) came to believe that certain mythic themes,
or *archetypes*, are actually built into the structure of the human mind, and
therefore inherited genetically.[3] Each person is born with a full complement of
archetypes in the form of the *collective unconscious*, from which all dreams,
symbols, religion and mythology arise. While the world's deities might appear
to be infinitely diverse, according to Jung they are really only variations on

quite a small number of irreducible archetypes. In his analytical work with his patients, his study of myth and occultism (especially alchemy) and his own experience of mental breakdown and recovery, Jung believed he had evidence that his hypotheses were based in reality, in objective, universally-true facts about the human mind.[4]

Anima and Animus

Given the era in which Jung was writing (he would have been brought up, so to speak, on astral theories of mythology), his antipathy towards women's rights (what he lamented as the "too masculine orientation" of modern woman[5]) and his faith in the inherent truth of alchemical ideas, it is hardly surprising that he should see the *solar masculine* and *lunar feminine* as part of the unchange-able nature of things. He enshrined this doctrine in his concepts *animus* and *anima*. While a woman's true feminine nature is inescapably lunar, and a man's solar, each sex contains, within its collective unconscious, an autonomous archetype of the opposite sex. In popular terms, a woman has a "masculine side" and a man a "feminine side." A woman has *animus*, a man has *anima*. Psychic wholeness, mental and social health, depend on an integration of these mascu-line and feminine aspects of the personality, a "befriending" of the unconscious power.

Just as the man incarnates what Jung termed the solar *logos*—disciplined intellect, "order, formulation, discrimination, generalization, consciousness"[6] so does woman incarnate the lunar *eros*, the soft, loving, passive, yielding, emo-tional, unconscious, fickle, whimsical, changeable principle. The integration in the conscious life of each sex of the opposite subconscious principle appears in myth or alchemy as the mystic marriage of Sun-god and Moon-goddess.

The Inescapable Moon

On the surface of it, this looks promising. Surely, then, a woman is really "solar" within her true self? Not at all. A woman's first duty, according to Harding in *Woman's Mysteries*, is to submit to her lunar nature, that principle which, she claims, "functions unerringly and inevitably... by which [women] are controlled from within."[7] Harding actually admits that the primitive Moon-deity was universally masculine, but this aroused in her no curiosity whatever about the feminine Sun, nor any awareness of her own self-contradiction:

> "The symbol which above all others has stood throughout
> the ages for woman, distinctively feminine in contrast to
> masculinity, is the Moon. In poetry, both modern and

classical, and, from time immemorial in myth and legend, the Moon has represented the women's deity, the feminine principle, much as the Sun, with its heroes, symbolized the masculine principle. To primitive man and to the poet and dreamer of today the Sun is masculine and the Moon feminine... the fact that the sun seems to mankind to be a symbol of male, while the moon symbolizes female is easily appreciated... the sun is... constant and reliable, but the moon is changeable... she seems to be dependent only on her own whim..."

—and more of the same.[8] Harding emphasizes that woman's essential femininity makes her "fickle and unreliable," that she is given to moods, whims and frequent changes of mind, to shadowy unconscious perceptions and intuitions. This is woman's Moon-goddess nature; for her to refuse to submit to it is pathological; objections and dissent only show that the woman is deluding herself through fear, and refusing to renounce her superior intellectual attitude.[9]

While a woman is permitted to integrate with her inner man, her animus, she must not take on, or live out the qualities proper to the opposite sex. This would mean her losing her femininity. Jungians diagnose such a woman as *animus ridden*. A courageous, independent, intellectual, strong-minded and emancipated woman is not that way because she is a woman. For the Jungian, there is no such thing as feminine courage or feminine rationality. These things are, by their very nature, *masculine* properties. Hence the concept *Sun-goddess* is a contradiction in terms.

The Rule of the Solar Male

Anthony Steven's *Archetype, A Natural History of the Self*, also claims that woman must keep to her lunar place, for the sake of our *political* health. According to him, the archetypes evolved by natural selection, like other components of the body.[10] In other words, as humans developed, there must very early have been mythic images detrimental to human survival. Individuals and religions with these dodgy archetypes were wiped out, and hence failed to transmit their heresies to succeeding generations. And since Sun-male and Moon-female are animus and anima, they must be essential to our survival. Thus to controvert them, to affirm *Sun-female* and *Moon-male*, is actually psychologically and biologically damaging, a blasphemy against Nature; the mythic equivalent of inverting the crucifix or saying the Lord's prayer backwards.

Thus the traditional dichotomies of male, light, rule, action and so forth versus female, darkness, passivity, intuition, together with the biological differences between the sexes and the supposedly universal masculinity of Sun-deities, show (according to Stevens) that

> "...male dominance is a manifestation of 'the psychophysiological reality' of our species... patriarchy, it seems, is the natural condition of mankind."[11]

As the wavering lunar sex, women lack the perseverance, aggression and ambition to rule. They have less capacity for innovation, and are "adapted to a less physically demanding mode of existence."[12] Quoting approvingly from Steven Goldberg's *The Inevitability of Patriarchy* (a book written in reaction to the growing women's movement), Stevens asserts that matriarchy can never have existed. While woman is permitted to seek to develop her masculine side, it is only for the sake of psychic wholeness—she may not do this before she has fulfilled her feminine role,[13] and Stevens makes it quite apparent that his Christian father-god (who apparently created the *yin* and the *yang* principles to operate unfailingly throughout the cosmos) has ordained that she shall not usurp the solar place of man himself. Readers may be surprised to learn that *Archetype* was written, not in Victorian times, but in 1986.

The True and False Feminine

Another Jungian work preaching the inescapably lunar nature of woman is Penelope Shuttle and Peter Redgrove's *The Wise Wound, Menstruation and Everywoman*, of 1978. Speaking of the "Great Mother" archetype, from which Jung believed all goddesses to derive, they say

> "All her manifestations are discernibly linked to this moon analogy... Moonlight seems to belong to woman and sunlight to the perfecting patriarch... the moon and its Goddesses have always and in all cultures been regarded as the image par excellence through which a woman may strengthen her sense of her own nature."[14]

This is untrue, for not all goddesses are the Moon, and not all cultures or eras had a Moon-goddess. The woman of ancient Japan, Siberia, India, Lithuania and many other cultures strengthened her self-image by relating to the feminine nature of a Sun-goddess. But this is a Jungian book, and so the feminine Sun has no archetypal validity, even though the authors acknowledge male Moons, and in some instances almost discuss the idea of the feminine Sun. They believe that the lunar identification of women is responsible not only for the menstrual cycle (a topic which we will discuss later) but also for the actual development of human thought and society. For this reason they consider it essential for women to submit to this Moon-principle. Failure to do so is the source of evils ranging from period-pains to nuclear warfare.

The dust-jacket of *The Wise Wound* carries this accolade from the poet Ted Hughes:

> "It is far and away the most radical and unarguable case for the real dignity and sacredness of woman, therefore of all processes belonging to her and related to her, therefore of the real feminine in spirit and the real feminine in nature, that I've read."

What exactly is this so-called *real feminine*, or as it is more frequently called, the *true feminine*? If the real or true feminine is incarnate in the Moon-attuned, lunar-identified woman—the woman who is irresistible to men, according to Harding[15]—then we are led to ask what the *unreal* feminine might be. If the true feminine is lunar, then could the *false feminine* be, say, *solar*?

Hughes' comment is certainly very Jungian—it implicitly relegates *dissenting* females to this realm of false femininity, the animus-ridden, the women who have lost their archetypal caste. Jung himself termed the *solar logos* in women "often only a regrettable accident,"[16] making himself eternally hated among feminists for suggesting that men were "not entirely wrong" in wishing to brutalize articulate, intelligent women into silence.[17] There is a vague hint here that the solar woman has indeed lost caste, like a Victorian prostitute or Hindu nautch-girl—by breaking sexual rules, she has forfeited her true womanhood and thus her right to be protected from male brutalization. The man, whether husband or animus, is the solar male with whom the lunar woman ought to mate. This is the nature of things—the real feminine woman accepts and submits to her lunar role and the heterosexual mystic marriage this implies. But when the solar is *feminine*—active, incisive, hot, autonomous. sexual, thinking, free—all the things patriarchy would that women were not—a kind of psychosexual perversion has taken place. The woman has, as it were, lost her solar lesbian virginity. She is a non-woman, the False Feminine. This is the Jungian legitimation of male hostility towards women who fail to live down to the cultural stereotype.

The Lunar Angel

There is a familiar, sinister ring to the idea that women who disbelieve, question or dissent from their archetypal lunar role thereby forfeit their feminine dignity:

> "The appropriate duties and influence of woman... are unobtrusive and private, but the source of mighty power. When the mild, dependent, softening influence of woman under the sternness of man's opinions is fully exercised, society feels the effects of it in a thousand forms... But when she assumes the place and tone of a man... we put ourselves in self-defense against her; she yields the power which God has given her... her character becomes unnatural."[18]

These words come from a Christian fundamentalist pastoral letter of 1837, but with only a little alteration they might almost have come from *The Wise Wound*:

> "The menstrual powers and influence of woman... are unobtrusive and private, but the source of mighty power. When the magical, psychic, intuitive influence of the menstruating woman over the logic, intellect and rationality of patriarchal opinions is fully exercised, society feels the effects of it in a thousand forms... But when she assumes the place and character of the Sun... we put ourselves in self-defense against her; she yields the power which the Moon gives her... her character becomes unnatural."

On this issue of what is natural, Jungian, Victorian and modern spiritual-feminist concepts of true femininity draw remarkably close. In 1842 an American woman, Eliza Farnham, received "by intuition" a revelation which she called *The Truth of Woman*, published twenty-two years later as *Woman and Her Era*. Farnham's argument was that woman was superior to man—biologically, mentally and in every way. Whereas man dealt with material things through his crude faculty of reason, woman's more refined and elevated intuition gave her the advantage, both morally and spiritually. Farnham might almost be called the mother of the modern feminist-spirituality movement. A Swedenborgian, she had occult leanings rather similar to those of modern Goddess-worshippers.[19]

In her views on women Farnham did not materially differ from antifeminists of the day, for they too attributed to woman a kind of spiritual superiority. In 1846 the antifeminist Ida Klug produced a statement to the effect that men were superior in "intellectual acuteness" and "cold inflexible inquiry," while women were superior in "love."[20] Precisely the same idea was to be enshrined in Jung's own identification of the feminine principle as *eros* and the masculine as *logos*. Such thinking formed the backbone of Victorian attitudes to woman and her relationship to men. A few years after Klug's statement, the poet Coventry

Patmore published the first part of his work on ideal Victorian marriage, *The Angel in the House*. It exalts woman as noble, loving, moral and pure—but at the same time inferior—a powerless child or imbecile. This concept of perfect womanhood was enthusiastically supported by the Church. Such a submissive, asexual woman enclosed, nun-like, in her separate domestic world was the same archetype (I use the term advisedly) as St. Paul's ideal Christian woman—her husband (or men in general) stood in relation to her as God stood to man,[21] as the Christ-Sun stood to the Mary-Moon.

Myth, Religion and Mother-Right

As Victorian woman sought emancipation, the demands that she keep to her "natural" place became more and more strident. To call on Christian doctrine and the authority of God was not enough—it became necessary for threatened patriarchal society to raise battalions from among the ranks of psychologists, biologists and anthropologists. In the process a new 'ology' was created—sexology—with theories of homosexuality which were used as weapons against the growing women's movement, against the passionate female friendships which had previously been acceptable, but in the context of women uniting against men, were now seen as threatening.[22]

Inevitably, mythology and the history of religion were pressed into service. In 1870 Johann Jacob Bachofen published his *Myth, Religion and Mother-Right*, which used mythological and other material to show that woman is inherently unfit to rule. For him, mother-rule was the material, animal, undifferentiated world of the beehive, the dark physicality of matter with its lunar and earthly nature, as opposed to the superior light, the *solar* light of masculine rule, inherited from the same patriarchal Greek culture which had itself overcome the Amazons, representatives of social and spiritual chaos.[23] For Bachofen, patriarchy was inevitable—it was written in the very nature of the human male, whose solar intellect was bound to unfold, like the flower from the bud, and overcome womankind.

The Development of Lunar Feminism

The founding fathers of communism thought Bachofen had got it right, insofar as the history of society goes. So too did some modern women, who discovered Bachofen via socialist feminism in the 'sixties. All kinds of other discredited theories became popular again at this time—everything from Velikovskian catastrophism to "hereditary witchcraft"—as a form of rebellion against established authority. By the mid-seventies women were attempting to reclaim the religious power of which they had been deprived by Christianity, Judaism, Islam and the other patriarchal religions. For the developing Goddess-movement the rediscovery of Bachofen was like a scriptural revelation. *Myth, Religion and Mother-Right* had been written with the purpose of maligning women, but in doing so its author had let the cat out of the bag. He had been obliged to reveal "herstory" as well as history.

The sense in which spiritual-feminist women took Bachofen had important consequences for the Goddess-movement. They saw his work as disclosing a lost world, a forgotten religious heritage, a Golden Age of feminine wisdom, the answer to that long-concealed secret — *what Woman really is*. And in doing so, *they accepted without question that woman is essentially lunar*, with every-thing that that means in terms of traditional so-called lunar attributes.[25] They did not question this division of reality into the solar and the lunar, male and female principles, but continued (along with everyone else in the Western world) to think that things had never been seen any other way. Their rebellion against patriarchal thinking was in no wise thorough-going. *They accepted patriarchal cosmology wholeheartedly.* There was no radical change or re-thinking of what patriarchal scholars and theologians had told woman about her place in the structure of reality. All that happened was that solar/male/good versus lunar/female/evil became *solar/male/evil* versus *lunar/female/good.*

The Results of Moon-Consciousness

A number of other texts were added to the Goddess-movement's canon of scripture. These included Neumann's The *Great Mother*, Briffault's *The Mothers*, Harding's *Woman's Mysteries* and *The Way of All Women*, Robert Graves' *The White Goddess*, Elizabeth Gould Davis' *The First Sex*, and Helen Diner's *Mothers and Amazons*. All of these books take it for granted that Sun-god/Moon-goddess is "that which has been believed by all people at all times and in all places."[26] In consequence the women's spirituality movement right at the very beginning made a doctrinal commitment to the proposition *The Moon is always female*, and made it a shibboleth of political orthodoxy.

The effects of this on the feminist study of myth and religion have been dire. Sceptical inquiry, careful reasoning, intellectual discipline and factual accuracy are anathematised as so-called *Sun-consciousness* — men's way of thinking — and thrown out of the window in favour of Moon-consciousness, "fantasies, intuitions and dreams...[which are] more legitimate and more to be trusted than Sun-consciousness."[27] As a result the modern spiritual-feminist texts — books such as Monica Sjöö and Barbara Mor's *Great Cosmic Mother, Rediscovering the Religion of the Earth* and Barbara G. Walker's *A Woman's Encyclopaedia of Myths and Secrets* characteristically make no distinction between fact and speculation. So intensely garbled and confused are both of these books (*Great Cosmic Mother* reads like a cross between Von Däniken's *Chariots of the Gods* and Sellars and Yeatman's *1066 and All That*) that it would take a work thrice their respective lengths to even begin to disentangle, refute and correct the misinformation they contain.[28]

Moon-consciousness, it seems, absolves women from any responsibility to distinguish between truth and falsehood. Question-begging, circular argument, deletion of the agent (very common), using the word "all" when "some" is correct, unwarranted conclusions, outrageous generalisation, equivocation, deleting personal pronouns, compounded errors, wishful thinking, and every classic variety of false-logic technique proliferate on every page, to say nothing of factual inaccuracies and information stripped of every vestige of its context — all these techniques are used to grossly distort and misrepresent the history and content of mythology. All is sacrificed to the doctrinal need to see the Moon as female, and to avoid at all costs being contaminated by any of those things deemed to belong to the solar principle.

Yet many women read and accept such books uncritically. The important point is that, having sold out to the notion that intuition is the sufficient, proper way for women to think, we have played right into men's hands. We have voluntarily taken on that feminine mind which patriarchy has long defined for us.[29] This is precisely why men who wish to keep woman in her place are so keen that the idea Sun-god/Moon-goddess (and all that means in terms of so-called solar and lunar attributes) should not be subverted. By designating the critical faculty *solar* and *masculine*, such men clearly hope to keep it for themselves, and to discourage women from thinking too much. By assuring women that their True Feminine nature is in the realm of the intuitive, the vague, changeful and mysterious, the *status quo* can be safely maintained.

Do We Need The True Feminine?

The debt which feminist spirituality owes to the Victorian concept of angelic womanhood and the theories of C. G. Jung is quite obvious in the literature, particularly in the conception of masculine and feminine principles as static, universal archetypes, the attributes assigned to them, and the idea that similarities between myths signify universal truths. Yet these roots in Jungian psychology are rarely acknowledged, simply because the roots of the Goddess movement are rarely subjected to critical examination.

Jungian psychology always shies off from context, history, politics and other developmental aspects of myth. For Jungians, Sun-male and Moon-female operate independently of any such context, as *absolutes*, eternal and un-changeable. To preserve this paradigm from contamination by context and contradictory evidence, Jungians (such as Harding) are obliged to distort mythology, artificially enhancing similarities and suppressing differences, offering as 'evidence' spurious symbolic interpretations. Mythology becomes destiny; mythological means biological means natural means inevitable.[30] The Jungian hypothesis is one strand of a long tradition which constantly, even today, seeks to prove that there is a natural place for woman. And as in Jungian psychology, such attempts usually appear in the guise of helping woman to discover her *true feminine* nature. Historically, they are closely associated with attempts to prove that black people, Jews and other "inferior" races are happier if they are kept in their natural place. They are typically found in conservative and reactionary religio-political movements. Jungian psychology, whatever else may be said of it, is one of the methods by which our patriarchal western society seeks to curb and direct women's powers into acceptable channels and so to preserve the *status quo*.[31]

The "collective unconscious" is quite superfluous as an explanation of the similarities between myths. These common elements can be explained perfectly well in much simpler, more naturalistic ways. Some diffuse over extremely wide areas via migrations, conquest, intermarriage, missionary activity and the aston-ishing network of very ancient trade routes.[32] Others arise independently as common solutions to questions about nature, or as practical, obvious responses to life-events, natural dangers, the need for food and warmth, and so forth. They are never culture-independent, but belong inseparably to a social context, continually shifting their meaning with time and changing conditions. We can trace recurrent themes, but these too are dynamic and provisional. We cannot extract an essence and call it "The True Feminine," because this is an attempt to fix—to make static and eternal—one particular cultural ideal of femininity. The concept *Great Mother archetype* disables us in the face of social change; belief in it inevitably closes off certain possibilities for women, and promotes a sort of nostalgia, a reaction against the challenges and change inherent in our modern condition. It is not surprising that the rise of interest in the Goddess or the True Feminine coincided with the Christian fundamentalist revival of the 'seventies. Both are reactions, giving security against violent change.

We do not need the True Feminine, whether defined by Christians, Mus-lims, Jungians or modern spiritual-feminists. Woman's real sacredness and dignity must never be allowed to depend on religious definitions, especially not on a compulsory identification with Moon-goddesses. The dignity of woman subsists entirely in her dignity as a human being. Here the occurrence of Sun-goddesses in world myth is useful to us, for it subverts not only the Moon-is-female dogma, but, also many other narrow concepts of feminine and masculine.

Eclipse of the Sun

Chapter 4
The Paths of the Moon and the Sun

"The Sun is simple; the Moon is complex."

—Aubrey Burl[1]

One of the many ways in which mythic stories are created is through the attempts of ancient and tribal peoples to explain natural phenomena. Such explanations often show evidence of a close, careful observation of the natural world, of both the heavens and the earth. *Sun and Moon myths are universal,* regardless of whether a particular culture has a developed cult of sky-deities.[2] Even where the Sun and the Moon are not deities at all, they figure in myth and folklore.[3]

The movements and changes of Sun and Moon provoke certain questions. Why does the Moon change shape—or is there more than one Moon? Where does the Sun go at night (and what is it doing while it's there)? Has the Sun died at night? If so, is the next morning's Sun the same one reborn—or is it a different Sun each day? (Is there an infinite number of Suns under the earth?) Why does the Moon vanish from the skies altogether for several nights? Why does the Sun change colour? And (in the north) why does the Sun fail to appear at all for part of the year? Immediately a calculated guess is made, myth begins to be created— and since that is, too, an hypothesis based on observations, poetic or mythic early thought shares common roots with scientific inquiry.

The Sun's Yearly Cycle

For people in the twentieth century West, largely separated from Nature's changes and cycles, the Sun appears more or less the same every day—it rises in the east, "crosses the sky," and sets in the west. Actually, the Sun doesn't do this. It is only our modern out-of-touchness with Nature that allows the Sun to be described as "[the Moon-goddess's] unvarying and shackled consort [who runs] his monotonous and always-prescribed path across the sky."[4] In most climates and latitudes the Sun's path and appearance is manifestly not identical each day. Equatorial countries may see the Sun shining every day from cloudless skies, and during the course of the year not changing a very great deal in its rising and setting places, but as we move north or south things are very different.

In the northern hemisphere the summer Sun rises in the *north-east* and, staying in the sky for rather a long time, gets right over to the *north-west* before setting. By mid-winter it rises in the south-east and, without climbing up very far into the sky, sets shortly afterwards in the south-west.[5] These movements are very wide-ranging—my living room faces north, but receives sunshine first thing on summer mornings and last thing on summer evenings. The to-and-fro arcs of the Sun, over the course of the year, trace a labyrinth-like pattern.[6]

The Sun also changes its appearance at sunrise and sunset, when it is frequently blood-red, orange, pink or deep gold, depending on weather conditions. These can also make the Sun appear pearly, silver or white, or even a bluish shade, when veiled by thin cloud. All of these changes are noted and explained in mythology, along with myths about the change in the Sun's *heat*. Just as the Moon's light waxes and wanes, so during the course of the day does the Sun's warmth. The heat of noon has led to a number of myths claiming the Sun stands still when it reaches the top of the sky.

Sun of the Seasons

Primitive and ancient peoples knew that the Sun's changes through the year were associated with the seasons.[7] Indeed, *the Sun is directly responsible for the seasons*; as the Earth travels around the Sun, over the course of the year first one hemisphere and then the other receives solar radiation more directly, due to the tilt of the Earth's axis. This alternate warming and cooling brings spring and summer, then autumn and winter.[8]

People who need to know about the seasons for survival are well aware that, when the Sun moves north, fine weather, warmth, the regrowth of plants and other beneficial things are near. When it moves south, the weather gradually becomes cooler and nature slowly changes again in the course of the year's eternal cycle. It is not true to say that the Sun and the seasons are only important in this way to agricultural peoples. Among cultures like those of the Inuit (Eskimo) and the native Australians, the return of the Sun after the winter is associated with the migration of certain birds and animals and the regrowth of important food-plants. Thus myths and rites concerning the Sun's reappearance are found in every culture, from aboriginal to agricultural and urban.

The Sun Stands Still

When the Sun reaches the furthest point of its journey north or south, it seems to rise from the same place for three or four days before gradually edging south (or north). Hence the term *solstice* (Latin *solsistit*, "the sun is made to stand still."). The solstices are universally celebrated, with a holiday lasting for several days—not only because the Sun "stops" for this time, but also to include other events of importance (such as a particular phase of the Moon, or rites appeasing or purging winter demons) and to give everyone the chance to perform necessary rituals before the Sun starts on its journey once more.

In some mythologies the Sun "dies" at Winter Solstice and is reborn as a young deity who grows to maturity over the course of the year. In others, the Sun is eternally young. The Sun-goddess characteristically withdraws into a cave, mountain or beneath the earth at Winter Solstice, and has to be lured out or released by certain rites or games. When we come to the Sun's complete absence for part of the year, we are obviously dealing with northern ideas.[9] *The Sun is seen to descend into the Earth*, and it fails to appear again until spring, its reemergence being accompanied by light, warmth and the rebirth of Nature.[10] During the Sun's absence, the Moon (which never vanishes for months like this) is imagined to be deputizing for the Sun-goddess in the upper world, while she stays at home underground.

Some cultures are very specific about the length of time that a goddess spends underground.[11] Such goddesses are routinely classed as "Earth goddesses,"[12] yet it is precisely the heavenly bodies which seem to descend into the Earth, and specifically the *Sun* which vanishes for weeks or months, bringing new life to nature when it returns.[13]

The Night Journey of the Sun

Every evening the Sun appears to have been overcome by the power of darkness, yet it always emerges renewed and triumphant from its mysterious and perilous night journey. Mythology everywhere attempts to explain what happens to the Sun after it vanishes. Sometimes it is thought to have sunk into the sea; it descends into the underworld waters where it swims east, or is drawn by waterfowl, or rides through the underground waterways in a boat or a golden cup. It has crossed the great ocean to its own home, the island of the dead, which lies in the uttermost west, or it has fallen down a rock pit, or gone down a hole, or vanished into a mountain cave. It sleeps on a bed just out of sight below the horizon, or it is in its house under the earth, or visiting the underworld to give light and warmth to the dead. And sometimes the Sun itself dies each day; it drowns in the sea, or its fires run out of fuel and have to be relit next morning, or the sea-water extinguishes it, so that a fresh Sun has to be made every morning. These myths are very diverse, but certain motifs do recur, because given a disappearing Sun (and, of course a disappearing and changing Moon) there are always some rather obvious suggestions as to what may have happened, i.e., mythologically reasonable ones. The Sun does actually *look* as if it has gone down into the sea, or as if it has descended into the earth. We do not usually find arbitrary or nonsensical ideas—the Sun has not exploded, been abducted by a camel train, or gone late-night shopping.

The Phases of the Moon

Just as rites everywhere celebrate or try to assist the miracle of the Sun's daily renewal, so also do they celebrate the Moon's monthly resurrection, after the three mysterious dark nights when it fails to appear. While the Moon has no causal relationship to the seasons, its twenty-eight-day cycle of distinct phases has one outstanding usefulness—it can be used to keep a precise tally of days. This in turn leads to the possibility of *naming* individual days, and hence weeks and months. Thus lunar calendars are characteristically employed to fix religious festivals of every kind. This does not, however, mean that the Moon was therefore the principal deity—at most, it means that the Moon-god or goddess presided over *time*. Nor does it mean that a deity whose festival was timed by the Moon was therefore a Moon-deity. If a culture knows nothing but a lunar calendar, then *all* deities necessarily have festivals timed this way—gods and goddesses of herding, war, weaving and everything else.

Why the Moon should change shape at all, is a question which most mythologies answer in terms of the absolutely obvious. The Moon is growing fat, then growing thin, just like a human being. Or it is gradually being eaten away by a disease, or nibbled by animals, or devoured piece by piece by a demon. Sometimes the Moon is imagined as a sort of vessel which fills up with a liquid (almost invariably water, semen, or a herbal sap which brings ecstasy and immortality) which is then spilt, or its contents used up. The Moon can also swell up with the souls of the dead (which the Moon-deity may actually devour) before they are sent back to Earth for reincarnation. The Moon quite often "shrinks" from fear, embarrassment, or in an attempt to hide, gradually showing its face when the danger is past. Another motif describes the Moon's phases as dismemberment of the deity, who is hewn to pieces with an axe or sword.

During the three dark nights, the Moon is absent from the sky in one of two places—either he is wandering about as an invisible entity on the earth itself, characteristically dallying with mortal women during their sleep (after this encounter they wake to find that they are menstruating—the Moon-god's attentions are very commonly seen in this fashion, as a kind of monthly defloration), or he is underground. Down there, he meets with and makes love with his wife (or sister) the Sun. Quite often the Moon is imagined to grow from a child to an old man over the lunar month, finally dying and spending three days and nights in the earth before being resurrected as a young child, the new crescent. Tribal myths explaining human mortality commonly make reference to such a belief.

Lunar and Solar Calendars

In the Indo-European and some other languages the word for Moon is etymologically related to words for *measurement* . The complications of the lunar cycles could only be worked out by the careful keeping of records, the construction of basic observatories, and taking of measurements. Simple tally-sticks marking the passage of solar and lunar days were not enough. But all the lunar measurements in the world could not solve one important calendrical problem—*the Moon's cycles do not determine the seasons*, and a purely lunar calendar will inevitably move out of synchronization with what is happening in Nature. The ancient Romans met this problem with their lunar calendar. By 50 B.C. it was so out-of-step with the seasons that the vernal equinox fell on the Ides of May, eight weeks too late.

> "It was necessary to make a fundamental break with tra-
> ditional reckoning to devise an efficient seasonal calendar."[14]

Lunar calendars are rare, because of this very problem. Almost all the calendars claimed by modern Moon-religionists to be lunar are in fact *lunisolar*, with various multiples of twenty-eight day months adjusted to fit the seasons by the addition of *intercalary days* . The claim is made from a point of view of religious ideology, but calendars are not holy or unholy, they are simply more or less useful. Calendrical reckoning is an immensely complex subject. Its perennial problems continue to tax human ingenuity.[15]

The Solar Trinity

Sun-goddess mythologies constantly attest to ancient and primitive observation of the Sun's daily journey, personifying her in rising, midday and setting aspects, remarking the daily increase and decrease of her heat and light. This is one of the many ways in which a *trinity* arises in myth, folklore and religion. Like the lunar trinity of waxing, full and waning Moon, it expresses a religious sense of completeness and balance, a satisfying feeling of beginnings, middles and endings, which assures the community and individual of continuing cosmic order. This triple rhythm is eagerly sought and commemorated in myth wherever and whenever it is found.

The agricultural day in particular was marked out by the Sun's three stages, so that we frequently discover rites or prayers for sunrise, noon and sunset. Where people have neither clocks nor sundials, the time of day is still judged by the position of the Sun relative to familiar objects—a large tree, hill, church spire or temple roof[16]—not so useful a method in the northern hemisphere! Until quite recently shepherds in Britain knew how to tell the night-hours by moonrise, moonset and the movements of the stars,[17] a skill also familiar to sailors and those nomads who travel by night. The pre-Islamic Arabs and the native Australians gave an important place in their religion to the stars, for in those countries the vast open spaces and clear skies emphasize the magnificence of the heavenly bodies. The Semitic and Indo-European tradition of beginning a 'day' from sunset (rather than from midnight, as we do now) originates in nomadic societies when people would travel during the cool night, pitching camp at dawn and resting, cooking, etc. during the day.[18] Thus the primitive Moon-god is very often the guardian deity of travellers.

Temples of Sun and Moon

When the positions of Sun or Moon were fixed by reference to features in the locality, the next step was to build something permanent, to align it with various solar and lunar positions, and so to keep a record of these patterns and perhaps obtain the favour of the deities at the same time. Many of the megalithic monuments in Europe appear to have been purposely aligned in this way, some to the Sun, others to the Moon and yet others to both, although the lunar alignments are less certain, because there are so many more lunar positions to choose from (and hence more chance of mere coincidence).[19] When such monuments are aligned to the Sun, writers always automatically assume the worship of a Sun-god.[20] Yet one of the most famous sites, the tumulus of New Grange in Ireland, is ornamented with what are clearly goddess symbols. On the four days of the mid-winter solstice, the rising Sun shines through a specially-designed quartz "roof-box" and down through the long, narrow passage to illuminate a triple spiral within the central chamber. The usual explanation is that this is a cosmic sex-act, the Sun-god (who seems to have a very long thin weedy penis) penetrating the vagina of Mother Earth—the tomb-mound being, of course, her swelling belly. The problem with this is not its sheer unimaginativeness, but its dead-end thinking—it fails to connect with any known motifs in solar mythology (the famous Sun-ray penis is a constructive interpretation, not found in actual mythology, where it is always the *storm-god* who fertilises the Earth-mother with *rain*) and helps us understand nothing about the possible meanings of this complex building. Martin Brennan's exquisitely illustrated *The Boyne Valley Vision*, which conveys the beauty of the tomb's many carvings far better than photographs, comes very close to an alternative explanation. He actually recounts part of Amaterasu's story, describing how this Sun-goddess withdraws into a cave at solstice-time and has to be lured out again by elaborate ritual and bonfires. Yet, later, he dismisses the idea that the triple spiral could be a goddess-symbol, because the greatness of New Grange shows that it must have been something much more important, i.e., than a goddess. Given such breathtaking misogyny, it is scarcely surprising that Brennan opts for the cosmic sex-act theory, although unlike the Sun-goddess myth it fails to explain, for example, why bonfires were lit opposite the entrance of New Grange, or what connection goddess symbols might have with the Sun in this context of a death-cult. When we realise that several primitive Sun-goddesses are believed to nurture the dead during the Sun's night journey through the underworld, the association with the the death-cult becomes clearer. As the reader will discover, the details of Sun-goddess cults cast a great deal of light on such puzzles as New Grange, whereas the reduction of the Sun to a male god having intercourse with the Earth *closes the question* and allows us no lateral, creative thinking. It helps us understand nothing—which is hardly surprising, because it isn't true.[21]

The idea that the stars and planets reach into our minds and affect our bodies is still current in twentieth century life. Is that belief founded in fact?

Eclipse of the Sun

40

Chapter 5
Holy Blood, Holy Moon

"The difference between science and codswallop is real, if not always that evident. Science is what impels us to find out if something might be or clearly isn't the case. Codswallop is what tells us that things can just as easily be one thing or another, and there's no telling which and so we might just as well forget about it and believe whatever pleases us the most."

—Ralph Estling

"Were the old religions expressive of objective scientific truth...? ...The evidence is that the woman's cycle is probably naturally related to the moon's cycle, but even if it were not, there are indications that she has the ability so to relate it, if she wishes."[1]

—Penelope Shuttle and Peter Redgrove

One of the most striking and recurrent elements in world religion is the association of women's monthly cycle with the Moon. In virtually every tribal culture, menstrual bleeding is imagined as the visible result of an invisible encounter—sexual intercourse with the Moon, who is almost invariably a *masculine* deity among primitive peoples.[2] He characteristically descends to earth during the three moonless nights to woo (or violate) mortal women, sometimes abducting them in their sleep and then returning them to earth after a night of passion, when they wake to find blood, as if they had been newly deflowered. Hence traditions arise which say that a goddess or woman renews her virginity each month. When, in later times, the Moon came to be thought of as female, such goddesses were confused with the Moon itself, although they are much more likely to have started life as the Sun-goddess whose love-affair with the Moon-god was regarded as the primordial mating. This was reenacted each month when both Sun and Moon were absent from the sky together, beneath the earth. In some of the tribal myths describing this encounter, the Sun smears the Moon-god's face with her own menstrual blood, thus causing the marks we see on the Moon. Whereas in earlier times each mortal woman was thus a Sun-goddess, visited once a month and mystically deflowered by the menstruation-causing Moon-god, her lover, in later times—with the reversal of Sun and Moon's sex—the association of Moon and menstruation became much more vague and general. Even Briffault remarks on the near-total absence of lunar motifs from many so-called Moon-goddesses.[3] The earlier causal relationship between Moon-god and menstruation has become an unclear "influence" or "control" or symbolic analogy. Although we find endless examples in world mythology of the Moon filling up (and emptying) with *water* or *semen* (or even souls awaiting reincarnation), we do not find examples of the Moon swelling with menstrual blood and discharging again.[4] *Clear causal relationships* between the Moon and menstruation always involve the Moon as a *masculine* agent.

But all this belongs to the realm of myth and old traditions. Is there any factual basis in Nature's workings, to account for the religious belief that the Moon influences menstruation? Before trying to answer this question, it is worthwhile to look at our popular beliefs about the Moon, not only those of modern Moon-worshippers but also of the man or woman in the street.

The Transylvania Effect

As everyone knows, the full Moon encourages certain people to turn into werewolves, while Count Dracula and his associates like to be out-and-about in the moonlight. Even normal people go funny at full Moon, and as for psychopaths and other unstable individuals, the full Moon provokes them to frenzy. Traffic and industrial accidents proliferate, bright students fluff their exams, women go into labour, marriages break down, gunmen go on the rampage, people dream more (of white animals, pearls, balloons, white grand pianos, etc.), suicides increase, people get sexually excited, dogs and cats come on heat, and there are more crimes of violence and admissions to hospital. This claimed lunar influence has been termed by some scientists *the Transylvania effect.*[5]

If it is real, then the Transylvania effect has important implications for our lives. This has led a number of scientists to study the purported connection between lunar phase and human behaviour. The overwhelming weight of evidence shows that the Moon has *no effect whatever* on madness, birth, accidents or any other aspect of human life. Professors of psychology Ivan Kelly and James Rotton, together with the astronomer Roger Culver, reviewed all the literature on the supposed lunar effect, including the work of scientists who claimed to have found a link. They conclude that there is no such thing as the Transylvania effect, human behaviour being quite independent of lunar phase.[6]

Invariably, when a study which claims to show a special influence of the Moon is closely examined, a number of typical flaws appear—the experiment is badly designed, so as to produce equivocal results, or the results have been improperly analysed, or those conducting the experiment (or taking part in it) have allowed their beliefs about the Moon to influence their collection of data.[7] Those who believe that the Moon influences humans have been shown to pay more attention to incidents that appear to confirm their belief, while ignoring the same incidents when they fail to coincide with the preferred lunar phase.[8] Such pseudoscientific data is easily shown up when other workers, recording impartially, *fail to replicate* the results of the experiment.

The Powers of the Moon

Spiritual-feminists and neopagans make some huge claims for the influence of the Moon on planet Earth and its living things. Virtually all of these are classic pseudoscience, muddleheaded and crackpot ideas which do not deserve serious consideration:

> "The ancient people believed, with their usual biological accuracy, that the Moon-mother created human society. If the moon were to vanish, all mental activity on earth would cease."[9]

There is no conceivable way that one could test such an assertion, since we cannot "remove" the Moon, and even if we could, the "cessation of all mental activity" would presumably mean we wouldn't be able to realise the result if true.

Such absurd claims rely for their success on mental activity having already ceased in the reader. Here, at the lunatic fringe of modern Moon-religion, the wilder the claim, the better:

> "Moon and menstrual experience are referred to in language,

science and mythology in terms which suppose them to be linked as the founders of civilizations and mental experience."[10]

The Moon is also supposed to cause the seasons and the weather, to be an absolute necessity for all fertility,[11] to shine by its own light,[12] and to cause the growth of plants. All of these are *untrue*—both the seasons and the weather are *solar*, not lunar phenomena, likewise the growth of plants; the Moon shines by its own light only in the same sense that it is made of green cheese and apart from certain marine animals whose reproductive cycles are linked to the tides, fertility is unrelated to the Moon.[13]

When writers make such claims, they attribute them to one of three things; lunar light, lunar gravity, or an unknown psychic force, *lunar energy*, which is supposed to emanate from the Moon.

Moonlight or Moonshine?

Many people speak of the Moon's phases as if the Moon *itself* really changes through the month, its actual substance shrinking or expanding. But the Moon stays the same, whatever its phase, and exactly the same "amount" of Moon crosses the sky. What we see from Earth is the changing illumination of the Moon, depending on how much of it is lit up by sunlight. As the Moon goes round the Earth and the Earth around the Sun, their changing positions relative to each other mean that we see first the crescent, then more and more of the Moon illuminated until full Moon, and then the sequence is reversed.[14]

Moonlight is always sunlight, weakened and slightly polarized by being reflected from the Moon's surface. Modern Moon-worshippers *moonbathe* at night, to allow the body to absorb so-called lunar energies. But, as far as light is concerned, there is no such thing as "lunar energy"—all moonlight is *solar* energy. Now, there is no reason why weak sunlight of this kind should have any special benefits, nor any reason why it should be able to compete with other sources of night-time illumination, such as fluorescent strip-lighting. The biologist Edmund Dewan, who specializes in studies of natural rhythms, used a shaded light-bulb to represent the Moon, in his study of the human menstrual cycle. His experimental subject found that her periods seemed to be regularized by sleeping in this "artificial moonlight" on the 14th, 15th and 16th days of her cycle.[15]

Leaving aside the objection that one would need to test a large sample of women under much more stringently controlled conditions than this, to be able to make any claims about night-time illumination and women's periods, this experiment does not tell us anything about the Moon, but about light-bulbs. It starts out from the assumption that an artificial light source, reflecting from walls and ceiling, accurately reproduces sunlight reflected from the Moon. This is not necessarily so. In any case, such light could equally well be acting to extend day-length—indeed, the action of day-length in causing hormonal changes is well known. Daylight stimulates the brain through the eye, causing the release of hormones which in turn affect the master-gland, the pituitary, which governs the reproductive cycles. Thus lengthening days, for example, brings about the hormonal changes required for birds to breed. In the northern hemisphere these changes therefore coincide with our spring and summer, with the plentiful insect food needed for the young, and the long days needed to collect it. These hormonal changes and breeding patterns *have* to be linked to the Sun's movements for natural, practical reasons of survival, and so it is with other animals who reproduce seasonally.[16]

The effect of day-length on human female hormones has also been realised. Women who suffer from depression during the winter months have been successfully treated using artificial ("full spectrum") daylight lamps. The depression is believed to be caused by hormonal imbalance resulting from lack of sunlight. If a woman is kept in total darkness for some time, her periods will stop altogether.[17]

It is sometimes claimed that Dewan's lunar light-bulb effect works equally well if the bulb is shut in a cupboard, purportedly because the bulb produces an unknown emanation like the unknown emanation from the Moon. Unfortunately this means that the real Moon must also be producing an "emanation" which passes through walls and doors—thus raising the question why the real Moon does not regularize periods no-matter-what. Moonlight and light-bulbs are quite redundant if the actual lunar influence is some unknown force passing through solid objects, and therefore easily penetrating drawn curtains, clothes or cloud-cover. (And what about the influence of the Moon in the daytime sky?)

Madame Minerva Gravity[18]

There *is* an invisible lunar force, but there is nothing unknown or mysterious about it—it is just plain ordinary gravity. Almost all writers making claims about the Moon's influence attribute it in large part to gravity, the idea being that the lunar gravitational pull, because it is powerful enough to raise vast bodies of water in the tides of Earth's oceans, must therefore have an enormous effect on puny little humans.[19] Our body fluids must surely be helpless in the grip of such a mighty force. No wonder the Moon causes madness and suicides!

This could hardly be further from the truth. In crude terms, the bigger the object, the bigger the Moon's gravitational pull on it. It pulls the Earth *fifty trillion times* harder than it pulls you. What you describe as your "weight" is really a measure of how much Earth's gravity pulls on your body. In comparison to this the Moon's tidal force on you is infinitesimally tiny—all in all, less than the effect of a mosquito sitting on your shoulder. Another consideration is the distance of the Moon—it's too far away to do more than this. Nearby objects in the room in which you are sitting exert a tidal force on you that is millions of times greater than that of the Moon. Even this book in your hand out-pulls the Moon by tens of thousands of times.[20]

The wateriness of human body fluids is also quite irrelevant, for two reasons—firstly, the Moon's gravity acts equally on solids and liquids alike. The reason the sea-tides are conspicuous is because water is fluid—it can move and we can see it move, in contrast to the solid earth which is also deformed by the Moon's pull, but only by about twenty centimetres in total—a bulge which we just don't see.[21] The second reason is that, like the Mediterranean with its almost non-existent tides, the fluids of the body are landlocked. They simply cannot respond in a tidal fashion, for there is nowhere for them to go—tides happen only in *unbounded* bodies of water which are free to slosh around. And as we have already seen, the Moon's gravitational pull on the human individual is so infinitesimally minute that it could not affect human body fluids in any case.[22]

It is important for non-biologists to realise that the bloodstream and cerebro-spinal fluid are not just haplessly sitting at the mercy of any external force—they are maintained by constant vigilance on the part of internal body systems, which do a very good job of keeping the inner environment in a steady state. This state of internal balance, the body's harmony, is called *homeostasis*, and its complex mechanisms evolved to preserve the organism against much more disruptive forces than the imperceptible tug of the far-off Moon.[23] There is a constant tendency in neopagan literature to speak of the Moon in astrological terms, as a strong, ineluctable force, a supernatural entity which has living things by the scruff:

> "The moon also controls the fluids of the human body, and
> the brain, as the moistest part of all, was particularly subject
> to its influences... We do feel the lunar tides in our bodies,
> and the water in our bodies 'sees' the moon as the crystalline
> structures of water alter or resonate with the moon passing
> overhead."[24]

All this is just so much nonsense, just plain *wrong* at every single point. The belief that the Moon "controls" us in any way can only be maintained by ignoring or rejecting Nature herself, and her actual ways of working.

The Moon and Menstruation

Exactly how similar is women's cycle to that of the Moon? Actually, it is a poor match. There are two sorts of lunar month—the sidereal month of 27½ days which is the time the Moon takes to orbit the Earth, and the synodic month of 29½ days, the extra time being needed for it to go back to its starting point relative to the Sun.[25] The menstrual month varies widely among individual women (short 14-day cycles and long 35-day ones are not uncommon) but the average, and the cycle enjoyed by a few women who menstruate perfectly regularly, is 28 days.

> "If the Moon's phases and the tidal rhythm has some con-
> nection with the menstrual rhythm, then they ought to
> match perfectly, but they don't... the length of the menstrual
> period is quite irregular in a Universe in which the cycle of
> the Moon's phases is very regular."[26]

The standard spiritual-feminist objection to this is that, as modern, unspiritual people, we are not *attuned* to the Moon. Women are said to suffer from variable, non-lunar menstrual cycles because we are divorced from the lunar rhythms, because we have been duped by the 'solar' intellect and hence cannot receive lunar benefits. This is a circular argument. Why do we not menstruate with the lunar cycle? Because we are not attuned to the Moon. How do we know we are not attuned to the Moon? Because we don't menstruate with the lunar cycle!

While some authors claim that there are "*huge* statistics [*sic*] claiming that menstruation is more common at new and full moon" (although the same authors fail to give huge examples of any)[27] impartial studies have failed to show any such correlation. Each day just under 4% of women potentially able to menstruate, actually begin a period. This percentage does not suddenly shoot up at new or full Moon.[28] Spiritual-feminist literature is full of anecdotes by indi-vidual women claiming that, by attuning to the Moon, they start to menstruate at New Moon, and that so would all women, if they approached the Moon with belief and respect.[29] There is, however, a simple explanation for this. The menstrual cycle, because of the close connection of endocrine system and brain, is very susceptible to emotional and psychological interference. Practically every woman has had the experience of her period turning up, out of the blue, to coincide with her holiday, or a special occasion. Anticipation, strong emotional arousal, intensely pleasant or unpleasant shocks, can all alter the menstrual clock. There is no doubt that women who make a fuss or obsess about the Moon's influence on their periods, performing emotional rituals and concentrated meditations to attune to its supposed force, will be able to alter their periods to fit their strongly-held beliefs. (One thing is certain, and that is that women who tried this and failed will not report their failure in the literature.) By exactly the same technique a woman could, in theory, time her periods to coincide with the arrival of her monthly bank statement, or the publication of *Good House-keeping*.

Myth and Menstruation

If menstruation is neither caused by the Moon, nor even associated with it in any natural, real or intelligible sense, then why the mythological connection between the two? The answer is that it is a *false analogy*, based on a superficial resemblance between the lunar month and the menstrual month.[30] When ancient and primitive peoples sought meaning, order and unity in their world, they noted these kinds of similarities and correspondences, not worrying at all about how approximate they were. The important thing was to organize Nature's profuseness and capricious behaviour into an intelligible system, in which everyone and everything had a secure place. This was based on the *seen* aspects of Nature. Nobody had any reason to suspect, say, the existence of an unseen and underlying biochemical world. Thus the ancients declared certain sorts of vegetable to be masculine entities, because they looked vaguely like a penis, or they said that bats were birds because they both fly. Even today, this simplistic and quite false way of thinking is given credence as disclosing real information about Nature. In the Orient, rhinoceros horn powder is believed to be a cure for impotence, because the horn is supposed to resemble the erect penis. In Europe, country women still think that if a hare crosses a pregnant woman's path, her child will be born with a hare lip. In the West, modern Moon-worshippers still think that the approximation between the Moon's and women's cycles means the Moon causes periods.

There is a way in which the modern person, faced with the facts of these old mistakes, can salvage something of her intellectual conscience, and that is by bringing in a *spiritualizing* explanation. Yes, the cucumber and the penis, the Moon and periods, the hare and the cleft palate, are really connected, but on a *higher level or sphere*. According to this idea there is an ineffable *masculine principle* which expresses itself on the "merely material" level as the vegetable marrow, Cruise missile, Christmas cracker, penis, clarinet, spear, gun, sun-ray and so forth. The *feminine principle* expresses itself as cups, pots, bowls, ovens, round fruits, wet things, the Moon and anything hollow or womblike.[31] When scientists investigate the actual workings of Nature—particularly when they discover that religious or paranormal claims are false—they can then be said to be operating on the "merely material" level, where they supposedly have no chance of comprehending how the Moon causes menstruation. This is the ideal let-out clause for anyone who wants to go on believing something in the teeth of all the contradictory evidence. It allows the individual to remove the Moon-and-menstruation question to a realm where it is quite safe from checking, testing or any kind of intelligent inquiry:

> "If you deal with some unknown, undetected force, you can make it responsible for anything at all, and there would be no way of telling whether some particular statement you make about it is true or false."[32]

It is rather as if the person who believed the Moon to be made of green cheese, were to say, when presented with incontrovertible evidence that it is rock, "Ah, yes, but the Moon is made of *psychic* cheese!" This is certainly one way of having one's cheese and eating it.

The connection between menstruation and the Moon is a product of human myth-making. I'll leave the last word to the science writer Isaac Asimov:

> "Perhaps it gives [women] a feeling of importance to imagine a connection with the Moon that men don't have. However, that's a non-existent connection, and it's my own opinion that women are quite wonderful enough in their own right to require no support from a superstitious illusion."[33]

Chapter 6
The Sun, the Moon and Mother Earth
Celestial Influences and the World of Nature

"Prior beliefs constitute the emotional commitment that
makes pseudoscientific ideas, no matter how preposterous,
appealing and satisfying. Believers are unconcerned about
the scientific absurdities of pseudoscience, not because
they are incapable of understanding them... but rather,
because they have been previously committed to a world
view in which meaning and purpose take precedence over
precision and accuracy. Thus, extraordinary explanations
persist because people want to believe them."

—Leonard Zusne and Warren H. Jones[1]

Ancient myth and folklore often attribute to the Moon roles in Nature which
we now know belong to the Sun. But, while myth and folklore are pervasive
and long-lasting, passed down easily by word of mouth and traditional usage,
scientific understanding of Nature's workings needs more time and effort to
grasp. Thus society is less permeable to it. Even today, otherwise well-informed
people take for granted folk-beliefs about biology which have no basis in the way
Nature herself goes about things.

Lunar Energy

A very popular belief is that the Moon, by producing some mysterious,
subtle "lunar energy," actually powers the life and growth processes of the

whole living world, in contrast to the Sun, which (especially in 'hot countries') is inimical to all life. At best, the Sun's role is confined to "helping" crops to ripen,[2] and "germinating the seed," although some writers even deny the Sun's role in germination.[3]

Traditional gardening and farming lore in many parts of the world reckons sowing, planting and harvesting times by the phase of the Moon. The waxing and full Moon are good times for harvesting and planting, because then the crop will increase with the Moon.

On the other hand, wood is usually cut, or grain harvested, during a waning Moon, because as the Moon empties itself of water (an explanation of its waning condition) so the wood or grain will be drier.[4] Peaches, cabbage, root-vegetables, etc., are gathered as the Moon is "filling up," to be bigger and juicier.

A moment's reflection should tell us that this is *sympathetic magic*, based on a false analogy between the Moon's perceived "increase" and the desired increase of crops. The magical idea is expanded in mythology into a personified Moon-deity, whose mysterious influence reaching Earth via moonbeams, or in the dew believed to drip from the Moon, puts the vital energy of life and growth into plants, or fertilizes mortal women.

Modern alternative writers on green religion and ecology also postulate *Earth-energies*, which are said to be inherent in the soil's property of darkness, or the Earth's occult powers. These energies are thought to cause seeds to germinate, and the Earth to bring forth vegetation.[5]

The Solar-Powered Cabbage

Is all this true? Does the beaming Moon nurture plants and make them grow? Does Earth's vital energy come from the Moon?

The short answer is "Not at all." The long answer would more than fill this book! The vital energy which powers the whole of the living world, which lies at the beginning of all food chains and hence of all ecological relationships, comes from the *Sun*. Humans have only recently learnt how to make use of solar energy, in the form of solar-powered cars, calculators and so forth. But we still cannot do what plants have been doing for at least six thousand million years, ever since algae first appeared in the sea—and that is to capture solar energy in food, to turn *light* energy into *chemical* energy.

This process is called *photosynthesis*. It starts off when sunlight shines on green leaves. The plant uses this solar energy to split the water molecule—giving hydrogen and oxygen. Now, oxygen is a plentiful by-product. The plant takes a little for its own needs, but the rest is just thrown out as rubbish. Well—not quite—for it is this oxygen which the whole of the rest of the living world needs to breathe. At this moment you are respiring using oxygen, say, from your house plants, from your front lawn, from the algae of the wide oceans, from the rain-forests of the Amazon—from plants all over the Earth. *Oxygen depends on photosynthesis depends on the Sun.*

Back to the leaves. The plant hungrily takes in carbon dioxide gas from the air (the same gas that you are busy breathing out, and the civilized world is busy producing at a faster rate than plants can cope with) and uses it, along with the hydrogen, like a biological Lego-kit. Every plant is programmed (by its inherited genes) with the biochemical know-how to build what it needs to live—glucose, sucrose, starch are some of the basics. Add minerals from the soil, and proteins and other more complicated things can be made. All of this activity is ultimately solar-powered. It all begins with that vital solar energy, transformed by the plant into chemical energy. The whole of the living world—everything that's not itself a photosynthesizing plant—obtains its energy at second-hand from plants.

That was the merest sketch of photosynthesis—a rather junior-school sort of account.[6] And now a simple version of the opposite, complementary process— *respiration.* While the obvious physical evidence of this is 'breathing,' actually all living things respire—it's a chemical activity which goes on in every cell of your body, making that one-time-solar-energy available for all your body's needs—keeping warm, thinking, blinking, running for a bus, mending a cut finger—absolutely *everything.*

Respiration needs oxygen plus a fuel for the oxygen to work on. For most humans and animals this means carbohydrates. The body cells quite literally burn this fuel to liberate the energy it contains[7]—energy which once belonged to the Sun. There's a by-product, and that is *carbon dioxide.* The same kind of process on a bigger, cruder, messier, less controlled scale—bonfires, power stations, motor-car engines—also frees energy for our uses and gives carbon dioxide, but Nature is unable to cope with this abuse of her natural systems, and we have the *greenhouse effect*—global warming—as a result. This is not due to any wickedness inherent in the Sun,[8] but to human interference with the natural balance.

When the natural world is in balance, photosynthesis and respiration involve plants and animals in a mutually beneficial swap— oxygen for carbon dioxide, carbon-dioxide for oxygen. Water, carbon-dioxide and oxygen are the fundamentals of life on Earth, but without solar energy they are useless.

Every living process depends on the Sun. If it were suddenly to "go out," or clouds of dust (e.g. the result of nuclear warfare) were to obscure it, a terrible winter would descend on the Earth, like that prophesied in old Icelandic writings, when the Sun-goddess *Sunna* is finally swallowed by the demon wolf, her pursuer.[9] Without the Sun's heat, our planet would freeze into a sterile wilderness. Our seasons and the whole world's weather-systems would be chaotically disrupted, for winds, sea-currents and climate are all dependent on the Sun.[10]

Without the Sun, plants could not photosynthesize—hence oxygen production would stop, carbon-dioxide rise unchecked, and food chains would be without a food supply. Without the Sun, all life on earth would perish.

The Fire of the Sun

Photosynthesis has tremendous implications for our everyday lives. As you read this book, every move you make and every thought you think is ultimately solar-powered. The warmth of your body is none other than that same energy, and if you are sitting beside a fire, that too is shining with the light and heat of past summer suns, whether of the Sun which shone millions of years ago on the coal-measure forests of the Carboniferous era, or upon the ancient seas, or that which shone on trees familiar to you in your own lifetime. The 'fire' in fuel, in coal or oil or wood, in human and animal bodies, in bread and butter and living plants, is not lunar but *solar*. In this case, the cultures who thought fire came from the Moon got it wrong, but there is good reason to believe that Moon-goddesses who personified fire, or owned it, were previously Sun-goddesses. There is one important property of fire which the Moon conspicuously lacks, and that is *heat*. For this reason Hebrew tradition, for example, said the Moon was made from light and the Sun from fire,[11] and northern traditions habitually make the Moon *cold*, the abode and source of ice and snow, while the Sun is *hot*, the source of earthly fire.

The Dual Character of the Sun

The Sun, as everyone knows, has a dual character. It is the great life-giver, it cheers people's lives, its warming rays bring joy to humans and animals alike. Yet it is dangerous, for its heat evaporates the water on which all life depends, and its ultra-violet rays disrupt parts of the living cell, causing mutations which can sometimes be useful in Nature, but which can also lead to cancer. For the same reason, sunlight kills bacteria, both purifying and bleaching materials such as cloth—hence strong sunlight was one of the world's first antiseptics. Sunlight is singularly effective in healing certain skin diseases. There are many examples of 'solarized' water being used to magically treat skin complaints, and our English belief in washing the face in the May-dew at the moment of sunrise to gain a beautiful complexion, comes from the same kind of thinking.[12]

There is a persistent notion that the Sun in the north gives life, but in "hot countries" (it is not quite clear what is meant by this—it seems be be a cover-all term for the sort of places white Europeans go on holiday) the Sun does exactly the opposite and destroys life. This is a false dualism. Life *everywhere* depends utterly on the Sun, even in the most arid and burning deserts. But life also depends utterly on water, which fierce sunlight rapidly evaporates. A *desert* is defined, not by the amount of strong sunshine it receives, but by its *lack of water*. Creatures which live in deserts have had to make a serious evolutionary compromise, e.g., the various sorts of cactus, which have reduced their water loss by giving up leaves. But they have to photosynthesize just the same—they need solar energy every bit as much as the birch trees of a Siberian forest. The result is a short, tubby, leafless *stalk*.

In the most arid of the world's deserts there grows a strange plant called *Fenestraria*. To reduce water loss it lives buried in the sand. Not a good idea for plant, as it needs the Sun to live, so Nature has provided it with a small, glazed window which peeps through the sand surface like the pavement skylight of an old-fashioned pub basement. (You can grow *Fenestraria* in a greenhouse, but it is so adapted to the blazing desert Sun that our northern sunlight is too weak for it, and so it has a tendency to rot.) Desert animals likewise show marvellous adaptations, preserving them against the fierce solar rays and reducing water loss, but every single one of these creatures receives its food and vital energy via a food-chain beginning with the Sun.[13]

In the actual tropics, where water is plentiful, plants cheerfully photosynthesize at a terrific rate without being troubled at all by the intense sunshine. The world's most highly productive land plants are tropical grasses, like maize and sugar cane. So long as a plant has sufficient water, "hot countries" and maximum sunlight are simply wonderful; life flourishes there in unbelievable luxuriance, the great tropical rain forests being the prime example.

The Sun at Night

There is another misconception about Sun and Moon that goes like this: things which happen during the day are vaguely "governed" by the Sun, or even more vaguely "associated with" the Sun, so those which go on at night must be "controlled" by the Moon. This is another false dualism. Sun and Moon are in no sense equivalents of each other—they do not have an equal and complementary role in Nature, neither astronomically nor biologically. By day and by night the primary energy source for all life is the Sun.

Now, it is a popular idea in folklore that the Moon makes plants grow at night. Plants do indeed use the hours of darkness to transport, metabolize and assimilate the chemicals they made during the day, but that does not mean that such activity is lunar-powered. On the contrary, like every other energy-requiring process in living things, the energy which drives it comes from the Sun. The plant uses that very energy which it captured from sunlight during the day. Plant growth which occurs at night, therefore, is due ultimately to solar, not lunar power.

Rising Sap

A rather similar idea is the belief that plant "sap," a vague general term (actually sap or fluid in plants is of several, importantly-different kinds), is somehow drawn up by the Moon, like the tides, so that plants get juicier as the Moon waxes and more flaccid as it wanes. Another false analogy.

Like human body fluids, those of the plant are not free to respond tidally, even if the Moon's gravitational force were immensely greater than it actually is. The smaller the living thing, the smaller the Moon's gravitational pull on it, and it isn't strong enough to raise a cupful of sap to the top of an average oak-tree, let alone affect fluids in something as small as a herb like parsley or lavender.

Water-movement and relationships in the plant rely on basically simple, mechanical processes. The Moon has about as much to do with it as the middle name of your Member of Parliament. Just as in the human body, the plant has its own internal harmony, with various ways of keeping that state steady, and it would be quite disastrous for the plant if the Moon were to affect its water-relationships in the way supposed. The waning Moon in particular would be a *killer*, plants would wilt, and there would be no way of reviving them. Wilted (flaccid) plants close their pores and are unable to take in carbon dioxide or do photosynthesis. A Moon which had this effect would cause a major ecological crisis for fourteen days out of every twenty-eight. Plants show *no evidence whatever* of evolutionary adaptation to such violent lunar disruptions.

"Sap" is actually of two basic sorts (in the sense that the layman uses the word). One is water, coming up from the soil through the tissues called "wood." Wood fibres are dead, like your hair or fingernails. To get the many gallons needed to the top of a tall tree, Nature uses a marvellous, simple, straightforward method called *transpiration*. This is solar-powered. Water evaporating from leaves in the Sun's warmth pulls up a long, connected series of water molecules (something like the water going up a drinking-straw) which runs right from roots to shoots—no fuss, no mess, and no lunar emanations required.

The other sort of sap circulates just below the plant's skin, in intensely-alive cells.[14] It transports upwards, downwards and in both directions at once all those chemicals the plant makes for itself from simple raw materials and solar energy. (If you peel vegetables, it's this living tissue and its goodness that can get wasted.) Now, this sap flow needs energy to work, but it isn't the non-existent "lunar energy," just the plain honest-to-goodness solar kind, captured during photosynthesis.

Herbs and the Moon

Folkloric herbalists and occultists are concerned to gather their herbs at certain phases of the Moon—when waxing, the Moon is supposed to encourage the maximum yield of therapeutic oils, etc., either by some unknown, untestable occult influence, or by "drawing them up" through lunar gravity, or just sympathetic magic—more Moon, more oils.

As we have already seen, the lunar gravity theory is a non-starter. But even if it were not, the products herbalists prize—such as oils, gums and resins—are for the most part totally immobilized in special cells. It is not in the plant's interests to transport them or let them flow around anywhere, for they are generally insoluble, and would gum up the works, like molten wax poured down a kitchen sink. In fact, two herbal products, the milky latex of (e.g.) the broken dandelion stalk, or the sticky resin of (e.g.) the sawn pine-branch, are used by the plant to plug the breaches in its defences. If such fluids were at the mercy of the Moon's gravitational pull, the result for the plant would be a sort of stroke—botanical thrombosis.

Few people who consult a herbalist in the Western world would expect them to grow and gather the herbs themselves. Most herbs are commercially produced. Here the emphasis is on practical knowledge of real biology—of what makes the plants grow best and produce a high yield of the vital chemicals. Lavender, rosemary and most other herbs are grown on south-facing slopes, to get the maximum sunlight. While sunshine, warmth and a dry summer encourage oil-production, direct hot sunlight also evaporates oils, so a compromise is reached and herbs are traditionally harvested on a fine morning, but before the Sun becomes too hot.

Mrs. Grieve remarks on the fact that Deadly Nightshade, a *very* "lunar" plant according to occult tradition, is particularly dependent on the Sun for the best production of alkaloids.[15] (Hecate must be slipping up somewhere.) This is not really surprising, since these chemicals are made, like all plant products, by an ultimately Sun-powered process. Commercial growers do not include the Moon's phase in their reckonings, for the simple reason that it has nothing at all to do with herbal yields.

The Role of Darkness

Related to the belief that "lunar energies" influence plant growth is the notion that "darkness" (again, the term is used very vaguely) is an absolute requirement for life, for example it is imagined in some sense to "nurture" the growth of seeds and babies, to be essential for germination and so forth.

Not according to Mother Nature. Apart from some specific instances (such as Ivy and Love-in-a-Mist) darkness isn't necessary for germination, as anyone who has ever grown mustard-and-cress on a flannel will be able to verify. Most seeds are quite indifferent to darkness or light, germinating equally well in either, while some species (such as lettuce, daisies and beech) actually *need light* to germinate. If sown in darkness, such seeds germinate very poorly, or not at all.

There's also the idea that the special property of earth which allows it to grow things in its "darkness." What actually makes soil such a teeming city of life (a teaspoonful of good garden soil contains literally millions of tiny living things, microbes and invertebrate animals) is its porous, crumbly quality, what biologists call its *crumb structure*. The air-and-water holding properties of soil make it a marvellous home for countless creatures, who in turn act on particles of clay, minerals, sand, dead leaves, and so on, to build up the crumb-structure itself. (Soil-science is a most complex study, occupying the life work of many biologists.) In terms of soil colour, dark soils are more fertile than pale, but the reason is that black soil absorbs the Sun's rays more easily, thus warming up earlier in the year and providing a better environment for seeds to germinate.

There is a lot of confusion about germination—some authors seem to think it's the same as spontaneous generation or even fertilization.[16] Germination is essentially the process of getting a young plant started in life, until it can capture Sun energy for itself. A seed is made up of a minute plant or *embryo*, and a food-store. (Next time you have a packet of peanuts, look for the embryos—they're the tiny crunchy bit between the two peanut halves, while the food-store is in the peanut itself.) The food-store is a kind of pack of baby-milk, which the seed brought with it from the parent plant, to serve as its first nourishment in life. But that food is dried, its energy locked up, and to liberate it the seed must have enough of three things—*water*, *warmth* and *oxygen*. This is why spring is the time of germination and new growth. Nothing to do with Moon or Earth energies. The soil warms up in the growing heat of the Sun, and together with spring rains or meltwaters, the growing process (i.e. *germination*) is triggered. Then it's a matter of the young plant getting to the sunlight as soon as possible. Once it has its first green leaves above ground, it is independent of its baby-food. Germination has as much to do with the Moon as it has with the stock market closing report.[17]

Mother Nature's Way

Nature works in a businesslike, practical, down-to-earth way, using quite straightforward, natural processes like photosynthesis and transpiration, in an elegant complexity of beautiful relationships. The marvellous cycles and rhythms of the living world are all powered by the vital energy of the Sun; even the high tides to which marine animals respond are *lunisolar*, the result of the combined gravities of Sun and Moon. The insuperable problem in postulating the Moon as promoter of growth is that the Moon produces nothing that living organisms can *use*. The largest living organisms are also much too small to be affected in any way by lunar gravity, as we have already seen. Likewise the bodies of living things are so constructed that their body-fluids are kept stable, so they could not respond to lunar gravity even if it were many times stronger. It is not at all that scientists wish to deny the Moon, or exclude it from their reckonings. As George Abell points out, "...scientists would be overjoyed to find a significant new [lunar] correlation and to achieve some professional acclaim for their discovery."[18] It is simply that proposed influences from the Moon are quite superfluous in explaining how Nature works.

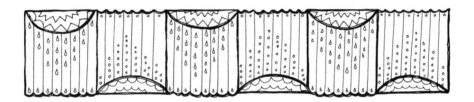

Chapter 7
Great Female Possessor of Noon
Japan

"This great deity actually is the Sun in heaven, which even
now illuminates the world before our eyes."

—Motööri

Amaterasu-O-mikami is the best-known of all Sun goddesses, due to her
position as supreme deity of a living religion, *Shinto,* the native faith of Japan.
Her name means "Great-August-Spirit-Shining-in-Heaven," or "Great-Heaven-
Illuminating-Deity," but she is also addressed by other titles less familiar to
Westerners, such as *Shinmei,* "Divine Radiance," and *O-hiru-me-no-muchi,*
"Great-Female-Possessor-of-Noon." And again, various esoteric sects of Shinto
have secret names for her, revealed only to initiates.[1]

The Land of Queens

Amaterasu's myth was only written down quite late in history, yet it is
replete with very archaic motifs inherited from Siberian shamanism by way of
Korea and other parts of South Asia.[2] In these ancestral lands there are also
found female suns, masculine moons and women shamans, along with traces of
an apparent matriarchate.[3] Japan's Sun-goddess cult might have vanished,
overlaid and suppressed by Taoism, Confucianism and Buddhism, had it not
been the family religion of the ruling *Yamato,* a patriarchal clan who adapted the
female Sun-myth for their own political ends. Such clans each claimed descent
from a divine ancestor—a deified natural force, in this case the Sun, or a
powerful shamaness who claimed to incarnate her and speak her wishes.[4]

When the Chinese discovered Japan in the second century A.D., they found such female rulers to be so usual that they called Japan "The Land of Queens." Annals record how, in the chief realm of *Yamatai* (recently rediscovered by archeologists on Kyushu, Japan's southern island[5]) the shaman-queen Himiko, "Sun's daughter," ruled by the strictest laws from her strong fortress-palace. She was unmarried—probably for reasons of ritual purity—and seems to have been a recluse. At any rate, only her court of ten thousand vestals ever saw her, while the active business of government was carried on by her brother. He moved freely between palace and people as a go-between for his autocrat sister, a practice which must surely have contributed to the downfall of the matriarchy. It was not a gentle and mild rule, but as strict and harsh as any other in that era. When Himiko died in 247 A.D., members of her court were ritually slaughtered to follow her to the grave—a barbaric practice which can be traced back through North Asia to the Tartars[6] and the Kurgan pit-grave culture of South Russia.[7] Indeed, this is one of several parallels by which ancient Japanese culture is distantly linked to the Scythians, Balts, Celts and other Indo-Europeans.[8]

Confucianism, with its decree that woman is inherently unfit to rule or even to have possession of her own person, was introduced into Japan in 400 A.D., at a time when the Yamato were attempting to take over the whole country. This had the predictable, depressing effect on woman's status. A century-and-a-half later matters took a further turn for the worse with the advent of Buddhism, and its unwholesome teaching that a woman must be reborn as a man to have even a chance of spiritual liberation. Yet, for a time, empresses continued to wield great power. It was an empress, *Gemmyo*, who first published Amaterasu's myths in the *Kojiki*, "Record of Ancient Matters," in 712 A.D., aided by *Hieda-no-Are*, an old court lady, one of the traditional reciters who preserved the oral traditions.[9] Eight years later the *Nihongi*, "Chronicles of Japan," retold the myths, adding all kinds of interesting variant readings.[10] In both the *Kojiki* and *Nihongi*, the Sun-goddess is shown handing down rulership to a grandson, not (as originally seems likely) to a daughter or female oracle. This patriarchal idea of the emperor as "Son of the Sun" came from the Chinese and Korean imperial cult.[11] The "Record" and the "Chronicles" show much other evidence of mythological tinkering, old myths rewritten to bring a primitive, shamanistic religion in line with Chinese imperial notions and Taoist cosmology.

The Great Sun Buddha

Buddhism came to Japan from Korea and, after initial resistance, was accepted by aristocrats and commoners alike. The Buddhist clergy set about identifying the Shinto *kami*[12] with their own deities, forming a blend of the two religions known as *Ryobu*, or "mixed Shinto." Soon Buddhism had the upper hand. Not only were the powerful oracular priestesses, or *miko*, downgraded from their earlier political and religious status, but Amaterasu herself was subjected to a sex-change. The people were told that she was really a male god after all, a version of *Roshana* (Indian *Vairocana*), the Great Sun Buddha.[13] In the fourteenth century Shintoists were to rebel against this masculine Sun, and Amaterasu's chief shrine was to become the focus of an anti-Buddhist purgation.[14]

Folk-Shinto

Despite theological manoeuvres, the concept of the Sun as a providential Great Mother goddess continued in Japanese tradition. The doctrinal changes which had such importance for the leisured and literate failed to impinge on the lives of the peasants, who went on practising the old shamanistic religion. Even today this still exists in remote areas and is called "folk-Shinto" by scholars. Female shamanism plays a central role—Carmen Blacker's definitive study describes several kinds of shamaness, including the *noro*, "a majestic sacral woman" who exercises spiritual leadership over a group of villages. She rides a white horse and is accompanied by her brother, who acts as her acolyte.[15] In such folk religion the Sun-goddess is an important deity, and reverence for the Sun is a fundamental part of religious feeling. Country people believe that she rules their lives, like the Baltic Sun-goddess *Saule* bestowing the blessing of food and harvest. Children are warned not to waste food, or she will see and be angry with them. There are folk-tales recounting her dealings with earth. The existence of sacred cypress-trees is explained in a story where the goddess sticks her chopsticks in the ground after enjoying her lunch—not as frivolous a tale as it might seem, for digging-sticks became trees in an Australian solar myth, and the Cherokee and other Amerindian Sun-goddesses stop at noon for a meal.[16]

Shrine-Shinto

The sophisticated, speculative kind of Shinto, whose elegant ceremonies are seen by tourists to Japan, is known as "Shrine-Shinto." It combines archaic elements with beautiful contemplative ideas partly drawn from Buddhism, and has many different schools.[17] Shrine-Shinto is not the same as *State Shinto*, that infamous support of fascism which the Americans made sure to suppress. State Shinto was a reactionary, revivalist development (rather like the right-wing Christian fundamentalism of modern America) based on the religious cult of the imperial household, which it reinterpreted in a fanatical, nationalistic way. Although it still has its supporters, it is incorrect to classify all devout Shintoists with those who use Shinto ideas to back fascism, or to depict Amaterasu as a war-god-in-skirts.

Apart from traditional varieties of Shinto, there are numerous new religious movements, such as *Sokka Gakkai* (or *Nichiren Shoshu*), which incorporate Shinto, Buddhist, Tantric and even Christian beliefs. In some of these sects the Sun is a male Buddha, in others she is "the Sunny Mother-Spirit of the Universe,"[18] and in yet others she is a sexless and ineffable divine principle, *O-tenten-Sama*, "Heaven-Path."[19] The spirit of Shinto is always a matter of feeling rather than belief, an aesthetic reverence rather than an intellectual assent, which makes it much easier for the Japanese to appreciate different religions than it is for Westerners. In Shinto, the worshipper seeks a communion with things as they are, with the mysterious power at the heart of nature, through calm and reverent contemplation which makes the heart receptive to the *mitama*, the divine presence.

The concept of *mitama* is rather like the Jewish idea of the Shekinah, the "glory" or remote acting presence of Yahweh.[20] Although the Sun is in the sky—and that Sun is Amaterasu herself (the reason we do not see her womanly outline, say Shintoists, is because of the radiance which she gives off) her power also acts on earth, and that spiritual emanation is her *mitama*. Like other Sun-goddesses, Amaterasu has two aspects, fierce and gentle, corresponding to the dual nature of the Sun which can be burning and destructive or mild and nurturing. Her *ara-mitama* or "rough spirit" is that violent force which possesses the shamaness, while her *nigi-mitama* or "gentle spirit" is her force of inspiration and blessing. Apart from this, the word for "Sun" and "spirit" and "fire" is the same, *hi*, thought of as the primal source of life and growth, the divine spark enspiriting all things.[21] In folk-Shinto the most fundamental shrine of the Sun-spirit is the wood of a living tree, while in Shrine-Shinto the great vehicle of the goddess's presence is the *yata-no-kagami*, the Mirror of Ise, the most precious object in all Japan.

The Mirror of the Sun

Amaterasu's mirror is venerated as the means by which, in the beginning of time, she was lured from the heavenly cave. This is the central event in her story, but first we must learn how Amaterasu came to shine on the great sky-plain.

The first parents Izanami and Izanagi coagulated the first solid earth out of the formless waters, and began to produce numerous divine children, of whom the most resplendent and illustrious was their daughter, the Sun. When they saw how her dazzling light illumined space in every direction they decide not to keep her, but to send her immediately to the sky-plain, there to rule over all. Now at this time the plains of heaven and earth were connected by a pillar, the roof-tree which stood at the centre of the couple's home. Amaterasu climbed up to heaven (the first sunrise) by climbing the pillar—or, in other versions, by the shaft of the *hiboko* or Sun-spear, or even by a ladder—motifs of ascent which come directly from the shamanistic tradition. Some scholars see Amaterasu as a deified shamaness, making the ritual ascent to heaven in typical Siberian style.[22]

Another version says that the Sun-goddess and her brother the Moon-god were washed from Izanagi's left and right eye respectively when he took a purificatory bath—a myth related to the Chinese story of the earth-giant *Pan K'u*, whose body became the universe, his left eye the Sun, and his right the Moon. Yet another version says that Sun-goddess and Moon-god were born from two white copper or iron mirrors, like the Sun-goddess and Moon-goddess of Altaic tradition. These origin myths link the symbols *eye/mirror/feminine Sun*, a complex which we will meet again in Ireland and tribal India.

The Moon-God

The Moon is masculine in Japan, and little-worshipped because of his association with death. Ideas of the feminine Moon which turn up in Japanese lore and art were introduced with Buddhism, and played no part in primitive Japanese religion. Stan Gooch's insinuation that *Benten* was the Moon-goddess of the Japanese Neanderthals is pure nonsense—Benten is a version of the Hindu *Sarasvati*, goddess of speech and music, and was imported with Buddhism.[23] The Moon was sent downwards by the primal couple to rule *Yomi* the land of the dead, hence his name *Tsuki-yomi*, "Moon of Hades" and his masculine character is emphasized in texts by the addition of *-okoto*, "male."[24] Shinto is so passionately life-affirming that anything which seems to endanger life or spoil bodily integrity is held unclean—birth, intercourse, menstruation, death and illness in particular. There are, however, traces in ancient belief which suggest that the Moon-god was once the Sun-goddess's husband, and that he enjoyed greater importance as a weather-deity, also (like other primitive male Moons) as the secret lover of women and cause of menstruation.[25]

The Impetuous God

Amaterasu's serene reign on the high plain of heaven was shortly interrupted by another god, the deity of storms, winds, earthquakes and chaos, her brother *Susanowo*. Consumed by jealousy at his sister's beauty and pre-eminence and resentful at his father's favouritism towards her, he refused his duty of ruling the ocean-plain and instead tormented the gods by incessantly whining and complaining. Without his care, earth's greenery withered and nature died. All Susanowo wanted was to go down to the underworld and see his dead mother. The god's functions and behaviour are so typical of the masculine Moon that scholars believe him to represent a primitive Moon-god, the weather-deity who is so often found as the Sun-goddess's consort, the personification of storm and rain who pits himself against the Sun's light. Susanowo's details are virtually identical to those of the Australian male Moon *Bahloo* and the Khasi male Moon *U Bynai*, both gods of aboriginal cultures, who like Susanowo are troublesome shirkers, pestering to go back down to earth, and offending their sister the Sun.[26]

The Trials of Amaterasu

Sick of Susanowo's bad behaviour, Izanagi banished him to earth, but the storm-god's restless urges were still unappeased. He went upon a mischievous "farewell visit" to his sister, a daring act which put the whole of nature in an uproar of dismay. The shaman-goddess *Ame-no-Uzume*, "terrifying Female," hastened to warn Amaterasu of the god's approach, for it seemed certain that he was coming up to the sky-plain to wrest power by force.

Amaterasu wasted no time, but dressed herself in her most intimidating outfit, that of a warrior, binding up her hair masculine-style with hundreds of sacred jewels, putting on armour and weapons, and taking in her hand a mighty bow. Japanese authorities point out that this was a typical shamaness's costume—and indeed, Amaterasu went on to perform a shamanic dance. Shaking the great bow like a shamaness inviting possession, she worked herself into a frenzy, kicking up the solid ground like powdery snow. By the time Susanowo came face to face with her, she had worked herself into the ground up to her thighs.

At this intimidating display, Susanowo proceeded cautiously, feigning surprise at his sister's hostility. He swore that he had only come to bid her fond farewell. We can hardly blame Amaterasu for treating the claim with suspicion, but Susanowo did in fact pass a test which Amaterasu set him, to prove his honesty—he managed to produce children from sacred jewels without female assistance, whereupon she felt it safe to trust him. Alas, her trust soon proved to be mistaken. The god was overcome with jealousy at the sight of the heavenly rice-fields, the result of his sister's patient work. He had only been allocated dry, stony or salty ground on the reed-plain (i.e. Earth) which he could of course have made fertile, but refused to cultivate. So he spitefully destroyed the Sun-goddess's fields, breaking up the paddies and letting heavenly piebald horses into the crop. Finally he relieved his bowels in the goddess's beautiful garden.

Amaterasu, the divine embodiment of patience and forbearance, refused to be provoked. Instead she readily forgave her brother—an act which was lost on Susanowo. Next he desecrated her palace, newly-built for ritual purity, by using her throne-room as a lavatory. Even as the long-suffering goddess retched with disgust, she made excuses for her brother, forgiving him everything.

The Withdrawal of the Sun

Since Susanowo had failed so far to provoke his sister, he redoubled his efforts and assaulted the Sun-goddess's holy stronghold, the weaving hall where she sat with her maidens, weaving the silken garments of the gods. Breaking through the thatch, he flung down a dreadful, polluting object—the flayed carcase of a horse—which so terrified the goddesses that they fell down from their high looms while the shuttles flew loose, wounding them in their vaginas. The younger sister of Amaterasu, *Waka-hiru-me*, "Young Sun Female" was so badly injured that she died. Thus the holiest sanctuary of heaven was invaded by death, defilement and fear, and the storm-god seemed at last to have overcome the peaceful rule of the Sun-goddess. In deepest anger she withdrew into the recesses of the rock-cave-of-heaven (which is supposed to lie in northern realms of ice and snow), [27] shut the door fast, and refused to come out.

The results of this were devastating. Deprived of light and warmth, the living world came to a standstill. The heavenly company were sunk in grief and depression, while evil spirits took advantage of the darkness to torment everyone, like swarms of pestering flies. The gods took counsel together in the cheerless darkness. By what plan might Amaterasu be appeased, and persuaded to come out and light the world again?

The Luring of the Sun

At length the Thought-Combining god devised a plan, a clever ruse, to tempt the goddess with lovely offerings, to rouse her curiosity and even her jealousy; in short, to try several methods all at once.

Thus a celestial *sakake* tree (*Cleyera japonica*) was brought from the heavenly mountains and, like a prototype Christmas tree, richly decorated with offerings of blue and white cloth, lengths of *magatama* gems (sacred jewels, shaped like bear's claws) and a splendid mirror, as flawless as the Sun herself, of whom, indeed, it was intended to be an image. The smith-goddess *Ishi-kori-dome* had forged it from copper in the shape of a sun-flower.

Then the deities assembled anxiously outside the cave. The shaman goddess Uzume appeared, dressed from head to foot in sacred herbs, her ritual costume,

Ame-no-uzume

and carrying a spear. Then, like the dancing shamanesses who claimed descent from this goddess, she invoked the Sun by kindling bonfires, and climbing onto an upturned tub, began her ritual dance, stamping and beating the spear on the tub. Inside the cave Amaterasu could hear the racket. She felt sorry for herself, and indignant, too—how could her friend be enjoying herself, when she was shut up here and everything outside was in darkness?

Meanwhile, Uzume was taking off her clothes. In a frenzy of abandonment she gave forth "an inspired utterance," finally pulling down her skirt to expose her sex. The assembled gods, thoroughly enjoying themselves, roared with laughter. This was too much for the Sun-goddess. Whatever were they all up to, out there? Overcome with curiosity she opened the door just a crack—exactly what the gods had hoped she would do. Immediately they pushed the mirror up to the cave-mouth, while Uzume called out, "I dance and they all laugh because there is an honourable goddess here who surpasses your splendour."

To her amazement, Amaterasu was face to face with the impossible—*another* brilliant, dazzling Sun-goddess! She flung open the cave-door and was instantly seized by a strong god. Others fastened a ritual boundary-rope (*shimenawa*) across the cave-mouth, to prevent her from ever going in again.

"Heaven above at length became clear, and all people could see each other's faces distinctly. They stretched forth their hands and danced and sang together, exclaiming 'Oh, how delightful! How pleasant! How clear!'"[28]

As the radiance of the Sun-goddess filled the universe, so did nature begin to flourish again. Shinto mystics say that the cave into which Amaterasu withdrew was the human heart and that she is still hidden there. The goal of spiritual endeavour is to open the cave so that the Sun-goddess, embodiment of peace, wisdom and goodness, may shine out.

The Great Shrine of Ise

After her re-emergence the Sun-goddess did not actually concern herself with earthly affairs, but ruled in bliss from heaven's high plain. The great mirror passed to her descendants on earth. She gave it to her grandson *Ninigi*, the mythical first emperor, with instructions that he should regard it as the Sun herself, keeping it always beside him. Thus for a time it was the personal possession of the emperor, until the accession of *Suijin*, a superstitious man who could not steady his nerves in the goddess's awful presence. He gave the mirror into the keeping of *Toyo-suke-iri-bime*, the Sun's high priestess and oracle, an office traditionally held by an imperial princess. She left the royal enclosure and established the mirror at a village shrine, altogether serving her goddess for eighty-seven years, surely a record in devotional attendance! Political disturbances forced the succeeding high priestess, *Yamato-hime*, to wander for twenty-seven years with the mirror tucked into her hair as part of an ornamental comb, before Amaterasu instructed her to stop at *Ise*, the beautiful land in which the goddess wished to dwell.[29]

The mirror has been there ever since, from the seventh century housed in a primitive shrine of the most austere beauty. No-one has seen the mirror for an indefinite length of years, but it is traditionally shown in art as an eight-petalled flower, eight or nine inches in diameter. The casket in which it lies is enclosed, mummy-like, in many layers of wrappings, on top of which a new brocade cover is added when the old looks less than pristine. Even this much is only seen by the emperor and his highest priests, and they are no wiser about the mirror's real appearance than anyone else. Knowing this, Jesuit missionaries asserted that Yahweh's name was inscribed, in Hebrew letters, on the back of the mirror! This illustrates not merely Jesuit subtlety, but also the serious problems Christians have with the idea of the female Sun.[30]

The Ise Pilgrimage

As I write I have on my desk an actual fragment of the Ise shrine. It is a kind of amulet, a fragment of cedar-wood carefully wrapped inside an elegant brocade case, which pilgrims to the shrine—as many as eight million each year—bring

AMULET
FROM ISE

back to place on the *kami-dana*, the home shrine. Visitors to Ise (pronounced *ee-say*) go mainly for religious reasons. This accounts for about five million; the rest go on day-trips, business outings, holidays and so forth, or are foreign tourists "doing" the shrine on a package tour. The Ise-jingu itself is really two shrines, the outer or *Ise-geku* dedicated to the harvest-goddess, the inner or *Ise-naiku* to Amaterasu herself, while in the grounds is a small shrine to Tsuki-yomi. Since the sixth century the shrine has been rebuilt on precisely the same plan every twenty years, hence the fragments of earlier shrines which are sold as charms, bringing (or so a Japanese lady assured me) "peace and happiness," the gifts of the benign Sun-goddess, if carried about on the person.

Westerners visiting Ise will look in vain for profusion of symbols, for gold sunbursts, splendour and ornament. The shrine is utterly plain—simply thatched wooden halls, built without nails in a prehistoric style, and enclosed by wooden fences. Yet even the most hard-boiled or jaded globetrotter is not uncommonly moved to tears by the intensely simple beauty of Ise, and the magnificence of its natural setting, "in a wood of marvellous antiquity and stupendous vigour,"[31] with its pure air, sparkling streams and woodland paths. In this lovely but remote land the Sun-goddess felt lonely, so she asked her priestesses to bring her the agriculture-goddess, Toyo-uke-bime, to keep her company. The Ise mystics say that these two are aspects of a single, monotheistic goddess, the Sun herself, the highest manifestation of the ineffable cosmic deity.[32]

The Sun Vigil

Personal devotions to the Sun-goddess are performed facing the rising Sun, to which the worshipper bows, reverentially clapping to call her attention and dispel evil. Another practice commonly found in cultures where the Sun is (or was) feminine, is the *Sun-vigil*. On certain nights of the old calendar, Shinto believers assemble at each other's houses, there to hold a special ceremony in honour of the Sun. Then they spend the night talking and worship the Sun as she rises. This vigil is called *hi-machi*, "waiting for the Sun [to rise]."[33] The idea that the Sun dances as she rises is commonly found in other cultures as an integral part of the Sun-vigil, but oddly enough in Japan she dances as she sets:

"On the actual day of the [spring] equinox, the sun is believed to whirl round and round at sunset."[34]

For the Japanese, sunrise is a time of joy and religious exaltation, recalling the time when Amaterasu emerged from the cave. Sunset is thought to be a sad event, so Japanese people do not understand why Westerners consider it so romantic.[35]

Closing the Cave

The simple fact that Amaterasu is a Sun-goddess, that from time immemorial the Japanese have seen the Sun as a female being and the Moon as male, ought to cause nobody any problems. It's just how things are in that culture. But this does not stop Westerners from rejecting Amaterasu and calling her the Earth, the dawn, the Moon, a serpent-divinity[36]— *anything and everything except the Sun*. It is also common to find that books by Westerners on Shinto describe it without mentioning Amaterasu or her myth *at all*, even when they mention the shrine at Ise! Attempts to erase and discredit the Japanese Sun-goddess are so numerous and various they are almost worth a book to themselves. (One of the most blatant of them is by a feminist author.[37])

But, as Professor Jean Herbert (whose work is based on what Shintoists actually believe, not on what Westerners think they ought to believe) points out, claims that Amaterasu isn't the Sun, or that she is unimportant, are quite false. As divine ancestress she takes pride of place on every *kami-dana*. The number of shrines to her, great and small, is enormous—Herbert gives, as a typical example, an area only ten by fifteen miles in which there are a hundred shrines to Amaterasu.

If the goal of the Shinto mystic is to open the cave and let the feminine Sun shine out in her full splendour, then that of many Western thinkers seems to be to lock her back in there, and throw away the key. If the Japanese Sun-deity had been a male god, would he be treated like this?

Chapter 8
Dearest Goddess, Mother Sun
The Baltic Lands

O Little Sun, God's daughter
Where have you stayed so long?
Where have you dwelt so long?
Why have you left us all alone?

—Beyond the seas and the hills
I've shielded homeless orphans
And kept the shepherds warm
...Many are my gifts.

— Lithuanian Traditional Song[1]

The religion of the pagan Balts—that is, the ancient Lithuanians and Latvians and the Old Prussians—survived longer than any other religion of Old Europe, partly due to the fact that the Christian missionaries (by whom the Balts were forcibly converted after long resistance) simply couldn't speak the highly unusual Baltic languages. The Latvian and Lithuanian tongues, closely related, are Indo-European, of a very archaic kind—so old, in fact, that their nearest relative is Sanskrit. Indeed, it is claimed that a Latvian or Lithuanian speaker can often make sense of a passage of Sanskrit without any previous knowledge of that language.[2]

The Dainas

The great national treasure of the Baltic countries lies in the oral tradition, an almost unbelievably rich heritage from which *over a million songs*, known as dainas (Lithuanian dainos) have been collected. These verses, some of which resemble Old Indian poetic forms, describe in great detail the attractive deities of the Baltic pantheon, the everyday lives, experiences and emotions of the common people, and their reverence for and delight in the natural world. (An estimated three-quarters of this poetic tradition is the work of women, or expresses a woman's view of life.) The collected dainas, held in the National Archives, represent only those songs which collectors managed to write down — undoubtedly many others have been lost or forgotten.[3]

It is because of the antiquity and richness of this tradition that it was one of the first to attract serious attention:

> "The Baltic description of the sun as divinity is so complete and specific that it was one of the first to be studied by scholars. Of greatest importance is the similarity in both functions and attributes of Saule and the ancient Indian god Surya. Similarities between the two gods [sic] are so great that, were not the two peoples separated by several thousand miles and several millenia, direct contact between them would be indicated instead of only a common origin."[4]

Mother Sun

Throughout Baltic tradition, without exception, the Sun is *always* represented as a goddess. She is *Saule* ("sun," f.) while the Moon is always masculine, the god *Meness* (Lithuanian *Menuo*, *Menulis*, m.) Among the grim and bloody deities of ancient Europe, Saule makes a refreshing change. She is a most delightful goddess, described and addressed in the songs in a loving and passionate way, vividly evoking that joy which northern peoples feel at the warmth and brilliance of the Sun. Thousands upon thousands of dainas attest to her central importance in the Baltic pantheon.[5] It is she who warms the earth, bringing about the growth of plants, guarding the crops from harm, and moderating the thunder-god's enthusiasm by contending with him during storms. As the all-seeing-one, she watches over shepherds and their flocks, sailors at sea, and all those who are homeless, lonely or abandoned, sometimes descending to earth as a woman in peasant dress and flowing golden hair, to take a direct hand in human affairs.[6]

Saule is omniscient, powerful and interfering. Endowed with human moral characteristics, she punishes wrongdoers and helps those who suffer or are ill-treated. A daina tells us how a peasant is being cruelly used by an overlord, who is about to beat him; he pleads with his master not to whip him in the evening, but in the morning after Saule has risen, for then she will see and will "weep bitterly" for him. (The peasant doesn't mention it, but he expects the Sun-goddess to avenge him by punishing the wicked lord.) Another daina tells of a poor woman who loses her lamb. She goes in search of help from the deities—first the morning star, who is too busy, then in turn to the evening star and the Moon-god, but they merely offer her excuses. Finally she asks Saule, who replies, "Nine days I'll search on your behalf, nor will I cease upon the tenth."[7]

Dear Little Red Sun

Saule's light and the vicissitudes of her appearance at different times and weathers were keenly observed and much loved by the Balts. The dainas abound in the most lovely descriptions of the Sun-goddess and her elegant outfits. Saule's colours are red, white, gold and silver[8]. She is often called *balta*

LATVIAN COSTUME

saulele, "dear little white Sun," or *skaisti saulele*, "dear little red Sun" (*saulele* is a special diminutive, a term of endearment which cannot be translated without adding a coyness quite absent from the original).[9] "White" in Baltic terminology also carries a symbolic sense, expressive of joy, goodness and especially of sincerity (compare the derivation of our word *candid* from Latin *candida*, "white"). Saule is depicted in the traditional Baltic women's costumes, in embroidered and woven solar symbols, and her special colours. Women in folk costume are called *Daughters of the Sun*, that is, younger or little versions of the Sun-goddess herself,[10] and they wear a type of beaded coronet decorated with Saule's colours and long ribbon streamers, which represents the Sun and her rays. The floral wreath, particularly that made of red flowers, is also a Sun-symbol. Such wreaths were anciently worn by unmarried girls, but at Saule's festivals all women would wear them, in an expression of joy and freedom—and also, perhaps, because such festivals as Midsummer included sexual licence, one of the aspects of Saule's worship which provoked Christian rage.[11]

Sun-symbols

Even though *Saules mate*, Mother Sun, was richly personified and meticulously described in song, she was not so depicted in art. Instead stylized forms—geometric shapes and sacred animals—were used to represent her. In jewellery, ceramics, weaving, embroidery and woodcarving, Saule's emblems—rosette, ring, wheel, floriated cross, rayed circle and others—appear over and over again from very early times.[12] She herself is addressed in song as *ridolele*, the "rolling" Sun, and is thought of as a wheel rolling through the sky.[13] The dainas evoke her

by many more images—rosy apple, golden crown, precious belt or necklace, golden goblet, glowing iron ring fresh from its forging, red rose high in a tree—and other poetic metaphors which, nevertheless, are not merely fanciful, but connect very closely with important motifs and meanings in Indo-European tradition. The imagery of solar light is evoked in the dainas by the most lovely imagery—sometimes light is amber, or liquid gold, or pieces of gold and silver strewn on the earth. Saule prepares her daughter's dowry by gilding the tops of the forest trees.[14] At sunset Saule weeps red tears, which colour the evening clouds, or fall as red berries in the woodlands.[15]

The Sun's Horses

Saule's sacred animal is the horse. In some contexts the mare stands for the Sun while the twin stallions which accompany the goddess in folk-art are the sons of *Dievs*, the sky-father. Like many other Sun-deities, the Sun-goddess rides across the sky each day in a chariot of gold and silver, or a sledge drawn by the twin sons of Dievs, personified as golden horses.[16] Saule drives nine chariots at once, or has a hundred steeds in hand. Occasionally she makes do with one horse—but even that is made of gold and diamond. The Sun and her horses are tireless:

> Saule, with her two gold horses
> Rides up the stone mountain
> Never heated, never weary,
> Never resting on the way.[17]

Like the ancient Iranians, the Balts perceived the sky as a stone hill, or a mountain of silver, on which the deities have their farmsteads and "silver-gated castles." The personified sky is Dievs, a farmer, hunter and most kindly king, the lover of justice and order.[18] (He is one of Saule's husbands, but sometimes also her father.) He has his own castle in the sky, while Saule's home is in the furthest west, beyond "the Way of the Sun."

In the evening, at the end of "the Path of the Sun," Saule goes home to her apple-island paradise, which lies in the west, beyond the rim of the world. This is the wished-for home of the dead, who reach it along the path of the Milky Way by riding horses, or by flying there in the form of birds. On the seashore of this golden island Saule washes the Sun-horses before tethering them to an iron post, or she sits in the branches of the *Saules koks*, the Sun-tree or cosmic tree, holding their reins.[19]

When the time comes to return to the east, Saule passes beneath the Earth, through the underworld waters. The Sun's night hours and her daily resurrection involve other goddesses, the Sun's daughters.

Sun's Daughter

Saule's character is dualistic, in that she is represented on the one hand as a mother, *Saules mate*, and on the other hand as a daughter, *Saules meita*.[20] The dainas make it clear that these are older and younger versions of the Sun herself, perhaps the morning and noontide suns, or those of spring and summer—or, as in other Sun-goddess mythologies, the mild beneficent Sun and the fierce, burning Sun.

In Lithuanian mythology, Saule's principal daughter is *Auszrine*, the morning star, goddess of dawn and spring.[21] (Her Germanic equivalent, whose name is etymologically identical, was *Eostre* or *Ostara*, after whom our "Easter" is named.) Mythologists term her the "Sun-maiden." Her sister is *Wakarine*, the evening star. In a Lithuanian *daino* the singer asks:

> "Dear Saule, Mother Sun
> Who lights your morning fire?
> Who lights your evening fire?
> Who spreads your bed at eve?"

(Saule replies:)

> "Morning star and evening star
> Auszrine lights the fire
> Wakarine spreads the bed."[22]

The daughter-suns look after Saule's palace and horses (not always conscientiously—the Sun-goddess sometimes has to scold them) and sometimes accompany Saule during her night journey, diving into the sea with the setting Sun.[23]

While Saule is imagined to swim back to the east, in many dainas she sails through the underworld in a golden boat. In others the Sun's disappearance into the western sea causes her death—she has drowned, and thus the stars, her children, appear in the night without her, and are thus termed "orphans." When Saule drowns, it is the Sun-maiden who rescues her. She pleads with the Earth-mother *Zemes-mate* (Lith. *Zemyna*) who is Saule's eldest daughter and the ruler of the dead. From her she obtains the key to the realm of the dead, and the Sun-goddess emerges from the earth, resurrected, the next morning.

> "Some people are saying
> That my dearest Goddess
> Has died by drowning
> Well, I just saw her
> Walking over the waters
> Sowing handfuls of gold and silver."[24]

In the First Spring

Saule appears to be a polyandrous goddess. Tradition gives her three hus-bands—*Dievs*, the sky-father; *Perkons*, god of storms and rain, and *Meness*, the Moon-god. There is good reason to believe that this three-fold husband was in earlier times a triple Moon-god, representing the waxing, full and waning phases.[25] The goddess bears children to each—all star-deities, with the exception of the Earth, who is her daughter by the Moon.

Latvian mythology tells how the bliss of the Baltic dreamtime, the "first spring" of the dainas, was destroyed by Meness' adultery with Saule's own daughter; here the Sun-maiden is promised to the morning-star god *Auseklis*, but Menuo seduces her while Saule's back is turned.

> "The Moon wedded the Sun
> In the first spring.
> The Sun rose early at dawn,
> The Moon wandered alone
> Courting the morning star.
> Perkunas was wroth,
> He cleft the Moon with a sword."[26]

The result of this, of course, is that we see "pieces" of the Moon, the lunar phases. The Sun's daughter gathers up the fragments of her lover's body, and puts them together again, but the Moon-god's face still bears the marks of his ordeal.[27]

In the Latvian version it is Saule herself who dismembers the Moon:

> "The Sun shattered the Moon
> With a sharp sword
> Because he stole the bride-to-be
> Of the morning Star [i.e. the god Auseklis]"[28]

In general Latvian tradition makes more of the tensions between Saule and her husbands; some dainas depict spiteful arguments between her and the Moon-god.[29] According to an alternative Latvian version, it is Saule who is the adulterer, first marrying Meness but later falling in love with Perkons. When the Moon-god finds out, he rejects her, hiding from her in shame and anger, and ever afterwards avoiding her company. This may at first look like a patriarchal reworking of the story, but it may equally well represent an older or even non-Indo-European element. It expresses the primitive idea that the Moon is not the real husband of Saule, a concept hinted at in the standard version—the Sun-maiden is betrothed to Auseklis, but the Moon-god gets there first. In tribal traditions the Moon-god secretly visits or abducts girls and has intercourse with them, causing first menstruation. He is also typically the "real husband" of women, mortal men being mere stand-ins. The adulterous Saule and the fearfully shrinking, hiding Moon are exactly reproduced in an Australian aboriginal myth.[30]

The Moon-God

In both Latvia and Lithuania the Moon was worshipped much less than the Sun, as the relative proportions of dainas and artefacts show. Nevertheless he was a loved deity and played an important role as a war-god,[31] as well as being the deity of healing, and influencing the growth of plants (or so the Balts believed). Many folk-prayers exist in which he is invoked for health, wealth and happiness. Like the tribal Moon-gods, he is a philanderer and potentially dangerous to young women, whom he may abduct in his chariot.[32]

Before the Moon's adultery, he used to travel the skies side-by-side with the Sun, but they divorced and chose to live separately. Now he rides through the night skies drawn by black horses, a handsome dark-haired man swathed in a star-strewn cloak, beneath which he wears the outfit of a prince or warrior.[33] The pagan Moon cult died out, but that of the Sun continued to our own times.[34]

The Storm-god

The other husband of Saule is *Perkons* (Lith. *Perkunas*), the god of clouds, rain and storms. When he rides through the dark clouds, we hear the rumbling of his chariot-wheels as thunder. Perkons is a lover of goodness and enemy of all those evil spirits who cause mischief and misery. He smites them with his copper axe, or whips them with lightning.[35] But his main office is the bringing of rain for the Earth's fertility, and many dainas invoke this blessing on the farmer's fields:

> "Out over the waves went Perkons
> And the rain has poured into the sea;
> The peasant prays to little Perkons:
> 'Go, Perkons, over the earth,
> Go, Perkons, over the earth,
> For the ears of barley have withered.'"[36]

His marriage with Saule is literally tempestuous, for the dark storm clouds and bright Sun always contend, and the dainas tell how Perkons ruins Saule's white laundry (the clouds) with rain.[37] During thunderstorms, children sing to the goddess:

"Come, dear Saule,
Bring us cakes
Drive away the dark clouds
With your whips [i.e. sunrays]"

or

"Mother Sun, to us here, to us here!
Father Cloud, to Prussia, to Prussia!"[38]

It is always Saule who is victorious in these celestial disputes. She is regarded as the creatress of the rainbow's colours,[39] an idea which reveals the Balts' careful observation of nature, for it is when the Sun shines during a rainstorm that the rainbow appears.

Perkons is sometimes mendaciously presented as "the Sun-god" by writers unable to come to terms with the feminine Sun. The assertion is made in contradiction of every known fact. Nor was Perkons the principal deity. "The sun, Saule, occupies the central place in the pantheon of Baltic gods... there is no reason to believe that [Perkons] is the main god."[40]

The Midsummer Feast

"In Lithuania it is supposed that, on St. John's Day, the Sun,
a female being, goes forth from her chamber in a car drawn
by three horses—golden, silver and diamond—to meet her
spouse the Moon, and on her way she dances and emits
fiery sparks."[41]

"St. John's Eve" or Midsummer Eve, was the scene of great festivities and a typical Sun-vigil, of a kind almost universally associated with the feminine Sun. Midsummer was Saule's great festival, the *Ligo* feast, named after the refrain of the many songs joyously sung to the goddess, lilting songs describing her dance, "swaying (*ligo*), rolling, hopping."[42] People were afraid to go to bed on Midsummer Eve, lest they miss the Sun's dance as she rose:

"The Sun dances over the silver mountain
Silver shoes she hath on her feet..."[43]

But there were many festivities to keep them awake. On a high place, a bonfire was raised up on a pole, and around this dances and hymns were offered to the Sun, thanking her for her bounty, seeking her aid, asking her blessings on the harvest. Flower wreaths, Sun-emblems, were an important feature of the rites. All shared in a sacramental meal including a special cheese[44] and mead, then "got up to amuse themselves" in the Biblical sense, sexual licence being a feature of the Ligo ceremonies. The rites culminated in the appearance of the Sun on Midsummer day, dancing on the hilltops, dressed in apple blossom from her western orchard and wearing a wreath of braided red-fern blossoms.[45]

The Winter Imprisonment of the Sun

The other principal festival of Saule was the spring feast, equivalent of Celtic *Beltane*[46] when the return of the Sun's warmth and the renewal of Nature were celebrated. Less is known of Winter Solstice; as among the Lapps and Inuit, the winter cold was thought to be due to evil spirits and/or the moon (the Moon is "cold" in contrast to the hot Sun) and so a goat was sacrificed to Perkons, who would then smite the winter-spirits with his axe.[47] Bonfires were lit to help the Sun.

In previous times the Winter Solstice was explained by a type of myth which regularly appears in the cult of Sun-goddesses. Jerome of Prague, a Christian missionary, who visited Lithuania in 1431, was scandalized to find the Balts worshipping a giant hammer. The priests explained that it had been used to liberate the Sun from a high fortress-tower, where an evil king had imprisoned "it," depriving the world of warmth and light. The rescuers of the Sun were "the signs of the zodiac," i.e. the stellar gods, the *Dieva deli*.[48]

Wherever the feminine Sun is found in Indo-European myth, and even in some cases outside it, we find the same complex—the spring Sun (or Sun in her maiden form), the withdrawal or imprisonment in a cave, tower, mountain or labyrinth, the involvement of a smith or specially-forged weapon (or imitation Sun) and the Sun-goddess's liberation by twin gods who are the morning and evening star.[49] Almost until our own time this myth was re-enacted each spring, in the form of labyrinth-games or dances, in Germany and other North European countries.[50]

The Fire Cult

The fire was the centre of Baltic domestic ritual. It was regarded as a goddess, a daughter of Saule. The first fire was brought from the Sun herself by the swallow, whose face was burnt red and its tail scorched through by the encounter. Hence the swallow brings with it the warmth of summer, and there still exists an archaic swallow-worshipping dance, often performed by Lithuanian folk groups.[51]

According to one account, the Sun-maiden is driven out of the house by Saule for loving the Moon. She comes to earth as the fire-goddess, six times a year sitting by the hearth in person, rather like the Celtic goddess *Brighde* who visits the hearth in Spring, in her role as fire-goddess.[52] A permanent resident next to the hearth, in a bed of straw, was the house-snake, the *Zaltys*,[53] considered a masculine force of fertility. He was beloved by Saule, who wept when a Zaltys died, and punished anyone who failed to treat it well.[54]

A Disappointing Goddess

I would like to impress upon the reader that these details of Saule, and her songs and cult, are only a sketch or brief summary of the wealth of lore surrounding this goddess. Let us be clear about this—here we have an Indo-European Sun-deity belonging to one of the most archaic Indo-European cultures, the pagan religion of which survived later than any other in Europe, and which is known by scholars to be authentic and scarcely Christianized.[55] No other Indo-European Sun-deity has such a marvellous and rich corpus of extant lore. And yet Saule (and indeed, the Baltic religions) are scarcely known.

The reason is quite simple. Saule is a great disappointment to the Western academic world. *She is the wrong sex.* Moreover, she fails to fulfil other criteria expected of the Indo-European (or "Aryan") Sun-deity.[56] Had Saule been a male god, she and the religions of which she was a part would have instantly been hailed as supremely important to the study of mythology. Indeed, she is—but prejudice eclipses this most lovely Sun.

Eclipse of the Sun

Chapter 9
Fair Maiden Bright Sun
Russia and Slavonic Lands

"Thou askest me of what race, of what family I am;
My mother is the beauteous Sun
And my father—the bright Moon
My brothers are the many Stars
And my sisters—the white Dawns."
—Traditional Song of Tambof[1]

Although the Slavs separated from the main Indo-European stock about two thousand years before Christ, there is no real account of their mythology until the sixth century, when Christian missionaries noted the worship of such gods as *Perun*, the storm-god and *Dazhbog*, the Sun.[2] After the Slavs were converted in the late tenth century, there was massive destruction of pagan artefacts—especially, of course, those made of gold and silver—but the peasants, who continued to practise the old religion until at least the twelfth century (and in some places right until the nineteenth) continued to make model sun-chariots of traditional prehistoric type as toys for their children.[3]

Bright Little Sun

The Christian mediaeval chroniclers only recorded the "official" Slav religion, the cult of nobles, warriors and rich men, which was not necessarily that of the common people.[4] Archaeology, folklore and language attest to an earlier tradition of the feminine Sun, who still survives in art and song along with her husband the Moon and their children the stars, just as in Baltic myth.

The Russian word for Sun, *solntse*, is neuter diminutive, but linguists say it derived from a preceding, ancient feminine word. "In many Russian folk songs a verb having the sun as its subject is put in the feminine form, and the Sun is *almost always* thought of as a bride or a maiden,"[5] while the Moon is customarily described as a youth, a father or a grandfather in Russian, Serbian, Croatian and Bulgarian folk-songs. Not surprisingly, the word for Moon is a masculine name, *myesyats*. When the genders of Sun and Moon were reversed (which caused certain mythological difficulties) the "Moon-goddess" continued to bear a man's name, which is a lot like calling her Queen Fred. The Sun became *Tzar Solnitse*,[6] a title which in itself is revealing, suggesting as it does that the masculinity had to be added on afterwards. The absurdity of a male name for the female Moon was partly rectified by borrowing the word *Luna* from Latin during mediaeval times, but the ordinary people seem to have been unconvinced by all these manoeuvres and went on singing about Sun-brides and Moon-husbands.

The Sun is personified as a young woman whose youthfulness is eternal, in contrast to her husband the Moon, who is a young man in his crescent phase, but who grows older and dies each month.[7] In a Russian story a man journeys to the world's end, where sky and earth meet, and understandably enough feels exhausted by his travels. There at the rim of the world is a cottage, at whose door he seeks refuge, but the old woman who keeps house there is rather reluctant to let him in. At length she admits him, but only on condition that he hides himself. Later, a young girl comes in, and the man manages to sneak a look at her. She is a creature of wondrous beauty, with wings like an angel, and a dress of dazzling brilliance which lights up the whole room. Her mother, the old woman, helps her off with her dress and hangs it on the wall. Then, when she covers it with a sheet, darkness falls. In the morning the old woman is up very early, giving her daughter breakfast before helping her back into the radiant robe. "Now, my dear daughter, my bright little Sun [Solntse]," she says, "It is time for you to be off about your business." And with that, the Sun flies out through the window and into the sky.[8]

The Sun-Goddess and the Cult of the Dead

The Sun-goddess is the deity who warms the earth, taking pity on the sorrowing, the oppressed and the orphan. A weeping maiden is compared to the misty Sun,[9] while a lament from the Arkangel district implores, "Warm, warm, O red Sun! Shine, shine, O bright Moon!"[10] and another Russian song requests, "Rise, rise, O red Sun, give warmth to us, poor sufferers." The Sun was also connected with the Slavic death cult, since the land of the dead, the mysterious island in the west, was also the home of the Sun. She showed the dead soul the way to travel. Funerals were held before sunset, so that the departing goddess would carry the soul down with her, below the rim of the Earth, or down into the underworld.[11] It was a Croatian practice to let the Sun's rays touch the corpse before burial—Ralston says to warm the body, but clearly the original intention was to allow the disembodied spirit to see and follow the Sun.[12] An old Russian funeral lament calls the soul a white swan, who flies

> "Beyond the high mountains
> Beyond the swift-moving clouds
> Into the arbour where sits
> The fair maiden Bright Sun."[13]

Like the Celts, Greeks and Balts, the Slavs believed that the western isle of paradise, *Bouyan* (from *bui*, "burning, ardent, fruitful, vernal") was ruled by a Sun-maiden, *Zorya*. Ralston calls her the dawn, or the springtide Sun, or even a "thunder-goddess," but Zorya is the same word as *Surya*, and can simply be taken to mean "Sun." The details of Bouyan closely resemble the Baltic isle, home of Saule. Zorya sits, not upon the cold grey stone of the Baltic or Swedish Sun-goddess, but upon the wonderful "fiery stone" *Alatuir*, which is either a crystal, like the Sun-stone of the Celts, or amber, well-known in northern lands for its solar connotations.[14] When Zorya sits (or sets) upon the stone she gets out her sewing and plies a red-gold thread —a variation on the theme of spinning sun-rays—or sometimes, like Saule, she perches in the top of the world-tree like a bird.[15]

The Sun Palace

Solntse's palace or castle very closely resembles that of Saule. She leaves it in the morning, opening the sky's eastern gates to pass through, and returns to it at nightfall, the gates of the west closing behind her. Thus the palace seems to lie beneath the earth, an idea confirmed by the fact that Sun and Moon are at home together there, and when they argue, we feel the repercussions as earthquakes.

The Sun-palace is the family home of the sky-deities, the place beneath the earth to which Sun, Moon and stars descend when they set. There live the Sun's daughters, *Zvezda Dennitsa*, the Morning Star, who gets the Sun's team of horses ready in the morning; *Vechernyaya Zvezda*, the Evening Star, who unharnesses, washes and feeds them in the evening; *Zorya Utrenyaya*, the dawn, who opens the eastern gates of light; and *Zorya Vechernyaya*, who closes them at sunset. In folk-art the two Zoryas are shown one on each side of the enthroned Sun, so that the group represents the solar trinity of rising, noon and setting suns, or conversely, setting, underworld, and rising suns, the "three little Zoryas" of twilight, midnight and dawn.[16]

Another feminine inhabitant of the Sun-palace is *Perperuna* the storm-goddess, who seems to be a twin of the storm-god *Perun*. In Lithuania she appears as "mother of the thunder," *Percunatete*, and fulfils exactly the same role as Perperuna, which is to bathe the hot and weary Sun when she returns from her travels.[17] This is not a frivolous motif. The idea of the onset of night being due to the Sun falling (or in this case, being plunged) into water and being quenched, or even drowned, is frequently discovered in Slavic and other folklore. It means that the fire must be relit, or the Sun reborn, every morning. Indeed, according to the myth of the fire-god *Svarog*, the Sun is a torch which the god lights each morning and extinguishes at night.[18] (The devotees of Mithra also thought the Sun's fires were extinguished in the sea each evening.[19])

The Slavic Moon-God

The Moon-god of the Slavs resembles the primitive masculine lunar god in many important respects. He is the renewer of life and health. The Southern Slavs ask him to take away their children's ailments[20] while a traditional Russian invocation to the crescent Moon says, "Young moon! God give thee strong horns and me good health!"[21] It was undoubtedly the self-renewing properties of the Moon which made him the pre-eminent healing deity.

The new Moon was a young man, who grew until he reached his prime at full Moon, and then declined and finally died.[22] In a lament for the Tzar Peter the First, the dead man is called "thou bright Moon," and is compared to the Moon having ceased to shine—but with the unspoken thought that, like the Moon, he will live again.[23]

Although the Moon-god shares the Sun-palace, he and his wife do not get on with each other, and thus they avoid each other's company for most of the month. Like the Baltic Moon-god, Myesyats is a philanderer, an incestuous father who seduces Dennitsa, the Morning Star, just as Meness seduces Auszrine.

But where the sex of the Sun has been changed, the Moon is left without a wife. This puts the myth out-of-joint, so he has to be given Dennitsa to start with—leaving him without his illicit lover, so that another has to be provided in the shape of one of the other star-goddesses. This is an excellent example of the way that tinkering with the sex of the Sun destroys the coherence of a myth.[24]

The Swans of the Sun

The marriage of Sun-goddess and Moon-god is a popular theme of Slavic folk-songs, providing charming imagery of the Sun as a young bride. The Southern

Slavs call the groom at his wedding "Mr. Moonshine"[25] while a Russian wedding-song describes the groom and his hoped-for sons as the crescent Moon and the stars, while the bride and her daughters-to-come are the Sun and her swans:

> "The red sun with its rays
> Is Anna with her daughters,
> Dear Ivanovna with her swans."[26]

The concept of sun-rays as the Sun's daughters, or as horses which draw the Sun through the sky, occurs in Baltic tradition, where the Sun's daughter Auzrine is "goddess of sunrays." Here, too, is surely a reference to the immortal women who in Indo-European myth and folklore appear as swans, transforming themselves into beautiful maidens who marry the sons of men, often with dire results but, at least in theory, with the promise of celestial happiness.[27]

Water-birds are closely associated with the Sun in many prehistoric artefacts, particularly those of the Urnfield cultures of Central Europe. The Bronze Age peoples who left these elegant works of art were the ancestors of the Celts, who strongly influenced the Slavs during the fourth and fifth centuries B.C.E. The Slavs themselves left traces of Sun-worship from the Bronze Age onwards, associating the solar disc with horses, who drew it through the sky during the day, and swans or geese, who bore the Sun across the underworld waters on its nightly journey from west to east.[28] Russian embroideries show a figure called *Baba* ("grandmother") with a rayed headdress and flanked by two horses, a folk-art motif also common in Baltic designs where it represents Saule and the Dieva-deli who draw her across the sky. (Western commentators routinely misidentify this figure as "Mother Earth" because the corn-dolly is named "Baba" in some Russian traditions, but this has nothing to do with either Baltic or Slavic tradition, which does not associate an Earth-mother with the "little sons of God.")[29] An ancient Russian tradition, which in some areas continued until just before the second world war, used the embroidered figure of the Sun-goddess and her horses as the icon in a pagan rite. A napkin figured with this design in red, was hung high in the branches of a solitary birch tree, the tree sacred to the Sun-goddess, thus "placing the Sun in the sky" (as in the imagery of the Baltic songs). Then people took hands in a ring and performed around the tree a horse-dance, stamping to imitate hoof-beats. The napkin which served as a banner of the goddess was an important ritual item in each bride's bottom drawer. It was handed down through the generations from mother to daughter as a precious and sacred heirloom, both in Russia and in the Baltic lands.[30]

Sometimes the birch-tree was replaced by a real girl wearing a crown of birch-boughs. Sun-like crowns appear frequently in traditional Slav costumes. In the Olonets district of north-eastern Russia, an area in which "the songs of old times have been best preserved," the women's headdress was an archaic type of coronet, with glass balls or beads. In Baltic costume a similar crown worn by women represents the Sun herself.[31]

Firebirds and Sun-Eggs

Solar emblems abound in Slavic folk-art, as well as in ancient artefacts, indicating a long and unbroken symbolic tradition. Apart from Sun-discs, lozenges, circled crosses and other aniconic emblems similar to those of the Balts, which date from the earliest Slav culture,[32] there are the golden palaces, horses, cockerels, apples and firebirds, familiar to us from Russian tradition.[33] The firebird is of particular interest. Although female, it seems to be a version of the long-necked, long-tailed cockerel which appears in folk-art, and which bears an uncanny resemblance to the "long-singing birds of eternal night" in Japanese myth and art. As a Sun-symbol, the cockerel is never the Sun itself. Its solar associations (as myth and folklore make perfectly clear) derive from its habit of announcing the Sun's reappearance. Long-tailed cockerels are kept at the Japanese Sun-goddess's shrine at Ise, because they once helped lure her from the cave.[34]

In the Ukraine, where folksongs still tell of:

"Bright Moon with his wife the bright Sun
And their children the bright stars..."[35]

...solar symbolism was preserved in the making of *pysanky*, traditional Easter-eggs coloured in exquisite detail by a wax-resist process, rather like Indonesian batik. Among the pagan Slavs, at the festival of *Krasnaya Gorka* ("red or bright little hill") which was ousted by the Christian Easter, a red egg and a round loaf represented the Sun.[36] They were taken to a high place and formed the central symbols of a *Khorovod*, a rite of choral ring-dances. The chief singer, a woman, holding the Sun-symbols, turned towards the east and sang of the destruction of winter and the coming of spring.[37] Pysanky eggs are blessed and exchanged in celebration of Christ's resurrection, along with an Easter loaf or cake which replaced the former Sun-bread, but their symbolism is, apart from the Latin cross, entirely pagan. So-called *solarium* patterns are most common. The eight-point sunburst, adapted (for Christian purposes) to its related form, a cross, with various intermediate forms, is a characteristic emblem of the spring Sun.[38] Floriated crosses and lozenges expand on this theme with the added sense of "flourishing life." In southern Ukraine the Sun-symbol is a rosette, and even a red rose-like flower.[39] (cf. the Baltic image of the Sun-goddess as a red rose at noon). Other designs evoke fertility—male animals such as stags and goats were once emblems of the old weather-god, while running vines, ears of wheat, houses, vases, trees and flowers all expressed in old times the desire for security and plenty. Then there are spirals, triangles, bands, ribbons and other geometric figures, as well as the "running flame" design found on the ritual hearths of Slavic prehistory, together with round dots which are "Mary's tears," formerly rain, the gift of "Aunt Thunder," whom the Slavs identified with the Blessed Virgin.[40]

Christian Ukrainian folklore makes the Sun a divine *mirror* into which "God" looks each day (the reflection of his glory makes it too bright to look at) to see the deeds and sins committed on Earth. When the

RUSSIAN HEAD-DRESS

mirror becomes fouled with sins, God wipes it, causing an eclipse. During the night, God looks into the mirror of the Moon. This is dimmer than that of the Sun because more sins are committed under cover of darkness.[41]

The Sun's Dance

The Slavs, like the Celts, Balts and others, knew the tradition of the Sun's dance, which in some areas was supposed to happen on Easter morning, and in others on Midsummer's Day. On Midsummer Eve the peasants would go up to a high place, there to keep a Sun-vigil with a bonfire, choral dances, and special songs and games. The latter included *zagadka* or ceremonial riddles, of which the oldest are about the Sun, Moon, stars and elements. In one riddle "a bird sitting in an oak tree" turns out to be the Sun, while a shepherd whose flocks hide at dawn is the Moon, and his sheep the stars.[42] A similar riddle makes the Sun-goddess a cow, the Moon-god her calf and a flock of goats the stars.[43] As in other Sun-goddess worshipping cultures, the rituals of the night culminated in everyone present anxiously watching to see the Sun rise, and hoping to witness her dance, in which she whirled about and emitted coloured sparks.

Winter Solstice and Holy Kolyada

Winter Solstice was also an important occasion, like other holy-days having its own special songs. Ralston says :

"In none of them [the seasonal songs] are the traces of the old religion more perceptible than in those songs which are sung at Christmastide... and which bear the name of *kolyadki*... at that time, according to popular tradition, the Sun—a female being—arrays herself in her holiday robe and head-dress, takes her seat in her *telega*, and urges her horses upon the summer track. And to this solar goddess the people have given the name of *Kolyada*."

The most likely derivations of *Kolyada* are from *kolo*, "wheel," or *kolada*, "yule-log." In former times this Sun-goddess was impersonated by a young girl dressed in white, who was driven on a sled from house to house, escorted by a group of attendants singing Kolyadki songs, and offered gifts by every house-hold.[44] It is clear that Kolyada is the reborn Sun of the Solstice:

> "On Christmas Eve was Kolyada born
> Beyond the rapid river."[45]

The "rapid river" is that which flows from beneath the *Alatuir*-stone of the western isle. Beneath its cold and turbulent waters lies the underworld, through which the Sun must pass each night. Another song describes how "Holy Kolyada" is sought everywhere on the Eve of Nativity (that is, the Sun is "lost" in the darkness of Solstice night). People seek her "through all the courts, in all the alleys," recalling the maze-games of Europe in which "Lady Sun" is hidden at the centre. Kolyada is finally discovered in the thunder-god's palace, where there are three rooms—one for the Sun, mistress of the house, one for the Moon, its master, and another for their children, the stars.[46]

Ceremonies of ritual bathing took place at the Summer and Winter Solstice ceremonies, because the Sun-goddess and Moon-god were believed to have washed themselves, deep beneath the earth, "in the coldest possible water."[47] In Poland, where feminine Sun traditions are also preserved (a legacy from the Old Prussians, who were related to the Lithuanians and Latvians), the Sun-goddess bathes in the river on Midsummer Eve, before she rises to dance and play in the sky. In Upper Silesia, cakes were offered to the Sun-goddess on Midsummer Day, while girls danced together in a ring "after the Sun" (i.e. clockwise), singing, "Play, Sun, play! Here are your little suns!" In Poland, as in Russia, both the Midsummer and Midwinter waters were made especially healing because the Sun had bathed in them.[48] (Compare this with the Armenian folktale telling how water in which Sun-goddess and Moon-god have washed, restores a girl to life.[49])

Sun Goddess and Storm God

While the Sun-goddess is ancient, she was rejected by the "properly con-stituted religious authorities," that is, the ruling class, who, probably under the influence of Roman and Byzantine patriarchy, perceived the Sun as the divine type of male gods, emperors and priests. Since she was acknowledged only by the common folk, she was excluded from the "official" list of deities compiled in Christian times.[50] The influences of Christianity and nineteenth century scholarship still combine to exclude the feminine Sun from popular accounts of Slav folklore. Authors, whether Russian or otherwise, tend to recount only those folk-tales and songs which depict the Sun as male, or they present the thunder-god *Perun* as the Sun. They speak, for example, of:

> "...the preponderant role played by the god of thunder: he
> is the god who is found at the dawn of the middle ages
> among numerous Slav races in the guise of the sun-god... "[51]

But Indo-European tradition distinguishes with absolute clarity between the deity of *storm* and that of the *Sun*. They are only combined—or deliberately and misleadingly confused—by mythologists who wish to obfuscate the plain fact of the feminine Sun. The god of thunder, storm and rain, *Perun*, is the equivalent of Baltic *Perkons* (although, oddly enough, their names are not etymologically related).[52] The idea that, as a sky-god, he must therefore be a Sun-god, is a misconception based on Max Mueller's theories. Modern scholars do not agree that he was the principal deity, regarding this as the product of mediaeval Christian preconceptions about "God." The Slavs had no centralized absolute authority, a state of affairs reflected in their pantheon which empha-sized numerous spirits of Nature, and guardian spirits of the roof-tree, thresh-old, cooking-stove, etc. "Perun cannot be considered the supreme god of the Slavs, but is rather a spirit to whom was given the governance of the lightning."[53]

Eclipse of the Sun

Chapter 10
Sun-Woman of Ireland
The Feminine Sun among the Celts

"Greeting to you, Sun of the seasons
As you travel the skies on high,
With your strong step on the wing of the heights.
You are the happy mother of the stars.

You sink down in the perilous ocean
Without harm and without hurt
You rise up on the quiet wave
Like a young queen in flower."[1]

—Traditional Gaelic Prayer

The prehistoric Celts were an Indo-European people who occupied much of Iron-Age Europe, first appearing in Germany and then from about the ninth century B.C., spreading as far as Spain, Britain and Asia Minor. Their wide dispersal in a vast range of different conditions was reflected in their religion, or rather, *religions*, for the Celtic deities were strongly localized. Each forest, spring, mountain, sacred tree, cave and so on had its own god or goddess, many of whom are known to us solely by a name in a Romano-Celtic inscription. There was no centralized religious authority (the Druids were a British invention, exported from there to the mainland[2]) and no hierarchy or common system of divinities.

The Romans standardized some aspects of Celtic religion by adopting certain deities, such as *Epona*, the Gallic horse-goddess who became a favourite of the Roman cavalry, and *Lug*, god of male skills (and cleverness in general), whom the Romans thought was Mercury. The characters and cults of such deities were altered to fit Latin ideals, as they were carried further from their localities by Roman troops. The Roman practice of "identifying" all Celtic weather-gods as Jupiter, all healing gods as Apollo and all warrior-goddesses as Minerva, to name but a few, has distorted our later conceptions of the Celtic religious mind, and given to Celtic religion a uniformity it did not have. The Celtic spiritual world was a multiverse, not a universe, and "Druidism," for example, was only one part of that world, not the whole of it.[3]

The Sun and Moon among the Gaels

The deities of Ireland and Scotland were very numerous and included the Sun and the Moon.[4] Both solar and lunar rites played an important part in folk-religion until as late as the early years of this century, often in a barely Christianized form, uneasily tolerated by the Church who frequently made attempts to control or suppress their more pagan aspects. The Sun was imagined to be a feminine being, a state of affairs which the Church tried to change—Saint Patrick told his heathen audience, "The true Sun is Christ"[5]—but the Gaels were never really convinced.

Irish and Scots Gaelic is full of feminine expressions for the Sun. "Sun" itself is *grian* (or *greine*), a feminine word. It appears in personal names, such as *MacGreine*, "son of the Sun" (fem. *Ni Greine*, "daughter of the sun"), while *Dia Greine* is the Sun-goddess herself,[6] and the term *grian ban Eireann*, "paragon of Irish womanhood," literally means "Sun-woman of Ireland." A verse of the traditional Irish love-song "Mary, My Darling," says:

> "If I were a fisherman...
> I should catch in my net
> The sun of the women of Ireland."[7]

(This is a reference to the idea that the Sun went down into the sea each evening, as well as to the Gaelic belief that she was swallowed by a giant fish who carried her to the eastern shore each night.)

The heroine of Irish legend is often compared to the Sun. She is for example *grian na maighdean*, "fairest of maidens," or rather, "the Sun among maidens." The archetypal peasant woman, the good lady of Irish folk-tale, is traditionally named *Mor* (anglicized as *Mora*), which when feminine means *the Sun*. When masculine it means a great person or number, but without any solar connotations.[8]

The Sun and the Fire

Earthly fire was thought by the Celts to be of a solar kind. It had been brought from the Sun by a sacred bird—the wren, who was scorched red by the encounter, or more usually the swallow (whose red face-markings and forked tail were the result of the Sun's fires) or the swift, who was burnt altogether black by the fiery goddess.[9] There is an obsolete Irish name for the Sun, *tethin*, which like the related word for fire, *teine*, is feminine, and both are related in turn to Scottish *teth*, "burning, scalding, intensely hot (as a person in a fever)." *Teine* is solar fire; the word is best known from *Belteine* or *Beltane*, the famous May-day feast of the island Celts. This name is commonly—and wrongly—construed by modern-day occultists as "the fire of Bel," a supposed Sun-god.[10] *Bel* is however not the name of a god, but simply means "bright, white, beneficent, beautiful" or, as Cormac's ninth century *Glossary* puts it, "goodly." It is etymologically related to Baltic *balta*, which carries a similar range of meanings.)

The Celtic festival of Beltane, and the later Gaelic Christian Easter to which some of its May-eve rituals were transferred, included a typical Sun-vigil on a high place, at which the Sun was encouraged to come out of the darkness, and grow in strength, with the help of a bonfire, and other lights. The culmination of the vigil was the sunrise itself, proof-positive of the rite's efficacy.[11]

The Sun's Dance

As the Sun rose on Easter (or Mayday or Midsummer) morning, everyone hoped that they might see her dance. She was supposed to give three joyful leaps, and then whirl round and round, emitting multicolours and sparks.[12] Despite the belief that to look at the dancing Sun brought a divine punishment—blindness—many people claimed to have seen it, and some still expect the Sun to dance on Easter day.[13] Campbell reports a sceptical Scotswoman, rebuking a friend who thought she might go up and see the Sun's dance, saying, "Fool! And dost though think to see the sun rise from there, when she rises beyond Edinburgh, and as many hills as there are in the way?"[14]

Another means by which one could see the Sun's dance was to view her reflection in a water mirror, a method by which the Sun herself was mystically brought to Earth. On Easter morning, people would fill suitable bowls with water and set them out on the threshold to catch the rays of the rising Sun. Then, by shaking the dishes so the water rippled, the Sun's light would *dance* on the walls and ceiling. This rite is interesting in that it not only combines both *fire* and *water* in typical Indo-European fashion, but also brings the Sun herself *into the house*, perhaps with the same kind of intention as that of the builders of New Grange, or protecting and purifying the house with the power of the goddess's beams.[15]

Sun-Wells and Sun-Stones

Many of the Irish holy wells and springs are still associated with Grian in living tradition. *Tobar na Greine* means "Well of the Sun." Such wells are particularly associated with the cure of eye-conditions, like the Sun-touched holy waters of the Balts, Slavs and Basques, and the making of ritual offerings of *grianchloichit*, "Sun-stone." To obtain the well's benefits, one must bring and then leave behind on a nearby "altar," or drop into the spring itself, pebbles of white quartz. (In Irish tradition all quartz stones are sacred to the Sun.)[16] The well ritual or *pattern* also included circumambulation, done sunwise (clockwise) and often on one's knees, or all-fours. Patterns still go on today, under Christian auspices.[17]

As the Sun-stone, the clear quartz crystal and the white were both thought of in some sense as crystallized solar light. This is made evident by the ritual use of crystal to sanctify water in Scottish clan tradition. Many of the hereditary clan talismans were large crystals—the *Clach na Bratich*, "Stone of the Standard," belonging to the Robertsons of Struan, was "a bright globular crystal" enclosed in a case of golden filigree.[18] This talisman is now lost, but the Crystal of Currahmore—bigger than an orange, and bound with silver—is still preserved, and was until the last century used to treat sick cattle. The crystal was dipped into running water through which the beasts were driven. Other similar talismans were dipped in water and the sick person or animal would then drink.

We can compare this to the Scottish Hogmanay (New Year) rite, transferred from Winter Solstice, in which a live coal from the hearth-fire was dropped into a bowl of spring water. The purifying and blessing virtues of fire and water being thus combined, the house and family were sprinkled to protect then for the coming year.[19]

The traditions of the Scots and Irish Gaels concur with that of the Hindus in assigning crystal to the Sun. The *Surya-kanta* or Sun-gem (Literally "the glitter of the Sun") is rock-crystal, believed to be formed from condensed Sun-rays. Set at the tip of a priest's wand, the crystal is dipped into water, thus imbuing the water with solar fire and making it holy.

The Waters of Sulis

Perhaps the best-known Celtic healing spring is at Bath, in Somerset, the ancient *Aquae Sulis*, or waters of the goddess *Sulis*. Her name comes from the same Indo-European root as Baltic *Saule*, Germanic *Sol*, Slavic *Solntse* and all the other Indo-European names for Sun,[20] as does the closely related Irish Gaelic *suil*, which means "eye," i.e. the Sun, the eye of the heavens.[21]

The waters of Sulis come out of the ground at a most pleasant and useful temperature—hence from early times these hot springs were used to treat the sick. As we have already seen, it is quite common for the Sun-goddess to imbue natural waters with her healing powers. Moreover, she is very usually thought to descend into water at sunset, down a hole or well into the sea, and thus pass

RARE CELTIC COIN
SHOWING FEMALE
SUN-FIGURE

beneath the earth on her night journey. In Arab tradition the Sun is a fiery spark which is quenched in the sea at night, while among the Balts the Sun and her daughters descend into the western ocean and sometimes have to be rescued from drowning. Evidently, it would be nothing unusual for the Celts of Aquae Sulis to think of their goddess going down into the spring and like a kind of celestial immersion-heater, warming up the Bath-water.

The museum at Bath Spa exhibits coins recovered from the spring into which pilgrims had thrown them as votive offerings. The display informs us that many coins bear a phœnix, a reference to the "unseen fires" which heat the waters in the underworld. While several authors remark that the divinity of the spring was clearly solar, only Markale manages to make the connection with the Celtic Sun-goddess.[22] When the Romans took over the spring from the

Celts, they replaced the Sun-goddess with a Sun-god, Apollo, carving his image on the temple pediment so as to leave the natives in no doubt about the sex-change.

The Abode of Women

While at night the Sun went down in the ocean depths, during the day she ascended to the mountain heights. Hence in Irish and Scots Gaelic we find the word *grianan*, which means "the abode of the Sun." In Scotland a grianan is any sunny place, but particularly on a height, and particularly a high mountain peak which first receives the light of the rising Sun. In Ireland a grianan is a Sun-room or Sun-terrace, of the kind which formed the topmost chamber of the Celtic house. Here the women of the clan enjoyed a little peace, away from the drinking, bragging menfolk in the chieftain's hall beneath. The grianan was *the abode of the women*, and such a chamber. apparently circular with windows all around, is known to have existed at *Tara*, the ancient seat of Irish kingship. Men were forbidden to enter the grianan—hence it often appears in legends as a place of imprisonment, where a beautiful princess is enclosed by her father, to prevent her from marrying the man of her choice.[23] At the same time the grianan appears in legend as the inviolate throne-room of matriarchal heroines. The fairy-queen appears in a grianan, where she herself shines like the Sun; in this context *grianan* is translated "fairy bower," but it is not a bower of leaves and flowers. The fairy grianan is built from bright crystal, *grianchloichit*, the Sun-stone.

Another kind of grianan is any type of earthworks or ringfort on a hilltop. An especially magnificent example is the restored Grianan of Aileach in County Donegal, a stone built ring-fort of about 1,700 B.C. Folklore tells how it was ruled by three "princes," *Ceachta*, "stars"; *Coill*, "Moon"; and *Greine*, "Sun"—except that Greine would have been a *princess*. Scholars believe that these names refer to an astral cult which went on there; perhaps such a grianan would have been a kind of observatory.[24]

Sun-women of Legend

Celtic scholars have identified some female characters in early Irish literature as versions of the pagan Sun-deity. Such stories as the great Irish saga *Cattle Raid of Cooley*, or *The Pursuit of Diarmid and Grainne*, are undoubtedly based on stories of the old gods, although few certain interpretations can be made. The mortal woman Grainne may be the Sun-goddess Grian under another guide, her name shuffled to mean "Hateful." Markale is certainly of this opinion, calling her simply "the Sun-goddess,"[25] and there are definitely some clear solar motifs in her legend. She puts her lover *Diarmid* under a *geis*, a taboo or ritual obligation, compelling him to follow her, but Grainne's husband pursues the couple so that they are forced to hide in a cave. The chase lasts "a year and a day," during which the lovers take a circuit of Ireland, seeking refuge in a different cave every night. Irish tradition points to these as the dolmens scattered around the countryside, table-tombs which are called "the beds of Diarmid and Grainne." A year and a day is the folkloric term for a *solar* year, that is, a lunar year of thirteen months (each of twenty-eight days) plus the extra day which the Sun takes to complete its annual cycle. This all sounds suspiciously like the usual Sun-goddess and Moon-god pursuit of primitive tribal myth, where the lunar god is forced to follow his lover the Sun, and even includes the idea that, when Sun and Moon are both absent from the sky at once, they are together as lovers under the earth.

The possibility that the Sun-goddess has two names accords with the dual nature of the Sun itself, its mild and fierce aspects, or (in the North) its strong summer or weak winter forms. The Scottish year is traditionally divided into two parts—the time of the "big Sun," which runs from Beltane (the first of May, the first day of Celtic summer) until Samhain (the thirty-first of October, the first day of Celtic winter) and the time of the "little Sun," which lasts for the other six months, the cold season, when the Sun is perhaps "hateful" because she withholds her heat.[26]

Celtic Sun-Mares

A number of important Celtic goddesses or "fairy women" take the form of a mare. As Anne Ross warns, it is an oversimplification of a complex mythology to routinely identify horses as solar.[27] Nevertheless, some are undeniably associated with solar motifs, in particular *Aine*, or *Lair Derg*, "The Red Mare." Aine signifies "brightness, heat, speed"; she is the mare whom none can outrun, and her principal feast was a bonfire-vigil held on Midsummer Eve on the hill of Knockainy, County Limerick.[28] Her husband is *Manannan*, the sea-god from whim the Isle of Man takes its name. He has several lunar features—he appears to be a multiple god, he gave the other gods immortality, and he owned magical swine which regenerate after death.[29] His symbol, the *tryfuss*, consists of three armoured legs which run "moonwise," that is, from right to left; it is the traditional emblem of the Isle of Man. Aine and Manannan may represent the Sun-goddess and Moon-god of a particular locality or clan. Similar horse-goddesses appear in other areas under different names; *Macha*, a fairy-woman, runs so swiftly that none can better her; she is forced to race against the king's horses while she is heavily pregnant, and at the finish line drops twins and dies in childbirth; *Rhiannon*, the Welsh version of Gallic *Epona*, has a closely similar myth; she also appears dressed in brilliant golden clothing, riding a white mare which cannot be overtaken. The twin gods which these mare-goddesses bear are thought by some scholars to be the same as the Vedic *Asvins* and the Baltic *Dieva deli*.[30]

The Feminine Sun in England

While the Irish and Scottish deities were little affected by Roman influence, in England Latin solar traditions replaced those of the Celts, as at Bath. Yet mainland tradition still retained some trace of the feminine Sun-cult, and when the Nordic invaders came in on the heels of the Romans, they brought with them their own Sun-goddess *Sunna*.[31] Thus in the beginnings of the English language the Sun was *she*, both mythologically and grammatically feminine. Right up until Milton's time the Sun continued to be thought of as a woman:

> "For yet the Sun Was not;
> shee in a cloudie Tabernacle Sojourn'd the while."[32]

But during the sixteenth and seventeenth centuries changes in the English language combined with Christian influence and revived interest in classical mythology to change the sex of the Sun. Bishop Latimer's *Sermon on St. Stephen's Day* of 1552 still calls the Sun feminine:

> "...Not that the sunne itself of her substance shal be darkened... "

By the 1607 edition, *her* had been changed to *his*.[33] After Milton, the Sun of literature and popular symbolism was merely a copy of the late classical model; the Sun-goddess of the West European pagans was gradually forgotten among English-speaking people, and it became "normal" for the Sun to be a masculine god. But, here and there, we find traces of the older cult, in folklore and custom, sometimes occasionally in language.[34] As a child I heard a farm-worker, an old Yorkshireman, refer to the Sun as "she." (The tradition of the Sun's dance was current in my home county, Durham, in the last century, as also in Northumberland, the Border counties and North Yorkshire.) Both Yorkshire and Lincolnshire also preserved until recently a curious custom known as *Wading the Sun*, which is clearly a variant of the Sun-mirror water-pot used in Ireland. A wide vessel or bucket was filled with water and set out so that it would directly reflect the rising Sun of Easter Day. As the Sun appeared all watched her reflection anxiously, to see if she *waded*, i.e. glimmered or trembled, an omen of rain; if that day's rain came in the morning, the spring would be wet and the autumn fine, but if the afternoon was wet that signified a rainy autumn and bad harvest.[35] As an example of the use of *wade* in the Yorkshire dialect, the author gives:

> "It'll rain afoor neeght, t'sun waded sadly ez sha peeped over Roseberry." (*Sha* = she) [36]

East Lincolnshire and Yorkshire are thickly covered with *Scandinavian* names, of which culture this feminine Sun may be an inheritance.[37]

Eclipse of the Sun

Chapter 11
Grandmother Sun, Good Lady
The Basque Country

To the present day, Basque tradition preserves the former pagan belief that the Sun and the Moon are female beings. The Sun was the goddess *Ekhi* or *Eguski*, while the Moon was the goddess *Ilargi* or *Iretargi*. Different areas of the Basque country each have their own, slightly different versions of these names.[1]

The Sun-goddess traditions of the Basques have many elements in common with those of the Celts, Balts and Slavs, suggesting that a strong Indo-European influence touched Basque religion. The Iberian Celts doubtless provided those features which make Basque Sun-rites so very close to those of Celtic Britain and Ireland, while Roman Mithraists introduced the theme of the Unconquered Sun. But the Basques retained their own unique language and culture, along with the feminine identity of the Sun. Pure Basque no longer exists—about 70% of the spoken language consists of loan-words—but it is known to be unrelated to any other European language; according to philologists, it dates from Palaeolithic times.[2] Its name for Sun and Moon have no known cognates in any other language, so perhaps these goddesses, too, come from that remote past.

Grandmother Sun

Folklore, folk art and prehistoric artefacts all attest to the great importance of the Sun in Basque religion. Even after their acceptance of Christianity, the Basques continued to worship their Sun-goddess in the guise of *Eguski-saindu*, "Saint Sun," imagining the *monstrance* to be a representation of her. For those unfamiliar with Roman Catholic ritual, the monstrance is a glittering golden sunburst, made of precious metals and gemstones, with a central window used to display the consecrated Mass-bread. In the ceremony called *Benediction* the faithful bow down before it in adoration. It is easy to imagine how in this way a pagan Basque could go on honouring her beloved *Eguski Amandrea*, "Grandmother Sun." The monstrance became a favourite theme in folk-art, depicted especially above the main door of the house (which traditionally faced east, towards the rising Sun) except that instead of the Mass-bread, with its design of a crucifix, the Basque stonemasons carved Equiski's own sign in the centre of the sunburst. (In modern times this symbol, a kind of curved swastika, is known as *La Croix Basque*, and is the national emblem of the Basque people.)[3]

Both Sun and Moon goddesses are daughters of the Earth-mother *Lur* or the storm-goddess *Mari*, who travels the sky producing hailstorms and electrical phenomena such as lightning and fireballs.[4] "Grandmother Sun, you return to your mother," and "Saint Sun, good lady, you turn towards your mother," are traditional invocations made to the Sun as she sets. At sunset the Basques imagine that the Sun-goddess lays her head on the breast of mother Earth, there to sleep. In Christian times Dame Mari has become identified with the Blessed Virgin, a confusion which effectively gives Jesus the Sun and Moon for sisters![5]

The Sun-Vigil

On Midsummer Eve the people would go up to a high place, sometimes a mountain-top in the High Pyrenees, a "Mountain of Noon" where the Sun was believed to touch the high peak as she passed over the sky,[6] or more usually, a convenient peak near the village. There they kept a typical night vigil culminating in sunrise, everyone present hoping to see the Sun dance above the hilltops. She was hailed with ceremonial songs and greetings, such as:

> "Sun, glorious little Sun,
> Give us victory!
> To you courage, and
> To us, life and health!"[7]

Folklorists have collected many of these Sun-prayers. The use of an affectionate diminutive for the Sun, as well as the four-line form which regularly occurs in these prayers, recalls the Baltic *dainas*.[8]

Once the Sun was up, everyone hastened to the nearest holy spring, fountain or stream to bathe, for immediately these waters had been touched by the Midsummer Sun and infused with her fire, "their usual virtues of fecundity and healing were infinitely multiplied."[9] Bathing in the morning dew was also very popular (in case you were wondering how one might collect enough dew to bathe in, the method is much simpler—one strips off and rolls about in a suitable,

monstrance

preferably flowery meadow). Again we find here that mystical combination of fire and water which so fascinated the Indo-Europeans. The resemblance to Baltic practice does not stop there, for the ritual baths which conferred general health and good luck upon all were specifically imagined to heal skin-diseases.[10]

The Ritual Fires

Fire ceremonies were an important feature of the Solstice night. Bonfires were lit on the high places where people would gather to see the Sun come up, then young people would seize brands lit at this new fire so that the hearthfires down in the villages could be rekindled. Flaming brands, bundles of straw and herbs, or torches of plaited tree-bark were waved in circles "in imitation of the Sun."

Since the Sun goddess was inimical to all evil spirits and sorcerers (the latter became paralysed if she shone on them during their rites) the Eve of St. John was the scene of great cruelty towards "evil" animals. Snakes, toads and black cats were burnt alive in the Solstice fires, sometimes first being enclosed in baskets— a practice very similar to that of the pagan Celts, who burnt both animals and humans alive in wicker containers. The Basques imagined that in this way they

BASQUE ROSARY-RING

were purifying and exorcising evil by the fiery power of the Sun.[11]

Symbols of the Sun

The herbs and flowers sacred to the Sun—fennel, lime, chamomile, houseleek and others—were woven into wreaths for the Midsummer festival, exactly as among the Balts. Houses were decorated with them—a practice thought to protect against fire and lightning. In particular the stemless thistle (*Carlina acaulis*), with its impressive sunburst form, was Eguski's own flower, the Flower of the Sun, and its petals were used in various solar rites. It had a lesser connection with her sister the Moon, but this had virtually no ritual importance, as Ilargi's symbol *par excellence* was the wax candle, the death-light.

The lintel of the main door in the traditional Basque house is decorated with sacred symbols—especially the tree of life, monstrance, Sun-wheel, "shepherd's rose" (six petals within a circle), Sun-thistle, crescent Moon, *la Croix Basque*, stylized flowers (rosettes), hearts and other traditional designs, most of which are Sun-symbols.[12]

Grandmother Moon

The Moon-goddess's name Ilargi means "light of the dead," a reference to the belief that she illumines the underworld when she goes down into the earth.[13] Undoubtedly, Ilargi was, like other Moon-deities, at one time not only the goddess of death, but also of rebirth. Basque lunar folklore is otherwise very similar to that of the rest of Europe. Some authors, such as Briffault, believe that the Basque Moon was formerly a male god, although Briffault was incorrect in his claim that the words for "God" and "Moon" are the same.[14] The Christian god is *Jaun-goiko*, "Lord of the Height" (the equivalent of the "High God" in primitive mythologies), whereas Moon is *gaiko*—nothing to do with height, but associated with *gauko*, meaning "of the night."[15]

Better evidence for a one-time male Moon comes from southern Basque stories of the marriage of Sun and Moon, but here we are much nearer to the Mediterranean, and sometimes the Sun is a male. The types of Indo-European motif which one might expect from Eguski's cult are absent, and the pair are more like Roman deities. One story, however, tells that the Sun wished to burn up the Earth, while the Moon wished to freeze it. Instead of arguing all the time, they decided to form a partnership and take turns at freezing and burning. Thus the Sun married the Moon.[16] There is also a trace of the idea that the Moon is a fecundating male god, for babies conceived during the crescent period will be male, while those conceived during the decrescent period will be female.[17]

A solar eclipse is caused by an argument between the Sun and Moon. The Sun vanishes because it has been momentarily vanquished, and is too humiliated to show its face.[18]

A Multitude of Deities

The definitive works on Basque mythology by Barandiaran and de Marliave disclose a religious world of great complexity, with a wide range of deities and rites largely unknown outside the Basque country, yet casting much light on similar practices in the rest of Europe which have become obscure. Most of the important Basque deities and sprites are female, and the pantheon is generally weighted on that side. While the Sun-goddess was held in great honour, the Basque deities, like those of the Balts, had no hierarchical arrangement and were equally important, each in their own sphere of activity.

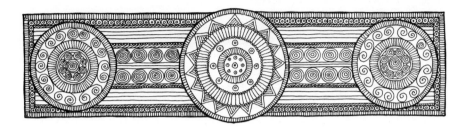

Chapter 12
She Who Makes the Day Glad
Germany and Northern Europe

"When ye see the Sun glad,
Ye own the fine day is hers.
Ye thank her, not God."[1]

—German mediaeval poem

In Teutonic and Scandinavian mythology, the Sun is always feminine, the goddess *Sunna* or *Sol*, while the Moon is always masculine, the god *Mani*. In Germany the Sun is still *Frau Sonne*, "Lady Sun," while the Moon is *Herr Mond*, "Lord Moon." Every time we use the words Sun or Sunday we refer to this Sun-goddess, for the Nordic invaders brought her worship to the British Isles and introduced her name into our language. Thus it was that, up until Milton's day, the Sun was called "she" in English, and why we still refer to "The Man in the Moon."

A folk-tale which is found all over Europe preserves a memory of the Sun-goddess and Moon-god. It was said that, once upon a time, an impious couple angered God by doing servile work on Christmas Eve, the man gathering wood and his wife spinning flax. God punished them by separating them for all eternity. First, however, he offered them a choice of freezing forever in the cold Moon, or unending fire in the hot Sun. The man chose the Moon, where we can still see him with his bundle of wood (and his dog, or his lantern) while his wife chose the Sun—and there she still sits behind her blazing spinning wheel which goes for ever round-and-round. She is the *Woman in the Sun*, the forgotten and eclipsed goddess.[2]

The Eddas and the Prophetess

In the various sources of Teutonic and Scandinavian literature the Sun appears as a goddess, a golden woman of great beauty and delight, in several respects resembling Baltic Saule. Important information on this Sun-goddess appears in the *Eddas*, Icelandic writings set down between the ninth and thirteenth centuries of our era. The *Elder Edda*, a series of anonymous poems on pagan lore, were used as a source for the Edda proper or *Prose Edda*, composed by Snorri Sturlusson in the eleventh century. He was mainly concerned with preserving the great traditions of Icelandic poetry, and did not hesitate to mix his own Christian beliefs with pagan themes, but the Prose Edda is still the most important sourcebook on the North Germanic deities.[3]

Sunna is given many poetic descriptions and names in the Eddas. As in other kinds of poetry whose intention was sacred, these names are not arbitrary and decorative—they connect with a network of other, mythic elements and meanings. The Sun-goddess is *the fair bride of heaven*. The elves call her *Elf-beam* (*Alfrodull*) or "Glory-of-Elves" or "She-who-shines-on-the-elves." She is the shining, "glittering" goddess, she of *Glitnir*, the heavenly palace.[4] Her character is "gracious," "sweet," "blithe"; she is "God-blithe," an expression referring to the beaming, "glad" or "smiling" Sun. She is the blithe Sun, "whereof the world had aye rejoiced."[5] She turns dwarves and trolls to stone by her glance, hence she is known as *Dvalin's Doom*, while other semi-divine beings call her *Everglow*, or *Fair Wheel* (*Fagrahvel*),[6] or *All-Shine*.[7]

The Elder Edda opens with the *Voluspa*, "What the Prophetess Says." a work detailing the world's origins and its final end. According to this the Sun and Moon simply appear, as the Sun-goddess "flings her right hand over the rim of heaven"; it is the goddess's beams, shining on the barren rocks of the new-made Earth, which bring forth plants:

> "From the south did Sunna
> Shine on the walls
> Then did the earth
> Green herbs produce
> The moon went ahead,
> The sun followed
> Her right hand held
> The steeds of heaven."[8]

But neither Sun-goddess nor Moon-god yet know their way through the sky:

"Sun, Moon's companion   out of the south
Her right hand flung   round the rim of heaven
Sun knew not yet   where she had her hall
Nor ever the Moon   what might he owned."[9]

The high gods then took counsel together and set the Sun-goddess on her eternal paths. Her own hall or palace. where she lives when not occupied with her task above, is in Hel, the underworld[10] like the other denizens of the sky who are seen to set below the horizon. There she sleeps on a bed of pure gold.[11] But she has to make the journey back to her starting point, driving her team along the road of the lower world from west to east.[12] In the morning she passes through the *jodyrr*, the "horse-doors," the gates which are set in the mountain-wall of the lower world, and her appearance is announced by the crowing of *Goldcomb*, the cockerel of morning.[13]

The Horses of the Sun

Both Sun and Moon cross the heavens in horse-drawn chariots:
> "Aarvak and Alsvidr
> Theirs it is up hence
> Wearily the Sun's wagon to draw."[14]

Aarvak ("Early-Awake") and *Alsvidr* ("All-Swift") are the Sun's horses, equivalent to the *Asvins* of Vedic myth. The gods have thoughtfully placed a "cooling iron" or "bellows" (*iskamol*) under the horses' withers,[15] and protected us from the goddess's heat by a shield:-
> "Svalin it's called,
> In front of the Sun
> A shield from the shining goddess
> Earth and ocean must smoke and burn
> If ever the shield should fall."[16]

Snorri's Edda explains why the goddess hastens across the sky:

> "The Sun moves fast, and almost as if she were afraid; she could not travel faster if she were in fear of her life. It is not surprising that she goes at such a pace. Her pursuer is close behind her, She can do nought else but flee."[17]

Behind the Sun runs a monstrous wolf:

"Skoll the wolf is named
That the fair-faced goddess
To the ocean chases. [or to the wood]
Another Hati is named...
He the bright maid of heaven shall precede."[18]

Skoll chases the Sun, and Hati the Moon. When they manage to take hold, we have eclipses, but the demons are not destined to destroy Sun and Moon before the world's final end.

The Fate of the Sun

The rule of the gods is destined to end in the cataclysm called Ragnarok, a great cosmic purification. The visible sign that the end is upon us will be seen in the heavens, for Sunna will be overtaken and devoured, turning first red, then black, resulting in a terrible winter (*Fimbulvetr*) lasting three winters long[19] (in the north, this adds up to about two years.) Then wickedness will prevail; nothing will be honoured or respected, sacred things will be despised and humans will live only for violence and greed. Finally Sunna's darkened wheel will vanish and the stars will tumble from their places as the keystone of heaven's arch collapses, and everything vanishes in the abyss. But the universe and the deities are destined to be reborn, the world reappearing as naked rock, as in the first time. Sunna will relive as her own daughter:

"Whence comes a new Sun
In the clear heaven again.
When the Wolf has swallowed the old,
One daughter alone
Shall that Elf-beam bear, before she is
swallowed by the Wolf,
The maiden shall ride on her mother's paths
After the powers have perished."[20]

Shining on the rocks of the new world, the maiden Sun will make them green again, as her mother did aforetime. She is called Sunna, and also bears the lovely name *Svanhild Gold-Feather*.[21] Hastings Encyclopaedia suggests that she is the same goddess as *Eostre* and the Baltic Sun's daughter, the young or spring Sun[22] who replaces her mother, the old Sun of the Solstice, or the Sun who descended into the Earth during the northern winter's darkness. During *Fimbulvetr* the old Sun-goddess goes down into Hel, where she sits by the river of the underworld. (There she is known as *Gjoll's Sunna*, after the river.) The gods ask her to recite, shamaness-like, the mysteries of creation (in the hope of restoring the cosmic harmony) but all she does is weep.[23]

Spinning Sunbeams

Several kinds of labyrinth or "paradise" hopscotch played in Germany evoke the Sun-goddess, a mysterious lady whom the players seek in the centre, or at the "top of the stairs." A Hessian version has the accompanying chant:

"Where does Auntie Rosie live?
—Up there, above.
What is she doing?
—Spinning silk.
How bright?
—As her own hair."

In other parts of Germany, *Frau Sonne* replaces "Auntie Rose" in this song, or sometimes the Blessed Virgin, who in German folklore was identified with the Sun.[24] The game recalls the spring labyrinth rites of Baltic, German and Swedish folk-tradition, where the young Sun-goddess was sought in her prison by the twin star-gods[25] as well as the Baltic image of the Sun-goddess as a red rose high in a tree.[26]

In Sweden, too, the Sun-goddess is a spinning woman who has to put in an early shift, getting the golden thread (sunbeams) ready for her dawning:

"Mistress Sun sat on a bare stone
And spun on her golden distaff
For three hours before dawn."[27]

According to German folklore, travellers who find themselves on the mountain summits at sunrise may meet a mysterious woman, white-robed, with golden hair falling to her feet, who sits and spins golden thread. She is a gift-giving goddess, and if she offers you anything you must take it, no matter how worthless it may seem, for when you get home it will have turned to pure gold. In folk-tradition she is one of the *Weisse Frauen*, the "White Women," beneficent spirits who are the descendants of the pagan Light-Elves,[28] worshippers of *Alfrodull*, the Sun-goddess Elf-beam. They bask in the light and warmth of the Sun's rays, becoming visible at noon as comely white-dressed women with long golden hair, boon-giving goddesses who help the poor, the oppressed and lost travellers.

The Eddic word for wheel, *hvel*, is the same as Saxon *hweol*, from which we get our word. Hweol also means a spinning-wheel. The Gothic rune *hv* is represented by a wheel ⊙, a sun-symbol which closely resembles the Egyptian hieroglyph of the Sun, ⊙, as well as suggesting a breast or eye, symbols of the Sun-goddess which are found in other cultures.[29] A blazing wheel, cast down a hillside or set on a pole, forms an important part of European folkloric ceremonies, particularly at May-time and the solstices, rites which come from archaic Sun-goddess cults of the North, but are now invariably attributed to male gods. In Teutonic tradition the Winter Solstice was sacred to the priapic god *Frey*, but berore this it belonged to *Freya*, who some scholars believe to have been a Sun-goddess. The blazing cartwheels which encouraged the Sun in these rites were imitation suns, designed to tempt the goddess *Fagrahvel*, Fair-Wheel, out of the darkness.[30]

The Darkened Sun

The Icelandic goddess *Sol* each day escaped her ravening pursuer by making it to the safety of the Forest of the Varns, which lay behind the western horizon.[31] Then she passed down through the western horse-doors to her own home in Hel. Teutonic lore gives an alternative nighttime destination for the goddess. Just below the horizon, she *sits down* in a golden chair or throne. Our word *sunset* comes directly from this tradition, *set* being merely an older form of the word sit. Thus when the Sun vanishes at evening, it's only because she has sat down behind the horizon, like someone behind a screen! And likewise, in the morning she *stands up*; she literally rises from her chair.[32] These mythological ideas have passed into our language, and we use the words *sunset* and *sunrise* quite unconscious of their original connotations. The same Germanic tradition that gives us the sitting Sun-goddess says that she takes a short cut back to the east by "*creeping* round the northern sea," i.e., on all fours! Of course, she has to creep, because if she stood up, she would appear above the horizon rather prematurely, in the middle of the night! (The northern sea-route is also taken by some of the Australian aboriginal Sun-goddesses.[33])

Sunna expresses her approval or disapproval by shining, or by withholding her light. When the Sun shines very warmly, according to a German saying, "Frau Sonne means well by us."[34] This is perhaps not only a courteous acknowledgement of the goddess's good favour, but also a hint that she shouldn't overdo it. The Sun-goddess can hide her face in anger or revulsion—Otfried's mediaeval poem *Evangelienbuch* contains a verse telling how Sunna, indignant at people's evil deeds, withdrew her light in disgust. This typical Sun-goddess theme, transferred to Christianity, gave rise to legends that she hid her face in grief at the death of Christ, or of a virtuous Christian man.[35]

Acknowledgement of the Sun's bounty was expressed in traditional invocations, recorded for example in this thirteenth-century poem:

"Hail to thee, Lady Sun!
Thou art all the world's delight!
When ye see the Sun glad

> The fair day to her ye ascribe
> To her ye give the honour
> Whenever ye see her beaming light."[36]

She was also invoked in prayers and charms. The *Merseburg Formula*, a ninth century chant for healing a sprain, names *Sinthgunt Sunna era suister*, "Sunna and her sister Sindgund."[37] Evidently, this referred to a well-known element of Sun-myth. Mythologists have disputed the identity of Sindgund, "companion," but most agree she is a star-goddess, the same as *Nanna Sintgunt*, who is described as Mani-the-Moon-god's daughter. She is said to "battle her way across the sky each night," a very apt description of a planet moving among the stars. (The idea that Sintgunt is a "Moon-goddess" is false.[38]) Sunna and her companion are clearly the same kind of pair as Amaterasu and her sister Waka-hiru-me, or the various Sun/ Sun's daughter dyads.

Oaths were also taken with the hand extended, palm upwards, towards Frau Sonne, inviting the all-seeing goddess to witness, as well as symbolically showing that one has nothing to hide. (This gesture is supposed to have been reversed to make the Nazi salute.) It seems that she may have inflicted fever on oathbreakers. A Pomeranian prayer, said facing the Sun as she rose, asked her

> "Dear Sun, come down soon, and take the seventy-seven
> fevers from me, in the name of the Holy Trinity!"[39]

In Bavaria it was traditional to take off one's hat to Frau Sonne at her rising. Here folklore tells of the separation between Sun and Moon. When the Sun-goddess married the Moon-god, he proved a great disappointment. She was a hot and passionate lover, while he was very cold, preferring to sleep rather than to make love. The Sun laid a bet with him, that the right of shining by day should go to the one who woke first. If this was a ruse to persuade her husband to rouse himself, it failed, and ever afterwards she shines by day, and he by night.[40]

Another Bavarian story says that the Moon-god once abducted a mortal girl, in typical Moon-god fashion. Not unsurprisingly, given his coldness towards her, the Sun-goddess was furiously jealous. She tried to get her revenge by stealing away the maiden's boyfriend. After a time the young woman and man met again, but she was in love with the Moon-god and had ceased to care for her former lover. As he wept, his tears became shooting-stars. This is a confused version of an earlier form in which it is the Sun-goddess and Moon-god who have ceased to care for each other, and the *Moon's* tears are the stars.[41]

The practice of keeping a Sun-vigil on a hilltop, with feasting, dancing, bonfires and blazing cartwheels, is found in many areas of Germany, for example, in Swabia, Saxony and Brandenburg. When the Sun arose, she was expected to dance and give "three joyful leaps." Teutonic lore also preserves the mystical connection of solar-fire and subterranean water, with a number of places even today bearing the name "Sun-Well" or "Spring of the Sun."[42]

The Charioteers of Sun and Moon

As the primitive Scandinavians anthropomorphized natural forces, they met a problem—how could the Sun be a blazing disc or wheel, and be a goddess at the same time? The Balts solved this problem in their lyrical poetry, making the Sun into an ornament worn by the goddess—a crown, belt, ring, etc. In the Eddas the story of Mundilfoeri's children is an attempt to deal with the difficulty. *Mundilfoeri* was a mortal man, but his name reveals him as a god, the one who spun the world or the heavens.[43] He had two children, a boy and a girl. They were so marvellously beautiful that impious pride took hold of the earthly man's heart, and in defiance of sacred taboo he named the girl *Sol* after the Sun-goddess, and the boy *Mani* after the Moon-god. Now, these names had been given to the great lights by the high holy gods,[44] and it was expressly forbidden to call mere mortals by these divine names.[45] The outraged gods deprived the blasphemer of his children and sent them to the heavens; there they drive the chariots of their namesakes until the end of the world.

Tolkien's Sun-Goddess and Moon-God

The English author J. R. R. Tolkien's work in Early English literature and comparative mythology eventually led him to compose his great fictional history, *The Lord of the Rings*, a tale of a far earlier world. He drew upon real languages and mythologies, particularly those which shaped English language and folklore, and thus in all of Tolkien's tales the Sun is personified as female.[46] *The Tale of the Sun and Moon* describes how the great golden ship of the Sun-goddess *Urwendi* is formed from a magic fruit. The ship itself, *Sar* ("Sun") or *Ur* ("Fire"), and the spirit who steers it, are female entities.[47] Readers who consult both this book and Tolkien's tale will be able to see how he employed motifs from a number of Sun-goddess mythologies. The idea of the Sun as a golden boat with sunrays for oars is not, as might be thought, Egyptian, but Baltic. The dainas describe Saule crossing the sky in this fashion.[48] The titles of the elvish Sun-goddess are reminiscent of Scandinavian ones—*Galmir*, "gold-gleamer" and *Gorwent*, "ship-of-gold." The storyteller adds "but her names among Men no man has counted them." Was Tolkien aware of the Sun-goddesses and the way they have been ignored? Commentaries on Tolkien's work also ignore the fact that he made the Sun female and Moon male,[49] while the popular way of explaining it is to claim that he deliberately reversed them, to emphasize that this is a magic world, where things are the other way round from "normal." But an examination of Tolkien's work indicates he based Sun and Moon on deities of northern mythologies, not on mere reversal.

Will the Real Sun Please Stand Up

Popular writers identify practically every male deity of northern pantheons as the Sun, on the slightest evidence or none at all. Odin is top choice, but Thor, Heimdall, Balder and nearly everyone else is proffered as the Sun at some point. The fact that such writers cannot agree on who is the real Sun (even though some, like Branston, remark in passing that the Sun was actually feminine, but withhold the details) shows that none of these gods have any claim to that position. (Even those modern "Odinists" who practise an extreme right-wing form of revived paganism dissent from Nazi belief and call Odin the Sun-god.[50]) There is a fundamental problem here—preconceptions of the Nordic or "Aryan" Sun-deity as a big blond warrior take precedence over the facts of mythology.

Chapter 13
Mother of the Merciful Rays
Finno-Ugria and Siberia

The Finno-Ugrian peoples of north and eastern Europe are united by the *Uralic* family of languages. They include the Lapps, Finns and tribes such as the Vogul, Ostyak, Selkup, Cheremiss, Mordvin, Pemyak and Votyak, together with the Hungarians. The tribes had their own, very archaic spirit-religions, to which they later added shamanistic practices from their Siberian neighbours.[1]

Sun-Mother of the Lapps

Among the Lapps the Sun is feminine, the Great Mother who blesses the land with plants and the reindeer with fertility. She is called *Baiwe* (*Beive, Paiva*). Uniquely among the Lapp deities she is never represented in human form, but as certain geometric shapes—on the sacred drum of the southern Lapps, for example, she occupies the central place as a lozenge with rays extending through the four directions of space. Other deities stand on her rays, drawing their sustenance from her, while the Moon, *Mano* or *Aske*, who is a masculine god, is represented as a crescent among the other deities.[2]

On the northern Lapp drums she appears as a rayed circle, sharing the upper level of the cosmos with the Moon-god. Another way in which the Sun-goddess and Moon-god are represented in ritual is in the form of a wooden ring, the Sun, and a wooden disc with a small central hole, the Moon.[3]

Mother of Animals

The Lapp Sun-goddess is the mother of all the animals, particularly the reindeer, on which the Lapps entirely depended.[4] She was offered only female animals in sacrifice—in theory, only white ones were ritually correct, but the goddess was satisfied with one of the ordinary colour, providing that a white thread was attached to its ear. Such rites were performed facing sunwards, with a Sun-ring fixed on a pole so that the goddess shone through it. This was evidently intended to trap or fix the Sun in one spot, for a Lapp who was lost in the wilderness would use such a Sun-ring, fixed on a handle, to sight the Sun and so magically prevent her from setting before he had found his way home. In this sense the Sun-ring had a similar function to the mirrors found in other Sun-goddess cults. When sighted through the ring, the goddess was symbolically present at the top of the pole; as it were, fastened to earth.

When a reindeer doe was sacrificed, the goddess received the blood, poured as a libation through the centre of a Sun-ring, and the bones, which were arranged in a neat ring on the ground, plus some token slices of meat, threaded on birch-twigs (the goddess's sacred tree). The family used up the rest of the carcass.[5] Offerings were also burned.[6]

While the Norwegian Lapps used a Sun-ring, the Scandinavian Lapps very inventively took long thorns and glued them all over a wooden ball—a unique way of making a model Sun, as far as I could discover, and one that shows that they understood the Sun to be a *globe*, not a flat disc. This image was set on a pole at the place of sacrifice.

Sun-Rites of the Seasons

In the far North, the Sun vanishes altogether beneath the earth for part of the year. Her return was greeted with joy, and in the beginning of February, when she was visible above the horizon for a good part of the day, each Lapp woman would bake a special cake to honour the Sun-goddess. It was kneaded from flour, reindeer blood and reindeer fat, and shaped into a disc. Then it was suspended by a string above the tent-door, so that the goddess would see it and be pleased. In this way each Lapp woman would ensure the Sun-goddess's favour for the coming reindeer-breeding season.[7]

It was Lapp belief—based on practical observation of Nature—that the Sun-goddess nurtured the reindeer by producing plants for them to eat. The Southern Lapps worshipped a special, springtime aspect of the Sun-goddess, whom they called *Rana-neida* or *Beive-neida*. She specifically presided over the nourishment of the winter-starved reindeer, in concern for them shining upon the south-facing hillslopes, warming them, melting the snows, and turning the winter-bleached earth green with new plant growth.

In an attempt to persuade her to bring an early spring, the Lapps set up special altars on which this Sun-goddess was represented by a spinning-wheel. The blood of the white doe was poured over it—or, if this rite was too costly, or the prayer to the Sun was an everyday one, it was sufficient to sprinkle a little blood on a spindle.[8] Or one could make a bloodless offering to this Sun-goddess of Spring simply by consecrating to her a spinning wheel and some flax; she was pleased with such an offering because she was herself a spinner, the blazing wheel of the sky who spun from her own substance the shining threads (rays) of sunshine. Thus the Lapp goddess closely resembles other spinning Sun-goddesses of the Northern lands.

Summer and Winter Solstice

Summer Solstice was Baiwe's principal festival. Then the people would weave Sun-rings or garlands from green grass and leaves, hanging them up to delight the goddess whose warmth brought such bounty. The rising Sun of Midsummer Day was greeted with an offering of butter, smeared on the doorposts, a share of the family's festival dinner which was a very rich concoction, "Sun-porridge," into which butter and other good things had been stirred. A sort of grace, recited by the father of the family, introduced this sacramental meal:

> "O Sun, pour your merciful rays,
> Over the reindeer
> Over the birch trees
> Over the [here came a list of all the things for which the
> family wanted the goddess's blessing.]"

After the meal prayer was offered again, this time for a happy milking-summer and for increase and protection of the reindeer. Baiwe also healed mental illness. [9]

The Midwinter rites were similar, but they also included an offering to the Moon-god, who particularly needed to be appeased during the cold weather. To please him and to ward off his baleful influence, a brass Moon-disc was hung in the smoke-hole of the hut.

The Sun-Goddess of Other Tribes

Among the *Votyak* the feminine spirits of nature far outnumbered the masculine ones. The Sun was *Shundi-mumi*, "Sun-Mother." [10] White animals were offered to her in sacrifice whenever anything threatened the already harsh lives of the people—sickness, drought, a late spring—and also at her annual feasts. Among the Cheremiss the Sun is *Ketse-awa*, "Sun-mother," and her cult closely resembles that among the *Votyak*. The Yurak Samoyed called the Sun-goddess the "kindly eye" while the Moon was the "evil eye," a dangerous spirit.

The Ostiak imagined the Sun to be a mother-goddess and the Moon an elderly male god. Fainting was believed to be a kind of visitation from the Sun-mother, upon which she would be given an offering of a cloth and a ring.[11]

The Feminine Sun in Siberia

Among the Siberian tribes, who practise a very archaic kind of religion known as *shamanism*, the Sun is very often a goddess and the Moon a god. In the bitter climate of North Asia she is welcomed as a warm, nurturing and beneficent force who in general receives a more active worship than the Moon, yet at the same time she is a formidable goddess who punishes oath-breaking with sickness. The Sun-deity of either sex has long, golden hair, streaming from heaven to earth. A vital energy radiates from the Sun-goddess and is commu- nicated to plant life by her radiant hairs—a mythic recognition of the Sun's essential role in the living world. The Siberian fire-goddesses, too, have long, golden tresses which represent the flames of the fire itself, its light and warmth, radiating through space, reaching up through the heavens and warming even the white clouds. Such fire-goddesses are clan-mothers, divine ancestresses.[12]

The Mirrors of Sun and Moon

Some tribes in the Altai, a mountainous region of central Asia, consider the Sun to be a goddess, *Kun*, while her husband is the Moon, *Ai-ada*. Another tradition from this region says they are sisters, mirror-goddesses who flew up from the primordial ocean when the high father-god stirred the waters. Previous to the goddesses' appearance people themselves (who in those days were luminous) were obliged to fly around to give the world light. Everything that happens on Earth is reflected in the Mirror of the Sun and the Mirror of the Moon, which is why we see marks on these heavenly bodies.[13]

Mirrors and metal discs representing Sun and Moon are important features of the very complicated shamanic costume. They are not merely ornaments but have a precise esoteric meaning and purpose. The Mongol shaman believes that he may view in his mirror a white horse, the spirit-horse who will carry him away, once he has fallen into trance. In his mystic journeys through the sacred levels of the cosmos, he will ascend to the Moon and Sun themselves. In the Yakur shaman's costume there is a metal disc, pierced with a central hole, representing the hole down which the shaman will descend to reach the underworld. The disc is called the Orifice of the Sun, because in just such a way does the Sun go down into the underworld.[14] This concept is also found among the native Australians.

Among the ancestors of the Japanese are known to have been peoples of the Altai. It is undoubtedly from this source that the feminine Sun, the mirror as her symbol, and the Siberian elements in her myth have passed into Japanese mythology. Early Japanese ceramics of the Yamato period, funerary sculptures depicting *miko* or female shamans in trance, show that a belled mirror was an essential part of their costume. Shamanic religions believe that sickness and misfortune are caused by the soul being stolen, or wandering, lost in the multi-level cosmos—hence the main function of the shaman, which is to freely travel all the worlds in search of the soul. To this end she has a soul-trap, the mirror. Once the lost soul is perceived in the mirror, it is recaptured. From this primitive concept came the idea that the dazzling Sun might too be "trapped" in the mirror, and hence retrieved, as the lost Sun-goddess was retrieved from her dark cave in the Shinto story. Other Siberian tribes, as well as aboriginal peoples of China and Korea, regard the Sun as a feminine being who is associated with the mirror.[15]

Bold Sun-Woman

Among some Mongol tribes the Sun and Moon are sister-goddesses, who look down from the sky at the beginning of time and decide that land must be created up from the waters. Various creatures essay the task, but only the Loon (*Gavia* species) or Diver is finally able to bring up mud from the depths to form land. After this the sister-goddesses discuss how they will light the nights and days. Unfortunately, the Moon-goddess has a very retiring temperament. She is bashful when people are up and about, so she waits until they are asleep in bed before showing herself. Even then she shrinks with embarrassment, trying to hide her face (this causes the Moon's phases), especially when she has to take the day-shift. Her sister the Sun is quite bold and open, striding over the day-sky quite happily.[16] Among many Siberian tribes the Moon is thought to deputise for the Sun at night, and to give light to the dead in the underworld, just like the Basque Moon-goddess.

Beautiful Sun

In the North East of Siberia, where the climate is very severe, live the Yukaghirs. Their Sun is a goddess, the celestial ideal of the beautiful woman. Mortal girls sometimes receive the compliment *Tudel yelóje titemei tat ômoc*, "She is like the Sun, so beautiful!" Mother Sun of the Yukaghirs, a kindly deity, is invoked for comfort and blessings:

"Mother Sun, warm us with your heat
Give us nourishment with your heat
Divert from us all evil,
Whatever may be its source."[17]

However, she inflicts punishments on those who sin against the tribe's moral rules. Other tribes who consider the Sun to be feminine include the Selkups, the Udegeis—whose Sun-goddess is wooed by the Moon-god—and some Buryats.

The Theft of the Sun and Moon Mirrors

Among some of the Buryats of Southern Siberia the Sun and the Moon are wife and husband, and they are represented once again by mirrors. The Buryat explain that the Sun and the Moon were once stolen by the Earth-god, who selfishly kept them shut up in a box. Thus the world was darkened, and it fell to Porcupine, the trickster, to see whether he could get them back. Porcupine, renowned for his cheek, went straight to the Earth-god's tent—a visit which put both under very strict rules of etiquette. Hospitality was so sacred that the Earth-god was obliged to treat Porcupine as an honoured guest, to offer him a meal and the choice of any gift he desired. Porcupine requested an "echo-spear" and a "mirage-horse," impossibles which, he well knew, the god could not provide. In such an event the host had to give his guest the most valuable thing he owned—and thus it was that Porcupine received the box with the imprisoned Sun and Moon mirrors. He flung them into the sky so that no-one could steal them again.[18]

The Moon-God

Like the masculine Moon of so many tribal peoples, the Siberian Moon-god is characteristically the lover of women, real father of children, and cause of menstruation. The Mongol emperor Jinghiz Khan's mother was impregnated by a Moon-ray. Siberian Moon-gods care for the souls of the dead who are to be reincarnated (it is sufficient simply for a woman to desire a child, and the Moon-god will visit her). He is also a healer, but of less importance in this respect than the Sun. Where both Sun and Moon are masculine—for example, among the *Koryak*, the *Chukchi* and the *Yakut*, the Sun is the Moon's elder brother.

Chapter 14
The Great Warmer
Alaska, Greenland and the Arctic

"There is joy
In feeling the warmth
Come to the great world
And seeing the Sun
Follow her old footprints
In the summer night."

—Traditional Eskimo Song[1]

The Eskimos own name for themselves is *Inuit*, meaning simply "The People."
Early European inhabitants of the North learnt the word *Eskimo* (or *Esquimaux*)
from Athapascan-speaking tribes of Alaska and Canada—it means "eaters of
raw meat."

Throughout the different Eskimo groups the Sun is always feminine and the
Moon masculine. In the absence of an Earth-mother, the principal Eskimo deity
is the water-mother *Sedna*, but in Alaska where Sedna is unknown, the Moon-
god is chief over all. The Eskimo deities are all imagined to have started off as
humans, living on Earth.

Sun-Woman of Greenland

The Sun-goddess is called *Malina*, and her brother the Moon is *Anningan*.
Once they lived contentedly, playing games together, but the time inevitably
came when they were no longer children. One night while they were romping
about in the dark, Anningan became sexually aroused. In his excitement he

seized his sister and raped her. The seal-oil lamp was overturned in the struggle; Malina's hands were covered in greasy lamp-black, and she smeared them over Anningan's face as she tried to push him away. Once he had finished with her, she ran and ran, further and further, up into the sky, where we now see her as the Sun.

Anningan, however, showed no remorse at all. He still lusts after his sister and chases her in a pursuit which goes on forever. So intent is he on the prospect of raping his sister again that he forgets to eat and so gets thinner and thinner, until at last he is forced to come down to earth and hunt for food. That is why the Moon is absent from the sky for three days each month—he is sitting patiently by a seal breathing-hole in the ice, waiting for the kill. When he has fed well on meat and blubber, the chase starts again, and the Moon-god gradually regains his former shape.

The Solar Eclipse

When the Moon is full, and at the height of his powers, he very occasionally manages to gain on Malina and rape her again, causing a solar eclipse. Not surprisingly, Sun and Moon hate each other. Moreover, they extend this hatred to all members of the opposite sex, rejoicing in the deaths of men and women respectively. When a *parhelion* is seen,[2] Sun-woman is thought to have decked herself with earrings or side-curls, in happiness at the death of a man, or the birth of a girl, but when a man dies or a girl is born the Moon-god pulls his hood over his face in grief, and we see this as a ring around the Moon.[2] Both the Sun-goddess and the Moon-god are baleful spirits who send diseases upon those who offend them[3] This is particularly liable to happen during eclipses, so that men are careful not to go out of doors during a solar eclipse, or women during the lunar eclipse.

The House of Sun and Moon

In the far north of Greenland the Sun-goddess is called *Sequinek* and the Moon-god is *Aningaan*. They dwell in a double house, partitioned so that the Moon and his wife *Akoq* (a mortal woman whom he abducted) can live separately from the blazing hot goddess. Intense light and heat come from the Sun's side of the house. Shamans who visit the Moon-god, their patron deity, have to be careful not to look at the Sun, or she will revenge herself by burning them.[4]

These ideas are very similar to corresponding Siberian tradition, but the Eskimo version meets with a slight technical problem—the concept of "earth," and a world in or under the earth, is absent from the lands of ice and snow. (This

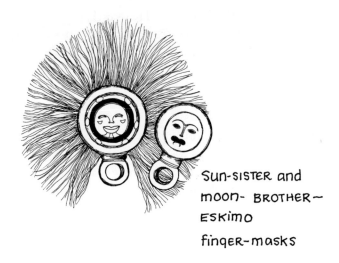

Sun-Sister and Moon-Brother—Eskimo finger-masks

is why the Earth-mother does not occur in Eskimo religion, her place being taken by the sea-mother *Sedna*.) The house of Sun and Moon is originally under the earth, accounting for the times when they disappear below the horizon, but because of the lack of "earthness" in Eskimo thought, the location of the Sun and Moon's house is either vaguely somewhere up above, or under the sea, or even on the Moon itself—resulting in various contradictions.

The Midnight Sun

During the summer the Sun never goes into her house—she is out both day and night, so the snow melts and the flowers grow.[5] But during the winter months she stays at home, and the Moon deputizes for her in the world above. He is also obliged to take driftwood home to her, to stoke her fires, because she is unable during the winter months to go out and look for it herself.[6]

It was the long polar darkness which encouraged the Eskimo to develop their art of storytelling, singing and games to a high degree.[7] One of the games which, played in the dim light of seal-oil lamps, helped while away the dark days, also had a ritual intent. "Cat's cradle," at which the Eskimos are renowned experts, able to make dozens of patterns, is thought to "net" the Sun and draw her back up above the horizon. Among the Copper Eskimo this game is forbidden during the light days. Instead, "cup-and-ball" is played to encourage the Sun to go higher and higher in the sky. Other groups such as the Iglulik Eskimo play "ring and pin" for the same reason.[8]

According to the East Greenland Eskimo, there are even more effective

Eclipse of the Sun

ways of getting the Sun to rise. They say that the Sun is a beautiful girl—at least, from the front view. Seen from behind she is a naked skeleton, because when she is at her lowest point, people cut her back with knives so she will rise again.[9] Other Eskimo say that she rises again in order to give warmth to orphans, like the Baltic and Slavic Sun-goddesses.

The Return of the Sun

After the winter cold and darkness the goddess's return is welcomed, for she brings warmth and growth, as well as the appearance of certain birds and animals. While in terms of *magic* and *ritual*, the Sun plays a lesser part in Eskimo religion than the Moon, in Eskimo *life* she is still an important natural force, reflected in the fact that Eskimo dance-masks often represent her.[11] An old Eskimo song says,

> "There is only one great thing
> to live, to see... .
> the great day that dawns
> and the light that fills the world."[12]

In fact, the return of the Sun is the one important seasonal celebration in the Eskimo calendar.[13] Her reappearance is heralded by the planet Venus, seen low in the western sky. This star is a masculine being, a bad-tempered old man who once imprisoned two children in a rock-cleft, because their noisy games disturbed his seal-hunt. Their angry parents chased him into the sky, where he became the evening-star.[14] He is eagerly looked for towards winter's end.

Among the Iglulik Eskimo, children go round putting out all the seal-oil lamps when the Sun reappears, lest she be offended. There has to be new light in the lamps, so fresh fire is kindled. In earlier times the West Greenlanders held a Winter Solstice feast, with special dances. Rituals for the return of the Sun also used to include the chasing away of winter spirits, embodiments of cold and darkness.[15] Knud Rasmussen collected details of the Sun tradition directly from a Greenland Eskimo man, *Maisanguaq*, who told him,

> "When Sun returns people call out, "Joy! joy! The Great Warmer has come; soon we shall be able to seek the sunny side!"

Her reappearance was then celebrated with feasting.[16]

Sun Traditions of the Copper Eskimo

During the summer the Sun-goddess is thought to draw closer to the earth and warm it, but in winter she goes under the sea, travelling far down into its depths. When members of the Canadian Arctic Expedition visited the Copper Eskimo in 1915, they were told that they would hear the Sun hiss as she set in the sea on her first day of reappearance (ninth of January)—presumably because her fires were so new and fresh.

In this tradition the Sun's face becomes covered with a black soiling during eclipse, and the shamans have to ascend to her and wipe it away. She shows her baleful nature by the parhelion, which warns travellers and hunters that they will not be able to get home, but will die a sudden death in the wilderness. Alternatively, the parhelion is a gale-warning—the Barrow Eskimo say that the extra suns are walking-sticks, which the Sun-goddess uses to steady herself in a high wind. (For other Sun-goddesses with walking-sticks, see the section on Australian traditions.) Evidently, the Sun-goddess is none too securely placed in the sky, because the rainbow is called *Aiyakutak*, that is, "the prop that keeps the Sun from falling."[17]

Sun Traditions in Alaska

Here the Sun-goddess is called *Akycha* or *Seqinek*, while her Moon-god brother is *Igaluk*. One of the Alaskan versions of their story describes the practice known as *Dousing the Lights*. The young people would gather together and extinguish the lamps, then select a partner at random in the pitch darkness, the idea being that no one should know who their partner was, nor should a fixed relationship develop. Such group-sex among adolescents was once a normal part of Eskimo life, but there were certain rules—incest was one of the greatest of all sins, so that those who fell within the proscribed circle of relationships were forbidden to play the game together. But Sun-sister and Moon-brother ignored the rule—with the predictable result. Sun-sister marked her lover's face with soot. When the lamps were relit, there was her own brother with a sooty face! Burning red and hot with shame, she seized her *ulu* (the woman's curved knife) and cut off her breast, crying, "Since my whole body tastes so good to you, eat this!"[18] Then she fled from the house, carrying a torch to light her way, and ran up into the sky, the wind of her ascent fanning her torch to a brilliant blaze. Moon-brother stumbled after her but fell down in the snow, quenching his torch so that it now smoulders with a dim light as he follows his sister through the sky.[19]

There are a number of slightly different versions of the incest tale. In some the Sun is raped by the Moon, while in others the pair willingly make love, only discovering their transgression afterwards. The Sun-goddess sometimes cuts off one breast, sometimes two; sun-spots are said to be the scars of this self-mutilation.[20] The Sun's light and heat sometimes emanate from her torch, and sometimes from her face, which burns with shame—in contrast to the Moon, who does not feel such shame "because he is a man."[21]

The Moon-God

As the master of magic and the teacher of shamans, the Moon is surrounded by a vast body of religious lore. He is the patron of hunters and travellers, and the deity who controls the weather. Snow, rain and ice are stored up in the Moon, from whence the god sends them to earth at his will. He presides over the Eskimo paradise, a place of carefree games, dancing, feasting and happiness, where he looks after disembodied spirits of humankind and sends them back to Earth to be reincarnated. In all these aspects the Eskimo Moon-god is the very type of the primitive masculine Moon.

His primitive character is also seen in his relationship to women. It is the Moon-god who is the real father of children. At new Moon he comes down to earth and makes love with mortal women, causing menstruation, indeed he will do this at the least provocation—in West Greenland young women are warned not to gaze at him in case he takes this as an invitation. (Rubbing the abdomen with saliva is supposed to keep him off.) A woman who wishes to have a child by the Moon-god may drink water upon which the full Moon has shone, while elsewhere the light of the Moon shining on a sleeping woman is thought to cause menstruation. Depending on the tradition in question, the Moon-god is imagined to be a good spirit, the friend and patron of women, or a dangerous and evil spirit, who hates women and will rape or abduct them.[22]

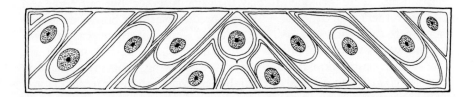

Chapter 15
Great Sun, Six-Killer
North America

"It is noteworthy that among almost utterly savage tribes in Africa and America, the moon is with them always regarded as a male, the sun as a woman; not until later are those relations inverted."

—Robert Briffault[1]

Sometime around 25,000 B.C., small groups of Asiatic peoples travelling on foot crossed over from Siberia into Alaska, at the point where the uttermost west of America nudges the far, far East. Today, the Bering Straits divide the two lands, but in prehistoric times fluctuating sea-levels allowed the wandering Palaeolithic hunters to walk straight over into their new world. The waters did not finally close over, dividing America from Asia, until seventeen thousand years later, by which time the ancestors of many native tribes, North and South American, had crossed from the Asian homelands and made their settlements. The vastness of the Americas allowed the different tribal groups to separate widely and hence to evolve a bewildering variety of languages and religions. But, time and again, we find elements of Sun-goddess cult which the Amerindians share with peoples of India, Japan and Northern Europe.

The Native American Sun-Goddess

When the western invasion of the New World began, there were many hundreds of tribes (not counting all the various tribal divisions and sub-groups), some of which were virtually extinct before the coming of the Europeans.

Numerous others were wiped out by the white man's diseases, his weapons and his greed. Yet others dwindled, were Christianized, and their remnant dispersed. Some tribes were unwilling to concede an inch of ground or thought to the white invaders, while others adapted to their ways, often incorporating their religion into their own traditional rites to form a distinctive hybrid, Native American Christianity.[2]

In recent historical times, when the American Bureau of Ethnology recorded what remained of native American religions, many tribes still regarded the Sun as female and the Moon as male. Sun-goddess and Moon-gods were chiefly found among the tribes of the Far North and the North West Pacific Coast— the Inuit (Eskimo), Tsimshian, Nootka, Tlingit, Coos, Chinook, Dene[3] and others. Elsewhere the Cherokee, Yuchi, Maidu, Caddo, some Apache groups and others thought of the Sun as a woman.[4]

But Christian influence was at work; the missionaries impressed upon their pagan audience that the true Sun, the Great Spirit, was really a man. It is undoubtedly this influence that has caused tribes to change Sun-woman's sex in modern times. The 1945 Smithsonian Report said that the Cherokee, Eskimo and Yuchi were the only remaining peoples to see the Sun as feminine.[5] Earlier records show that once things had been different. They also show that, within the same tribal grouping, some sub-groups saw the Sun as male, while neighbouring ones had different myths, depicting it as female. The white anthropologist often recorded only the tradition of the masculine Sun, because it accorded with his European preconceptions, and ignored the feminine Sun-tradition. Another source of such cultural imperialism is the so-called *New Age*, a quasi-religious movement based on theosophy, pop-psychology and flower-power. In recent years it has done much to misrepresent Native American traditions, to the grief of tribal elders. Because of its ultimate origins in Renaissance occultism, the New Age imposes Western ideas of the male and female principles on all religion. Thus New Agers regard the Sun of *all* Amerindian tribes as masculine, regardless of what tribal tradition actually says.

The Sun-Goddess of the North West

Along the North West coast, the mythologies reflect the traditional life of fishing, hunting and gathering—hence they are preoccupied with the animal world, rather than the forces of the elements. Nevertheless, Sun and Moon were important. The Sun, with her reliable warmth and kindly benevolence, did not require rites of appeasement, and when people prayed to her they did so without the intervention of a shaman.[6] The Moon was the master of magic, spirit of the mysteries of generation and renewal, and the arts of the shaman. He caused menstruation by having intercourse with mortal women. The Nootka of British Columbia regarded the Moon-god and Sun-goddess as principal deities, the Moon governing rain and snow while the Sun governed warmth. The Tlingit also held Sun and Moon in honour, but Moon was a rich chief, surrounded by his wealth, the stars, while Sun was a poor woman, appearing in the day sky all alone.[7] Nevertheless, her warmth was believed to animate all creatures in the day, while her husband watched over them at night.

Coos Sun-Woman

The extinct *Coos* of Southern Oregon said that the Sun-goddess was not always so mild and beneficent. Before their culture-hero visited her, she was intensely dangerous.

A young man came of age, and brought back to his father's home two most lovely wives. The old man eyed the girls lustfully, and an evil plan took shape in his mind, for he was a sorcerer. He plotted to get rid of his son and take the young women for himself. In what must have been the world's first space-shot, he sent the lad rocketing up to the sky-plain on a flying fir-tree.

The sky-plain proved to be a land of strange inhabitants and many adventures. Our hero was first of all welcomed by the Blue Cranes, friendly beings who gladly offered him their hospitality, but warned him that Sun-woman stopped each day at their house on her journey across the sky. The Blue Cranes gave Sun-woman her lunch, which consisted of human stomachs, for the goddess was a fierce cannibal. Undeterred, the hero decided to stay. It was not long before a tremendous noise, a fierce red light and a blast of terrific heat warned everyone that Sun-woman was approaching. The young man hid himself. As soon as he had seen the goddess sate herself with her grisly meal, he came out and accosted her before she could leave.

The young hero was undeniably handsome; Sun-woman was soon won over by his charm and seductive talk, and agreed to make love with him. As his penis was made of ice, this romantic encounter cooled Sun-woman's heat and violent temperament quite considerably. Since then, she has behaved with greater clemency towards human beings. In this story the hero has affinities with other Moon-gods of the far North, who are characteristically the producers of ice and snow. It is interesting in its association of heat and fierceness with feminine sexuality and the woman-Sun, the hero's icy penis and sexuality being the cold element which cools Sun-woman's ardour, i.e. satisfies her desire. Here too we find the common motif of the dual personality of the Sun-goddess—on the one hand, her violent devouring tendency, with its burning heat, and on the other her mild, beneficent personality.

In another version of the Coos myth, Sun-woman wishes to marry the hero, but sadly she cannot, for she is unable to stay at home and keep house for him. So, instead, she gives him her sister the Moon, who is at least able to be at home on occasion.[8]

Chinook Sun-Woman

In a Chinook version of the sky-plain story, the hero marries the celestial woman and falls under an enchantment, by which he is made to forget everything of his earthly life. His wife gives birth to Siamese twins, but on the sky-plain this is no tragedy—such children separate naturally as they grow up. Unfortunately, the couple's happiness was soon to end. The hero caught sight of his old home, far way below, through a hole in the clouds, and thus the spell was broken. His desire to return to earth was overwhelming. The sky people tried to stop him, but he let himself down by a magic rope, leaving behind his unhappy wife and children. Meanwhile, Blue Jay Bird had tried to separate the twins by cutting them with his beak. Their mother returned to find the two little boys lying dead. Thus bereft of both husband and children, she departed in her grief and rose up to the far reach of heaven, there to become the Sun.

On rare occasions, the Sun-goddess appears with the corpses of her boys, an astronomical effect known as a *parhelion*, which creates bright spots within the solar halo, or an illusion of multiple suns. Sun-woman is reminding the world of her sadness, for the parhelion is an omen foretelling the death of a chief. This tradition comes from the lore of the *Clackamas* Indians, one of the Chinook tribes.[9]

Maidu Sun-Woman

The Maidu Indians of California viewed the Sun as a fierce female and the Moon as a male, her husband. At first they lived together in a solid stone house, and the creatures on Earth dwelt in darkness. Nothing would persuade the pair to come out, and even the strongest could make no attempt on the stone house. It was left to the cunning of Angle Worm and Gopher, who cleverly introduced fleas through a little hole which the worm drilled, until Sun and Moon were tormented with itching bites. They came out and went up to the sky, where Sun-woman refused to travel with Moon-man. "I will go by night," said she, but it proved useless because the stars constantly harassed her for sex. Thus it was that Sun came to travel by day and Moon by night.[10]

The Sun-goddess was violent and hostile. She built herself an impregnable house of ice, like a great mountain, in the far north, from which she emerged to capture human beings, kill them and eat them. She stole Frog-woman's children one by one, until it seemed as if there would be none left. In desperation Frog-woman waited at the door of her house until Sun-woman came by, and swallowed her whole, but the goddess's blazing heat burst poor Frog-woman's body open. Taking pity on the frog, Sun-woman put her together again and gave her life.[11] This story appears to combine two separate strands—frogs and toads commonly represent the Moon, and as such cause solar eclipses by swallowing the Sun, in several mythologies. At the same time the Maidu myth contains the theme of the Sun dismembering the Moon (the frog) and putting it back together again, an idea we also find in the Sun-goddess mythology of the Balts.

Other Californian Indians knew of a feminine Sun. According to the *Achomawi* of Shasta County, the Sun-goddess crossed the sky in a regular fashion each day until she took it into her head that it would make a nice change just to roll along the ground. So one morning, instead of rising up high, she just fell down and started tumbling along. She didn't get far, which was as well for the Earth, for otherwise it might have been set alight—Mole saw her, and with a great effort pushed her back into the sky. This is why Mole's hands are pink and bent backwards.[12]

Sun-woman of the *Lake Miwok Indians*, Lake County, withdrew, like the Japanese Sun-goddess, into her stone house, and shut the door fast. Hawk, chief over all, complained to his people about the lack of light and warmth, so Coyote the trickster told the two Dove brothers to go and get Sun-woman out. Their methods were rather less subtle than those of the Japanese *kami*—they simply smashed the house wall with sling-shot, so that the Sun-goddess in fright rose up *through the smoke-hole.*[13] Several elements of the typical Sun-goddess mythos are here—the female Sun enclosed/withdrawn/imprisoned in a stone enclosure, the absence of light and warmth, the release by two gods (who in this case break down the house with sling-shot, as the Baltic "little sons of god" broke down the tower with a hammer) and the new sunrise via a hole which is symbolic of the Centre.[14]

Mewan Sun-Woman

The *Mewan* of California tell how the world was once in total darkness, save for a faint glow in the east where Sun-woman lived. They greatly desired her light and warmth, so they sent two men to persuade her to come and light the Earth, but Sun-woman was happy in her own home, just beneath the ground. She refused to return with them to the land of the Mewan. When the men went home without the Sun-goddess, the tribespeople were in despair. They next sent a big crowd of men with ropes, who bound her and drew her into the upper world, forcing her to come back with them. The Sun-goddess's body is covered all over with brilliantly shining abalone shells, which are so bright that we cannot look at her directly.[15]

Cherokee Sun-Woman

The tribe we know as Cherokee are really called the *Ani Yuwiya* in their own tongue, that is, "real people" or "original people." The Creek Indians called them "people of different speech," *Tsalagi*, which the Ani Yuwiya converted to *Cherokee*. Today the various branches of the Cherokee form the second largest Indian nation of the U.S.A., with their own written language which was developed not by missionaries but by *Sequoyah*, one of the tribe.[16] Before the arrival of the Europeans the Cherokee lived in the eastern woodlands, and today still occupy ancestral lands in Oklahoma, Carolina and Tennessee. Their religion blends Christianity with native beliefs and rites in a relaxed way, without theological tensions. The chief of the Etawah Cherokee, Hugh Gibbs, says:

> "Mankind itself was created by the female sun. She along with the male moon (her brother) are God's greatest angels— before man."[17]

The Sun Decrees Death

The Sun-goddess is known by three different names. She is *Igaehinvdo*, which means simply "Great Sun"; *Ulenanunhi*, or "the Apportioner," for she measures out the length of each day, and *Sutalidihi*, "Six-Killer," a reference to the six occasions on which she tried to kill humankind. For the Cherokee these correspond to the six world-ages, each of which was ended by a purification, linked in myth to an episode in the Sun-goddess's story.[18]

Ulenanunhi is the sister of the Moon, who is masculine, the god *Geyaguga*, and the Earth-mother *Elihino*. In the beginning of time the Sun-goddess lived in the underworld while the creatures of earth were obliged to put up with endless darkness. Eventually, the animal elders tried to rouse the Sun. When Opossum tried to pull her up by his tail, it was burnt off (which is why opossums have no tail) and when Vulture tried to push her up with his head, he scorched off all his feathers (which is why vultures are bald). Finally, Spider-woman, cunning and wise, made a strong web and drew the Sun into the upper world. Another version of this story makes it a fire-fetching myth, where Spider-woman brings fire from the Sun-land.[19]

The Sun-goddess created humans in order to give bodies to their spirit-forms, and at first it was her intention that they should live forever. But when she examined the earth, she found that it had limited resources and could not possibly sustain everyone forever. So she decreed that every person should eventually die.[20]

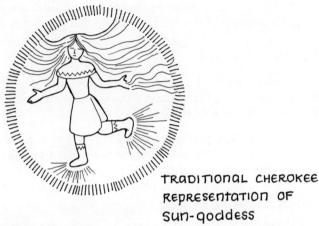

TRADITIONAL CHEROKEE
REPRESENTATION OF
Sun-goddess

The Great Sky-Arch

When the Sun was first made, she was so fiercely bright and hot that earth's creatures suffered terribly. The animal elders decided to raise her even higher, so, heaving and pushing, they raised her hand-breadth by hand-breadth until at last she was seven hand-breadths under the great sky-arch. For this reason the sky is called "The Seventh Height."[21] Now she travels the sky every day just beneath the arch, and gets back to the East by going over the top of the arch every night.[22] As the arch is made of solid stone, this is why we don't see her crossing the night sky (a similar route is taken by the Australian Sun-goddess *Pukwi*[23]). The sky-arch is of a rather hazardous construction, being suspended so that it swings slightly, leaving a small space where the end of the arch meets the horizon. This is the dangerous gap through which the Sun squeezes each morning and evening.[24] Every night, Ulenanunhi pays a visit to her original home underground, like the Sun-goddess of Australian tribes.

Sun-sister, Moon-brother

Ulenanunhi had a lover who made his night visit to her once a month, but she could never discover who he was. So one night as they were making love, she rubbed his face with ashes. When she met her brother in the morning she was astonished to behold his dirty face—and he, seeing the recognition in her eyes, fled in shame. He is the Moon, and because of his shame keeps as far away as he can from his sister the Sun, making himself thinner and thinner to try and hide from her as she approaches him in the west. However, he does visit her in the underworld once a month and thus is missing for three days (the dark of the Moon). During a solar eclipse he has become so bold that he is daring to confront her in broad daylight.[25]

The Sun's Revenge

Cherokee rites and myths emphasize the dual nature of the Sun-goddess. While her vital role in life and growth is acknowledged, she is also held to be a fierce and temperamental deity.

> "We Cherokees are told that the sun is female because everything in the universe needs her to grow... like any pretty woman she likes to be talked to, petted, fussed over and looked at; she likes this and will not burn up the earth."[26]

Thus rituals are directed towards keeping her happy, in case she destroys the maize-crop by burning it to a crisp, and even more, to stop her destroying humankind.

Lack of human admiration of her looks is an issue with this goddess. One myth tells how she hates humans because they cannot look at her without screwing up their faces. She complained to her brother, the Moon,

"My grandchildren are ugly; they grin all over their faces when they look at me."

The Moon had little sympathy with this point of view. As far as he could seem, humans were very beautiful. This was because of his milder rays, which allowed people to gaze on him pleasantly.

In a jealous rage the Sun-goddess sent down terrible rays of heat during the noon-hour each day, so that people were stricken with deadly fever, and died in their hundreds. Soon every family had lost loved ones and it seemed as if the angry goddess would not stop until she had killed everyone. So the people decided to kill the Sun-goddess.

The Death of Sun's Daughter

The Sun-goddess had a daughter, a younger version of herself, who lived in the middle of the sky, right under the sky-arch. Each day as she crossed the sky, the Sun would call in her daughter's house to eat midday lunch (this is why the Sun "stops" overhead at noon). The people knew this, and so they sent two men, who had been magically turned into venomous snakes, to wait at the door of Sun-maiden's house. When the Sun came out after her meal, her fierce light blinded one of the serpents and completely intimidated the other, so they never got the chance to bite her, and crawled off in shame.

On the second attempt, a man who had been turned into a rattlesnake was too hasty, and mistakenly struck at Sun-maiden when she peeped out to watch for her mother. The results were disastrous. When Ulenanunhi discovered her dead daughter lying in the doorway, she went into the house and shut the door fast. In her grief she would not come out, and the world was plunged into darkness. Now things were worse than before, and powerful medicine had to be made to persuade the Sun to come out again.

Seven men were chosen to go to the Ghost-country, the land of the west, carrying sourwood rods and a wooden box. They set out to bring back the Sun's dead daughter, not in itself a difficult task because of the strong magic they took with them, but dependent on one taboo; the box which brought back the dead must not be opened even once, or the Sun would never see her daughter again.

In the Ghost-land Sun-maiden was discovered dancing with the other dead people. When the seven men tapped her with the rods, she fell in a swoon and was easily put in the box. Then, with the lid tight shut, the men set off for home as fast as they could go, trying hard to ignore the cries from Sun-maiden who was by now pleading to be let out. For the men who were carrying the box, this was by far the most difficult part of the journey, especially when she cried out that she was hungry and thirsty.

At length they approached the settlements, but now the girl sobbed in an agonized voice that she was suffocating—could they please just raise the lid a little to give her some air? The men were afraid that they were going to arrive at home with a corpse, so they eased the lid just a crack. There was a fluttering sound, and the girl shot out of the box in the form of a Redbird, and escaped into the thickets. So, when they got home, all they had to give the Sun was an empty box.

> "So now we know the Redbird is the daughter of the Sun, and if the men had kept the box closed... we could bring back our other friends also from the Ghost-country, but now when they die we can never bring them back."

The Sun-goddess was devastated by the loss of her daughter. She wept so much that the world began to fill with her tears, and now after being burned by heat and fever, it looked as if people would be drowned. So they chose the most delightful young men and women to entertain her with their best songs and dances. It was to no avail, and the Sun stayed withdrawn in her grief, until at last "the drummer suddenly changed the song, when she lifted up her face, and was so pleased at the sight that she forgot her grief and smiled."[27]

In the"medicine wheel", the cyclic system of symbolic correspondences which symbolises the religious path for North American tribes, the Cherokee associate the Sun, the direction east (called "Sun-land"), the colour red, and the virtues of success and triumph. Beneficent spirits dwell in the east and also in the south, which is "Mountain Land."[28]

Sun-Goddess of the Yuchi

The *Yuchi* Indians belong to the same language group as the Cherokee, Iroquois and Caddo. Their principal divinity is the Sun-goddess *Tsoono* (from *tso* , "Sun"), the heavenly ancestress of the tribe. She is called "The One Who Is Breath", "Maker of Indians," and *Wetana*, the Great Spirit. At the beginning of time she presided over the council of the animal elders, who sought the earth, for all at that time was water. After several failed attempts by other creatures, Crawfish dived down deep and brought back yellow mud, from which the earth was formed.

Thus the new world developed and became the home of many creatures, but they were not happy. The earth was a dark and gloomy place. All of them wished for light but did not know where to find it, so they asked Panther to run across the sky. He provided no light, so in succession they asked Glow-worm, Spider (or Star) and finally Moon, but even he could not provide enough light. Then just as they were on the point of giving up, the Sun herself arose and the whole sky burst into light. All the creatures sang for joy! They watched as she climbed higher and higher, and the world grew brighter and brighter, until at noon she stopped on her way. Then all the creatures agreed that it was best for the Sun-goddess to have the role of light-giver.

Son of the Sun-Goddess

One day when the Sun-goddess was going down the path to get water from the creek, she shed a drop of menstrual blood on the ground. She did not notice this, and when she came back up the path, she gathered it up and returned home. The blood-spot became a baby boy, *Tsoya'ha*, "Son of the Sun." He lived in the sky with his mother and became the ancestor of the Yuchi themselves, who spent some time in the sky-world with Sun-mother before coming to live on earth. When, under Christian influence, the Yuchi reversed the sex of Sun and Moon, Tsoono's drop of menstrual blood was taken away by the male Sun. After four days it became a boy, and the Sun-god claimed that it was *his* son. Yuchi who have *dark* skin, were said to be descended from this Sun-god, who visits Yuchi women and impregnates them; these motifs, like the four-day wait before his "son" appears, come from the "Sun"-god's original lunar character.

The Solar Eclipse

The Sun-goddess is menaced by a monstrous demon toad who tries to swallow her. When it succeeds, we have an eclipse. As soon as the solar disc began to be obscured the Yuchi people would start special rituals to save the Sun, decorating their bodies with red designs and firing arrows at the Sun to drive off the toad. During the eclipse they wept and wailed that their mother was dying, but once the rites were seen to be having their effect, great rejoicing broke out everywhere.

The Sun herself is imagined to have taught the Yuchi all their rites and ceremonies. When she crosses the sky she pauses each day at noon, and surveys the whole Earth, checking to see whether the holy ceremonies are being continued, according to her instructions. The central square of every Yuchi village was laid out for ritual purposes with a central fire, which represented the Sun, and around which dances, songs and chants were offered to her and other divinities.

But, say the Yuchi prophecies, all ceremonies will come to an end, for not a single Yuchi will be left on Earth. The Sun-goddess will come from the East to seek her children, but, finding that they are dead, she will cover her face and go backwards to the East. Then universal darkness will prevail.[29]

Eclipse of the Sun

Chapter 16
Tales of the Sky-Women
South America

Many of the native tribes of South America perceive the Sun as feminine and the Moon as masculine. It is also very common for both of these deities to be masculine, in which case they are usually brothers—one strong and cunning, the Sun, and the other weak and foolish, the Moon, who gets into various scrapes resulting in his changing phases. And again, there are other tribes who do not personify Sun and Moon at all, but think of them as inanimate objects, particularly feather ornaments or playthings, with no influence at all over life or human concerns. Their light is taken for granted, and they are not objects of religious attentions. Such an attitude is natural for those peoples whose "sky" is the dense forest canopy, peopled by animals, birds and invisible spirits.[1]

Sun Sister, Moon Brother

Where Sun and Moon are personified, the Sun-sister/Moon-brother incest myth is common. That of the Panama Indians, for example, strikingly resembles the same myth among the Cherokee and the Eskimo. Sun-sister is sexually abused and raped in the dark by an unknown assailant. She manages to mark his face with *genipa*-juice (a blue dye used as body paint) or with ashes, or menstrual blood. In the morning her brother's guilt is thus exposed for all to see. He then flees to the heavens to become the Moon, to be chased forever by his angry sister, the Sun. Among some tribes this myth has been quite transparently reversed. The *Tomunda* tribe, for example, say that the brother was visited in the dark by an unknown woman, who debauched him, and to discover her identity, he marked her face—she then became the Moon. It is always among the most isolated tribes that the Sun continues to be female.

The Sky-Women

In the heart of South America, the region of modern Argentina called the *Gran Chaco*, the *Toba* people once preserved an extremely primitive way of life, with formidable jungle skills which allowed them to thrive in this "green Hell," as white invaders termed it. The Toba warriors held off the white men as long as they could, but even their war-craft gave way at last before guns and germs. Like the other Chaco tribes, the Toba were isolated and their beliefs uncontaminated by outside influence. Their Sun-goddess *Akewa* is a type of celestial woman often found in South American tradition—usually called "sky-women." they are more advanced than the menfolk on earth, because they possess the secrets of religion and culture (particularly fire), but they have frightening toothed vaginas and threatening, large clitorides. In order to subdue and possess them, mortal men must break the teeth on sticks or stones, and cut out their clitorides. Such myths are used to justify the genital mutilation of women among tribes like the *Chipibo*. This tribe believe that "the world and its contents are the work of a celestial woman, who is undoubtedly a personification of the Sun."[2] Since the takeover by men of women's ritual power, however, all things celestial or bright have been assigned to the men, and what used to be masculine—darkness, animal-like brutishness—to the women.

Sun-Goddess Akewa

The Toba say that Akewa once lived in the sky along with her sisters, the radiant sky-women, all of them round and fat and beautiful. One day they desired to come down to earth, in curiosity wanting a closer look at the brutish and ignorant menfolk (who at that time had no female company), so they lowered a rope from the clouds and slithered down. Alas, the men were lying in ambush, and as soon as they thought that all the women had come down they sent up their accomplice, a falcon, to cut the rope. The Sun-women were stranded on earth. But the men had made a mistake, for Akewa had been tardy in coming down the rope and, alone of all the Sun-women, she was left in the sky. We see her now as the Sun, a fat woman who walks across the sky each day surrounded by clashing iron weapons (her rays) with which she wards off the demons who try to swallow her. Occasionally she is overcome by a giant jaguar, but he is forced to regurgitate the burning-hot goddess. (This is an explanation of eclipses.) Akewa grows older during the course of a solar year, and then young again. When she is a young woman she walks quickly across the sky, and the days are short, but as she grows older she slows down, and it takes her much longer to cross the sky—hence the long days of summer. Clearly, Akewa is at

mother-goddess, venezuela

her youngest when the days are shortest, which means that she must be reborn at Winter Solstice. Like the traditions of the Cherokee Sun-goddess, this shows an understanding of the connection of the Sun's cycles with *day-length*. It also challenges the narrow thinking which attributes all changing-of-age and measuring-of-time to Moon-deities.

At the end of the day Akewa slides over the rim of of the world and down into the abyss at the world's end. (Presumably she walks back to start during the night.) Her Moon-brother sleeps in the sky, the changing phases we see from earth being due to the position in which he lies—sometimes we see the whole of his huge belly, and other times only parts of it. The Moon is a dozy god, so the demon jaguar often takes him unawares—which is why the Moon is more often eclipsed than the Sun.[3]

The Universal Mother

Several Carib tribes and others in Paraguay and Brazil have a Sun-goddess who is the *universal mother* type of deity, somewhat similar to female creatresses and ancestresses of Australian religion, in that she makes or births animals, plants, ritual objects, songs, dances and so forth. Among other tribes this universal mother is not identified with celestial bodies or the earth, but is simply a creative goddess.

It is interesting that Roman Catholic missionaries choose to ignore this goddess and instead identify their god with the tribal thunder-god, regardless of his role in mythology. One would imagine that the Virgin Mary might be identified with the Sun-mother, but the priests tell the natives that she is the same as (or like) Mother Earth. The problem is not simply that the creatress is female, but that she is the Sun—thus making her doubly unacceptable to Christian Sun-god theology.

The Moon-God

As usual among aboriginal peoples the male Moon is associated with mortal women, causing menstruation by his sexual attentions. The Uaupe Indians of the Upper Amazon call first menstruation "defloration by the Moon."[4] Several other examples are given by Briffault.

The Sun-goddess *Akewa* is pestered by her brother, the Moon, who trails after her through the sky, constantly trying to seduce her and repeatedly making her offers of marriage. She is disgusted by these incestuous suggestions. Refusal has no effect on him, so she endeavours to keep him off by flinging hot ashes (from her own fires) in his face. An exactly similar story is found among the Khasis in northern India.[5]

Chapter 17
Goddess of Life
Australia

"Sun-mother and Sun-daughter made themselves Dreaming
for us, so we would have light every day to move about.
Without the Sun we would starve to death."

—Arnhem Land Aborigines

"The sun has no place in Australian conceptions of the
supernatural...when personified it is regarded as a female." [1]

—Robert Briffault

Australian aboriginal culture is rich in a great diversity of beautiful legends,
sacred "Just-So" stories which make the primeval mythic world, the *Dreamtime*,
present in the "eternal now." All native Australian myths are directly associated with specific natural features—a star, for example, which may seem neither
particularly bright nor significant to a western observer, may be an important
character in a myth—and the trees, rock, springs and pools, Sun and Moon,
birds and animals of every kind, are all woven into a complex, all-inclusive
system of stories. These are not merely about things supposed to have happened
in the past. Nor are humans detached observers of the natural world. Their
everyday lives, tensions and concerns form an integral part of the Nature myths,
often in a deeply moving and humanistic way. It is through rites, ceremonies and
sacred recitation that the stories are activated and made continually present in
the living landscape.

Among virtually every single Australian tribe the Sun is feminine and the

Moon is masculine. (Sun-gods and Moon-goddesses are the rarities here, and many show features suggesting that they were introduced from Pacific mythologies.) It is impossible to give more than a sampler of the sheer richness of the feminine Sun tradition. Her myths are very various and picturesque, but two common images of the Sun-goddess can be traced—she is very often a spirit-woman carrying a blazing torch, or else a spirit-woman whose brilliant body (or eyes) burn like fire. In the Dreamtime the Sun-goddess emerged from underground, and each tribe holds sacred the place at which she is said to have appeared. It is important to remember that Australia is an immense continent with a wide range of climatic conditions, from lush jungle to snowy mountains, from burning desert to temperate lowlands, and the different tribal traditions reflect this variety. (The popular western view of Australia as just an arid red dust-bowl, peppered with a few gum-trees and peopled by Sun-tormented aborigines, is a Hollywood stereotype.) Native Australian tradition expresses joy and pleasure in the Sun as it does in the other aspects of Nature; in no sense is she rejected as a force hostile to life.

Yhi, the Goddess of Life

The Sun-goddess of the Karraru (south-western Australia) is the creator of all living things, the "goddess of life," Yhi. The following story was told by Kardin-nilla ("Rushing Stream") a sixty-five year old woman of the tribe:

In the beginning the earth was dark and silent. There were creatures underground, and Sun-woman, but they slept inert. It was the spirit-man Baiame who woke Sun-woman up, and when she emerged from the ground and opened her eyes, great light and warmth came from them.

Yhi settled her camp on the Nullarbor Plain, and then went off on a journey. As yet there were no plants, but as she walked, trees and plants grew up from her footprints. She kept on walking west, went over the edge of the world, and kept going until she reached the other side, and after many such journeys the earth was covered in vegetation.

However, she felt the need to go back down to her old place, and when she got underground, her heat and light brought the insects to life. When she went home to her camp on the plain, she stayed there for two days, and thus for all that time there was no darkness. On her next journey she went to the mountains, where her heat melted the ice and snow, releasing fish and reptiles and creating streams and lakes. These images are clearly based on careful observation of the Sun's effects on cold-blooded animals, who rely on the Sun's warmth for their metabolism (which is why snakes, lizards and insects sunbathe, and are more active in sunny or hot weather).

After bringing birds and animals to life from the caverns of the underworld, Yhi informed them that she was going back to the spirit-land, and so saying, she vanished into the west. They were terrified by the return of darkness, but overjoyed to see the Sun returning in the east a few hours later. (The dawn chorus is explained by the aborigines as the birds' greeting to the Sun-goddess.) Yhi took pity on those anxious ones who felt each night that she might never come back, and to console them gave birth to a daughter, the Moon, who would take the Sun's place at night. She also created the morning-star from a fragment of her own bright self and gave him to the Moon for a husband. Their children are the stars, and when any living thing dies, it too goes up into the sky and becomes a star. According to the storyteller, the progression of the seasons and the alternation of day and night are directly governed by the Sun-goddess. [2]

Yhi the Primal Genetrix

Another version of Yhi's story from Central Australia says that she is the first creator of all, producing everything from her lifegiving rays. Her son is the father-god, whom she delegates to care for her creation before she withdraws to the sky, whence she gives the world light and heat. However, she is obliged to interfere because he makes such a complete mess of things. The Sun-goddess advises him on his activities and puts right his mistakes, warning him "I alone can give power. I alone can act, and no-one can dispute my doings. I walk up and down upon the earth, and the dust and water give forth life." [3]

Despite the father-god's ineptitude, he is permitted to create male humans, an event which takes place while the Sun-goddess stands still, directly overhead. (After this, she never again stops on her daily journey.) There are no women, so Yhi creates the first one by shining on a yucca-tree, but she turns out to be a zombie-like creature without faculties, and her husband has to care for her and teach her over many years. [4] Sexual attraction between male and female creatures is caused by the Sun-goddess. [5]

Yhi's Son, the Moon-God

In some versions of Yhi's myth, the Moon-god is her son. He is a fat, dull-witted and merry man "with short legs, and arms that were very thin, and a big head with shining eyes." [6] The Sun-goddess has an incestuous desire for the Moon-god, pursuing him incessantly. He is filled with horror at her attentions, not it seems because she is his mother, but because she is promiscuous, taking and discarding lovers quite heartlessly, and even threatening to kill him if he does not give into her demands. Yhi tells the spirits who hold up the sky and earth that they must not let the Moon-god escape, as he slips through the gap between Earth and sky, or she will throw them down and there will be a cosmic catastrophe. On occasions she does catch him and try to kill him, whereupon there is a lunar eclipse, but the other sky-spirits intervene to preserve the Moon's light.[7]

Like so many of the aborigine deities, the Moon was a spirit-man of the Dreamtime, *Nullandi*, a cheerful person who retained his optimistic nature when he became the Moon, *Bahloo*. He is rather similar to Japanese *Susanowo*, a rude and boisterous character, resentful of his duties in the sky. He would much rather go down to Earth, where his favourite pastime is chasing women and girls to make love to them. But everyone knows about his amorous nature, so that women avoid him and often make fun of him, or lead him on and then playfully rebuff or trick him. He is hurt by their practical jokes and their unwillingness to have sex with him. In embarrassment he goes away and hides, shrinking with shame, until after a while his happy nature gets the better of him and he grows again in shape and confidence. Intercourse with this Moon-god results in menstruation.[8]

Wotjobaluk Sun-Woman

The *Wotjobaluk* of Victoria tell of a time before the world knew daylight, when everyone had to use bark torches to find their way about. A woman left her little son sleeping while she set off with her torch and her digging-stick to look for yams, but in the darkness she got lost because she was so engrossed in her task. To her surprise she found she had gone right over the edge of the world. Alas, when she went beneath and came up again on the other side, the little boy was nowhere to be seen. Taking her bark torch, she went up into the sky and became Sun-woman, who still seeks her son, day after day, carrying a blazing torch with which she lights the earth and the underworld. Another version of this tale, in the same tribal group, gives it a happy ending—Sun-woman finds her son in the west, and this is why she goes down at night, to nurse him. (Several other tribes give this as a reason for the Sun's nightly descent to earth.)[9]

Yulengor Sun-Woman

The Sun-goddess does not always pass under the earth at night in the conventional way. According to the *Yulengor* people of the Northern terri-tory, she goes west and then takes a short-cut north and east, keeping just below the horizon so we do not see her.[10] (Exactly the same route is taken by the Scandinavian *Sunna*, except Yulengor Sun-woman doesn't seem to travel on all fours!) The *Tiwi* tribe, also in the Northern Territory, explain that their Sun-goddess *Pukwi* is a black woman who gets back from west to east by travelling invisibly along the Milky Way at night. She emerged from the sky itself in the Dreamtime, tumbling down into a pond where she became a turtle, but a bird killed her and then she rose back up to the sky to become the shining Sun.[11]

mother-goddess,
PREHISTORIC ABORIGINAL painting

The Rays of the Sun

The *Yulengor* say that their Sun-goddess was created by the ancestral sisters, the *Junkgowa*. They gave her many legs (rays) for walking so that she could accompany them on their journeys, but before they could set off she gave birth to a son, and now she has to return each evening to the west to nurse him.[12] Sun-woman of the *Murngin* (Northern Territory) also goes west each evening because she can hear her children crying. Her husband is the Moon, and their twin sons are associated with rain-production taboos.[13]

Among the people of Queensland it is said that the Moon-god created a woman with two legs and innumerable arms; this is Sun-woman who sleeps underground at night, and in the morning when she wakes she has a good stretch, so that her arms (her rays) appear above the horizon before she does![14]

Sun-woman's rays are not always her arms or legs — according to the *Worora* of Western Australia, they are her walking-sticks! Sun-woman, Sun-daughter and the star-girls spend time together diving in search of water-lily bulbs. When Sun-mother takes her walking-sticks and tries to climb through the pine-trees, she gets stuck in the branches, so Sun-daughter takes the sticks and goes on up into the sky, but at the zenith she is bitten by a rattlesnake (exactly like Cherokee Sun's-daughter) and develops a fever, becoming very hot indeed (this accounts for the Sun's noontide rays). During the course of the afternoon Sun's daughter gradually cools down again, until at evening she stands up; all the walking-sticks roll down out of sight, over the edge of the horizon, and it immediately becomes dark.[15]

Aranda Sun-Woman

The association of the Sun's heat with fever is also found among the *Aranda* of Central Australia, who invoke their Sun-goddess *Tchintu* to bring down a deadly fever on an enemy. A charm modelled from gum-resin, string, rat's teeth and red down is concealed on a track where the enemy walks. It has to be handled with very great care, or it will work its magic on the user himself, instead of the victim, who is supposed to be struck down when he treads over it.

The Aranda also call the Sun-goddess *Alinga* or *Ochirka*. She emerges from the underworld each morning carrying a blazing torch (or "fire-stick") which dispels the darkness and gives warmth to the world, then she climbs up to the highest point of the sky. When her torch begins to give out, she goes back to her old place, the hole from which she first emerged in the Dreamtime. This is marked by a sacred rock, at a place near Alice Springs. (A gifted medicine-man, looking down the hole, is able to see her, but to ordinary people the hole appears quite empty.)[16]

The people of the Bandicoot totem lay special claim to this holy place. They tell how the Sun emerged from the earth as a spirit-woman accompanied by two Sun-sisters, the Panunga women (both called Ochirka), one of whom had a new-born child. Sun-woman went on, into the sky, but the two women settled down with the Bandicoot people, teaching them the songs, dances, rites and other observances and secrets of the Sun-goddess. The Sun-totem rites include special mother-and-child ceremonies in which Sun-emblems are worn by participants.[17]

Sun-ceremonies among the men employ a headdress or model of the Sun, a light round frame of twigs covered in concentric circles of red and white down.[18] Another object sacred to the Sun-goddess is a flat stone disc, marked with a central red spot which is said to be her navel, and around which red rays are painted. The neighbouring *Kaitish* tribe, who call the Sun-goddess *Okerka*, honour a sacred tree which marks the spot where she emerged. Should anyone destroy this tree, the Sun-goddess will burn up the Earth in her anger.[19]

The Sun is menaced by an evil spirit, *Arungquiltha*, who hates the light and desires to obscure Sun-woman forever. When he causes an eclipse, the shaman-istic elders take from their own bodies mystical, invisible rock-crystals, which they fling towards the Sun, thus driving the demon away.[20]

The Sun, Sister of Everyone

Among the Aranda, the Sun has a definite genealogical relationship to members of the group, for she is a totem ancestress, and the tribespeople are able to describe their exact relationship to her. The *Wurunjerri* of Victoria take a more general view, saying that she is "the sister of everyone." (This Sun-woman gets from west to east during the night by a northern sea-route.)[21] The *Dieri* of South Australia call the Sun-goddess *Dietyi* and say she is one of their own tribe, the daughter of a young Dieri woman who mated with one of the *Mura-Mura*, "the ancient people" or ancestral spirits, and after her birth sank to the Earth in shame. Dietyi sets each evening down a hole called *Dityi-minka*, "Hole of the Sun", near Lake Eyre, then travels underground to reach the east.[22]

The Fire of the Sun

The heat and light of the Sun often come from a torch which the goddess carries, or a fire which she lights. The *Wiimbaio* of South-East Australia say that their Sun-goddess *Yukowarri* was in the sky all day, proving a nuisance, so the father-spirit ordered her to burn up all her fuel each day. So it is that Sun-woman has to come down to earth each night to seek wood, and she relights her fire when she gets back to her camp in the east, at the end of the night.[23]

Fire does not usually come to earth from the Sun—in aboriginal myth it is generally the other way round; the Sun is kindled from earthly fire which was passed on to humans by animals, stolen in the form of a secret, or accidentally obtained from grass and forest fires. A few myths say that humans chipped a piece off Sun-woman as she went underground in the west, or climbed a string to the sky and borrowed from the Sun's fires.[24]

Other aboriginal traditions say that the body of the goddess herself blazes

155

with fire. In Catherine H. Berndt's account of native Australian myths, our Sun is the burning hot daughter of an even more fiery Sun-goddess, whose body is like that of the mythic Rainbow Serpent, brilliant and shining. Sun-mother is much too dangerous for us to see, and so she stays below ground while her fiercely-hot daughter crosses the sky each day. The aborigines say, "Sun-mother and Sun-daughter made themselves Dreaming for us [i.e. immortal] so we would have light every day to move about. Without the Sun we would starve to death."[25]

The *Pongi-Pongi* who live in the swamp plains west of Darwin also have a fiery Sun-goddess. The deep pit from which she emerges each day, and into which she descends each night, is on a desolate plain scorched by the heat of her daily appearance. Nearby, the shaman who is head of the Sun-totem makes his camp and guards the sacred place. Sun-woman's hot breath is responsible for drying up the earth and the water-holes. She is a dangerous goddess who chases and burns up anyone who dares to annoy her. The Moon of the same tradition is masculine, a man who once tried to seduce his daughters, but drowned in a lake. He was reborn as a crocodile, who grows fat through eating the spirits of the dead, but each month he falls from the sky, drowns, and is reborn as a crocodile again. When a rainbow circle appears around the Moon, the tribespeople say that the spirits are dancing their reincarnation ritual.[26]

The evil spirit of this and related tribal traditions is a man called *Wulgaru*, who is able to force Sun-woman to sink down quickly into the earth by magic chants. To counteract his evil spell the tribespeople sing their own magic songs to Sun-woman, encouraging her, and urging her to hold her fire-stick higher in the sky.[27] In areas of Australia which experience a cold season, Sun-woman is loved and appreciated; on the northern coast, when the rains come, bringing migratory ducks and geese who take advantage of the brimming lakes, the aborigines say that they have come to welcome "Old Sun Woman." Goannas who have been hibernating in the ground during the cold weather are woken up by Sun-woman, who drives away the cold-weather spirits with her blazing torch.[28]

Sacred Tablets of the Sun

An important feature of native Australian rites are the sacred tablets, poles or boards called *tjuringa*. They are commonly marked with grooves and engraved designs, in concentric circles, groups and running lines, which are traced with a fingertip while a sacred story is recited. The designs are not representational unless specifically described as so by the storyteller, and even then their unusual meanings cannot be interpreted by the non-aboriginal. (The concentric designs are often wrongly interpreted by Westerners as "moon-spirals" or "earth-currents" or "sun-symbols.")[29]

The tribes on the western shores of Carpentaria Gulf and the upper reaches of the Victoria River bring out the Sun-totem tjuringas at sunset, exposing them to the full light of the setting Sun. She is believed to be a woman with a fiery exterior who walks across the sky each day, returning to the sacred place at night. When the Sun's disc is just about to touch the horizon, the totem elders raise their hands to her and bow profoundly. This worship is thought to bring fertility to food animals and plants on which the tribes depend.

The same tribes have a masculine Moon who was once a human man. He was chased right off the earth by a demon dog, so that he had a very long walk home through the sky, and so was extremely thin when he got back. To assuage his ravenous hunger, he went on a night-hunt and soon grew fat, gorging himself on opossums. Unfortunately, the giant dog discovered him again, and this time he was too fat to run away. The dog tore him apart and ate him, piece by piece, but so savagely did he shake him that an arm-bone came free and was flung up into the sky. The dog was enraged that the Moon had escaped in this way, and soon the arm-bone began to grow and the Moon-man regenerated. He had gained immortality, and he got his own back on the dog by turning it to stone (a natural rock formation held sacred by the tribes).[30]

The *Aluridja* who tell this story share with the Moroccans and the Chinese the idea of *multiple suns*, imagining the Sun to be an indefinite series of women who take it in turns to cross the sky.[31] This explains why, unlike the Moon, the Sun never seems to tire or grow old.

The Sun-Goddess Visits the Dead

The *Narrinyeri* of Encounter Bay, Victoria, explain that the Sun is a beautiful woman who goes underground at night to visit the dead, an event to which they eagerly look forward, parting ranks and standing respectfully to each side to let her pass through. Sun-woman has a lover among the dead, whom she visits each night. In the morning she arises wearing a fine red kangaroo-skin, his gift to her for the favours he received during life. (This is why the Sun is red when she rises.) When Sun-woman returns from the underworld, people on earth beg her to stay with them forever, but she never can, for she has to make ready again for her night journey.[32]

The Native Australian Moon-God

Wherever the masculine Moon is found, he is always the patron of the native Australian woman, the "real husband" and real father of children, who receives souls of dead people (although some tribes give these souls a different destination) and sends them back to earth to be reincarnated. Some of the stories depict the Moon-god as a type of fool who misbehaves and gets into scrapes, particularly with the women whom he chases and woos. Intercourse with the Moon causes menstrual bleeding. Many stories also relate the Moon-god's myth to those explaining death and immortality.[33]

Chapter 18
She Who Darts Forth Her Rays
Arabia

"The mother is the true representative of the Sun."

—Hugo Winckler[1]

In Southern Arabia the Sun was believed to be a goddess, *Shams*, while the Moon and the Morning Star were always held to be masculine divinities.[2] As with all the pagan Arab deities, Shams' mythology was never written down but passed on in an oral tradition of recitation—just as the later Koran was passed on, before it was made into a book. The chief sources for our knowledge of Arab deities come from pre-Islamic votive inscriptions and existing folk traditions. In mediaeval times Islamic scholars wrote about pagan Arabia, but the actual record of archaeology shows that they misunderstood the nature of the deities.[3] Influenced by Syrian and classical ideas, they changed the Sun to a male and the Moon to a female, imagining that all goddesses were lunar—an error disproved by the pagan inscriptions themselves.[4]

The Arabic Trinity

The pagan Arabs were very fond of pairs, triads and multiplicities of deities. In South Arabia the principal deities formed a trinity of Sun-goddess, Moon-god and Morning Star god. According to the individual tribe, these gods and goddesses had local names and epithets. For example, in the Hadramaut, a mountainous region now in modern Yemen, Shams shared the honours with *Sinn*, the Moon-god (her husband) and their son *Athtar*, the Morning Star. *Shams-umm-Attar* means "Shams the mother of Attar (Athtar)," but is sometimes misinterpreted to mean that the Arab Sun-goddess was called "Attar."[5]

To all the Arabs the Sun-goddess was simply *Shams*; unlike the Moon-god she did not have specific tribal names and connections, although the tribe of *Hamdan* was especially devoted to her worship.[6] The northern Arabs changed her into a male god under Akkadian influence, for the Babylonians too regarded the Sun, *Shamash*, as a goddess in much earlier times. While they retained the masculine Moon,[7] her one-time consort *Sin*, they converted Shamash into a god. The job was not particularly well done; prayers and hymns to this "Sun-god" contain incongruous feminine imagery. A tablet found at Sippar, the god's cult centre, describes the way in which he opens the gates of heaven and appears in the east "like a wife pleased and giving pleasure."[8] At the same time as the Sun's sex was being reversed, so too was that of the Morning Star, giving the feminine *Ishtar*, equivalent of *Athtar*.

The Two Suns

Shams was generally described by paired epithets which evoke the contrasting aspects of her nature. (This is a common practice where Sun-goddesses are concerned, being found as far away as Ireland and Japan.) The people of Saba called the fierce Sun *Dat-himyam*, "She who darts forth her rays," while the milder Sun was *Dat-badan*, "She who is remote." At Saba the Moon-god's tribal title was *Ilqumuh*, "Il (the Moon-god) is power." He and the Morning Star god formed a trinity with Shams.

At Qataban the Sun-goddess was worshipped in her rising, noon and setting aspects. In the morning she was *Mashraqitan*, "she who rises," at noon she was *Atirat*, "bright," and in the evening *Mahrudawu*, "she who declines." When Muhammad gave his followers instructions for the five-times-daily Islamic prayer, he forbade them to worship at dawn, noon and sunset, because of the importance of these times in Sun-goddess cult.[9] Indeed, in South Arabia the Sun-goddess was one of Allah's chief rivals, and great efforts were made to stamp out her worship.

Some of the paired epithets give a tantalising hint of Shams' vanished mythology. In the Hadramaut she was *Dat-himyam*, but also *Dat-husul*, "she who is rejected," while elsewhere she was *Tanuf*, "sublime," and *Tadun*, "despised." Scholars suggest that these contrasting titles evoke the summer and winter suns—not a particularly satisfactory theory for Arabia. They may refer to the Sun of the day-sky and the Sun as she passes beneath the earth—her nightly underworld journey may have been seen as a form of humiliation, like the ill-treatment of Ishtar the Morning Star when she descended into the realm of death. Or there may be a trace here of the "divorce" concept, when Sun and Moon, once happily married, quarrelled and had to go their separate ways. Shams may have been despised and rejected by her Moon-god husband. Another real possibility is that the title "rejected" expresses the hatred the Arabs felt for the Sun-goddess in the burning desert. Such a dangerous, destructive goddess evidently required appeasement, as the active pagan cult of Shams indicates.

While the Sun was the burning power of the desert wastes, she was also welcome for bringing warmth after the bitterly cold night, and Arab tradition to this very day preserves an ambiguous attitude towards her. Pagan inscriptions honour her with titles which suggest a sense of delight in the radiant goddess: *Dat-zahran*, "She who appears in her splendour"; *Samhayat*, "celestial"; *Dat-rahban*, "She who is broad." Inscriptions invoke her by many names as a powerful and beneficent goddess. She sometimes appears as twins, *Shamsay*, her dual aspect conceived as two goddesses, like the twinned Sun-mother/Sun-daughter of Baltic and other mythologies. (The inscriptions which refer to pairs of women as tribal chiefs may be associated with the Sun-goddess dyad.)[10] And she even occurs as a plurality, *Ashams*, a reference to the belief that each morning's Sun was a brand new one, who travelled the sky just once before being extinguished at sunset, and so on in an endless procession of Sun-goddesses. This concept still survives in folk tradition.

Shrines of the Sun

The temples of the Arab deities were quite simple—excavations have uncovered types of rectangular sanctuary built around an altar and spring, or well, with an adjoining room which may have been the living quarters for the shrine guardian. Important shrines were controlled by individual clans, the priests and priestesses taking up office in a family line, learning the skills of divination, oracular possession, and the correct ways of leading worshippers in the rites, from their father or mother. Nomadic Arabs would come to the shrines to make sacrifices of camels or sheep, which were afterwards shared in a communal meal, in which the deity was thought to participate. The usual preparations for such a communion feast included rites of ablution, circumambulation, chanting, prostrations and so forth, all orchestrated by the tribal priests or priestesses. Before the worshipper left, he or she might give an offering (absolutely anything seems to have been acceptable, but fabrics, weapons and jewellery were commonplace) or seek the deity's will via an oracular priest or priestess. Divination and oracles were extremely popular in the cults of all the Arab deities.

Personal devotions to the Sun-goddess consisted of prayers and prostrations, performed on the roof-terrace under the open sky. The desert nomads would worship the Sun as she rose. Even in the last century the Bedouins of Central and East Arabia, ostensibly followers of the Prophet, would recite chants of invocation and adoration to the Sun from the moment her disc first appeared above the horizon, until she rode free of the ground. Likewise the Arabs of Moab would raise their hands to the rising Sun and address her with traditional prayers. In North Arabia the *Ruala Bedouin* curse the Sun as she rises, for they believe that she means to destroy them—a rite also noted by Herodotus, who reported that certain Arabs curse the Sun at its rising and setting because of its wasting heat.[11]

The Arabs did not make anthropomorphic images of their deities until very late in history, under classical and Babylonian influence. They preferred the *baetyl* or sacred stone (*bet-el*, "house of the god") which they imagined to be a vehicle for the divine presence. This was set on a platform or "throne"—in the absence of a baetyl, the empty throne was worshipped because the invisible deity was sitting there. Shams was provided with such thrones on the flat roofs of houses. Her power and force thus shone down into them, as into the roofless shrines of the tribal Indian Sun-goddess.[12] Aniconic symbols—painted, carved, or worked in jewellery—were also very popular. Shams was represented in an amulet consisting of a Sun-disc with a woman's henna-decorated hand appearing from it. This was taken up by Islam as "the hand of Fatima," although nowadays the Sun-disc is usually omitted.

The Sun-Goddess in Morocco

Details of Arab belief about the Sun and Moon are widely preserved in the traditions of the uneducated, whose folk-religion escapes contamination by the sophisticated, scholarly dogmatisms of the theologians. In Morocco there are some interesting pagan survivals. The Sun is a heavenly woman, *Chems* (the same word as *Shams*) but she flies up from Hell each morning, as a fiery spark from its roaring fires. At night she descends to Hell once more to lie and sleep. An alternative version says that she falls into the sea each night so that her fire is extinguished—thus each day sees a fresh new Sun.

The Hamadcha people tell a story about the Sun-goddess which has parallels in North American and Slavic mythology. At the beginning of time, Chems only shone on a tiny portion of the Earth, while the vast majority of people suffered in cold and darkness. So a delegation from the dark world went to beg light from the lucky ones who enjoyed Chems' beneficence, but they could only advise them to seek help from a holy man, *Sidi Ali Ben Hamdouche*. The wise man listened carefully to their complaint. Then he spoke to the Sun-goddess, saying, "Wherever I go with my stick, you must follow." As he walked all over the Earth, Chems followed him, spreading her light and warmth over every place and people. This is how Morocco comes to have its glorious sunshine, and how Sidi Ali Ben Hamdouche came by his title *Gouad Chems*, "conductor of the Sun." He is thought of as an Islamic saint, the special patron of the Hamadcha, but he is undoubtedly an Islamicization of the Morning Star god, who appears before the Sun and "leads" her on her way. [13] Other holy men, such as the patron of Marrakech, *Sidi Ben Abbes*, were thought to have power over the Sun, being able to stop her in her course.

sun and Lion, from Islamic banner

If the Sun becomes pale, or an eclipse is seen to begin, a special prayer is recited to revive her, because like the Ainu of Japan, the people imagine the Sun-goddess is fainting. During a total eclipse the Sun has been swallowed by an evil demon, an event permitted by Allah so that mortals will have fair warning of his wrath. After a while the demon cannot stomach the fiery Sun and so is obliged to vomit her up again.

In Morocco both the Sun and the Moon are female. The Moon is a beautiful young woman who is newly born in paradise at the beginning of the month. As the Moon-goddess grows to womanhood she blossoms and becomes full, then grows older and older, becomes wizened with age, and finally dies. After her death she goes back to paradise, while people on earth say *Chahr Mat*, "the Moon is dead," a term meaning "the end of the month." There is an endless succession of moons—the one we see at the beginning of each month is not the same woman. The dead moons are all up in paradise, caring for the souls of deceased humans. This association of the Moon with dead souls and the afterlife is very archaic and is more often found in association with the *male* Moon of tribal religions. Indeed, the Moroccan Moon-goddess's name is revealing, for it is masculine, *Chahr*, i.e. *Shahar*, the common name for the male Moon in most parts of Arabia.[14]

The Sun-Goddess of the Bedouin

The Ruala Bedouin, the only true Bedouin tribe of North Arabia, have an implacably hostile attitude to the Sun. They see her as a mean, bony and tough old woman who hates them and wishes to kill them all. She has no mild aspect, unlike other Sun-goddesses. She is eternally angry and passionate and she burns with an insatiable sexual appetite. In contrast, the Moon, her husband, is the friend and protector of the tribe. They imagine that he condenses water into dew and rain, and causes the growth of plants. Under his mild light they feel safe from prying and threatening enemies. Thus the Moon is their principal deity, and when he reappears as the new crescent they raise their hands to him in adoration, calling him lord, benefactor, powerful, saviour, guide of travellers

The Moon-god is a lithe and cheerful young man, his only misfortune being the fact that he is married to the Sun-goddess. After one night spent with her he is so traumatized that it takes him a whole month to recover. (It is the waste of his vigour which causes him to shrivel, resulting in the lunar phases, an idea similar to that of the Hindus and the ancient Iranians, who imagined the Moon to contain semen.) When Sun and Moon were first married and the Moon-god discovered the extent of his wife's sexual demands, he refused to have intercourse with her. In a fury she attacked him, and in a hand-to-hand fight each put out one of the other's eyes, leaving a scar which we see as Sun-spots or as one of the marks on the Moon. Now the Moon and Sun travel separately. The Moon-god avoids having sex with the Sun-goddess, except for once a month—a situation which does nothing to help her vile temper.

The Bedouin say that, were it possible for the Sun to regain her youth and bear children, she would be much kinder. As things are, she hates all life. She attacks the Bedouin with her rays, attempting to shrivel their skin and give them thirst and fever. When she finds the corpse of a human or animal, she turns it to a deadly poison. Even the plants are objects of her violence. It is the Bedouin's hope that one day the demon *Al-hawt*, who is part-fish and part-woman, and who constantly pursues both Sun and Moon, will finally rid them of the hated Sun. But to their everlasting disgust, and exasperation, the demon woman, unable to digest the hot, bony Sun, vomits her up again. Solar eclipses are therefore occasions of joy and hope; unlike most peoples, the Ruala actually encourage the demon who is eating the Sun, instead of attempting to drive it off![15]

The Coming of Islam

By the time of Muhammad in the sixth century A.D. the Arabs had been absorbing foreign influences for a long time—Roman, Hellenic, Jewish, Christian and other ideas had left their mark upon a paganism which teemed with goddesses, gods and spirits. The most important deity *of the individual tribes* themselves continued to be the Moon-god, under his various tribal names. These often make reference to the belief that the Moon was the real father of children, and hence of every tribeswoman and man. For example, the people of Hadramaut called him *Ab-sinn*, "father Moon," and claimed that they were his children.[16]

This multiplicity of Moon-gods, as it appears to us, poses no problem for those who imagine the Moon to be a plural deity. There was also a tendency towards lunar monotheism among the Arabs, for the Moon who is *many* is also *one*—as well as intertribal rivalry which must have involved conflicting religious claims over the Moon's special patronage of any particular tribe. The high god of the Semites was *Il* or *El* or *Allah*, all of which simply mean *god* but in some contexts *Il* specifically refers to the Moon. This is the same deity who became the monotheistic god of the Hebrews, with his special patronage of *their* tribe alone, and his later connotations of "father of all mankind" which really come from the remote archaic cult of the fecundating Moon-father. Abraham ("father of many"—a name which itself suggests the old Semitic Moon-god) was instructed by his god to go out into the desert, from a city which was one of the great centres of Moon-god worship, Ur of the Chaldees. The Moon-deity here was *masculine*.[17] The primitive Semitic speaking peoples knew nothing of any cult of "the Great Moon Mother"[18]—this is a modern idea based on mediaeval Islamic sources, late Graeco-Syrian cults and Western mis-identification of the various Morning Star goddesses as the Moon. To the Semites, the Moon was always a male god, the special patron and protector of women, even when the Sun had been changed to a male.

Although members of the Christian, Jewish and Islamic religions hotly refute the idea, it is almost certain that their monotheistic god derived from the masculine Moon of the tribes. Before the birth of Islam, Allah played a minor role among the many Arab deities, but a monotheistic trend developed in his cult, during the century before Muhammad, which was to lead to Islam.[19]

Al-Lat, Greatest of All [20]

In pagan times *Allah* had a female consort or counterpart, *Allat*; just as he appears to have been a Moon-god, so does she appear to have been a Sun-goddess, of the "Sun's daughter" type.[21] Inscriptions speak of her as the Sun and also as the Morning Star,[22] and in some she appears alongside Shams, forming a pair of solar goddesses. She is best-known for her association with the stellar goddess *Al-Uzza*, "the mighty" and the goddess of retribution and destiny *Manat*, "apportioner." This triad of goddesses originally came from north Arabia, and their famous cult centres in the south were only established after Southern Arab traders went north.[23] On the eve of Islam they had been subsumed by Allah's cult as his three "daughters." and received ardent worship at Mecca. There the Quraysh tribe worshipped al-Uzza as their chief goddess, alongside *Hubal*, god of the Ka'abah.[24] Al-Lat's cult centre in the south was on the green hill of At-Taif, in the fertile hill country, surrounded by luxuriant orchards, gardens and cornfields. The Thaqif tribe who guarded the shrine had accumulated immense wealth from pilgrim offerings. Al-Lat's baetyl, a cube of white quartzite stone, was housed in a rich temple, which Muhammad eventually forced the goddess's devotees to destroy with their own hands.[25]

Such was the devotion that the Arabs paid to the three goddesses that at first Muhammad was unable to make any headway, so he included a favourable reference to them in the early Koran, making it easier for the goddess-worshippers to accept Islam:

> "Have you considered Al-Lat and Ul-Uzza and that other, Manat, the third idol? These are the sublime princesses [or swans or cranes] and truly their intercession may be looked for."[26]

You will search the Koran in vain for this reference today. It was later removed, because the Prophet believed that Satan had whispered the words in his ear. It was replaced with:

> "Have you considered El-Lat and El-Uzza and Manat, the third, that other one?... They are naught but names... Allah has sent down no authority concerning them."[27]

The former approving words about the sublime princesses are traditionally called by Muslims "the satanic verses."

The Sun-goddess was seen as a demonic rival to Allah, and so her worship had to be suppressed, but the importance of the Sun in Arab life continued as before, a constant theme along with the Moon and stars in folk tradition and heterodox Islam. One of the ways in which Muhammad tried to discourage Shams' cult was by altering the calendar. That of the pagan Arabs had been lunisolar, but the Prophet forbade solar reckoning, even the use of intercalary days, and instituted a strictly lunar calendar.[28]

He taught that Sun and Moon were created by God as slaves, objects put to forced labour in man's service, and that every night the Sun was obliged to prostrate herself at the foot of Allah's throne.[29] Even today the devout Muslim will say, when looking on Sun or Moon, "God is greater," to quell any feelings of religious exaltation which might count as worship. Folkloric practices, such as bowing to the Sun as she rises, are expressly forbidden (but continued nonetheless), and whereas the Koran and the theologians say that the Sun is male and the Moon female,[30] the peasants and nomads continued to see things the other way round. The nomads always retained a freer conception of womanhood that that generally found in Islam. Their women go unveiled, and proverbial lore and history speak highly of them. Briffault records an Arabic saying, "The dignity of woman is as the brightness of the sun in the heavens... as to sovereigns we owe respect and consideration to women."[31] Lunar metaphors are used in speaking of men—Muhammad's face was traditionally compared to the brightness of the full Moon.[32]

The concept of the Sun as a mixed blessing is clearly marked in Arab lore. On the one hand she is the giver of warmth, a female being of beauty and splendour who tempts the faithful to idolatry, and on the other she is a demonic force of fire, death, thirst and disease. Even in this role she is ambiguous, for she purifies the earth with her fiery beams and hence is *barakah*, "holy," (Lit. "blessing"), and transmits *rahmah*, or the "mercy" of Allah.[33] She is imagined to rise each morning from the grave of the Prophet (this is clearly a reworking of the primitive idea which has the goddess emerging from a hole or "deep rock pit") which seems a rather honourable sleeping-place for a goddess supposed to be despised. Any ground upon which the Sun shines is regarded as ritually pure, and only needs to be cleared of obvious debris before being used for prayer. (Sun-purified ground needs no prayer-mat.) The powers of the Sun-goddess at noon are invoked by Arabic magicians for purificatory and other purposes, and children ask her for strong shining white teeth.[34] The Moon is more important in magic and occultism than the Sun. The peasants near Jerusalem in the last century would repair to the Well of the Virgin to sing this rain-chant:

"O Lady, O Moon [*Bedr*]
Water our crops with moisture!
O Lady, O Spring of Siloam,
Water our shrivelled seeds!"

Here the Moon has been feminized, but its name, *Bedr* (or *Badr*) is still masculine.[35]

Spiritual-feminist writers often say that the symbol of Islam, the star-and-crescent, was in some sense stolen from the Arabian Great Mother, but in reality it combined the two celestial symbols of divine *masculinity* for the Arabs; the feminine cult among Semitic peoples was primarily that of the Great *Sun* Mother, not the Great Moon Mother.

Chapter 19
Shakti Power of the Sun's Light
Tribal India

Before the advent of Indo-European speaking peoples from the north, India was inhabited by many different tribes. Some of these, like the *Khasis* of Assam and the *Mundas* of Bengal, spoke Austro-Asiatic languages. They were the aboriginals of India. In later times the land was settled by the *Dravidians*, who built great cities in the north—Mohenjo-Daro and Harappa, for example—before being forced away to the south by later invaders. The most important Dravidian group today are the Tamils of South India and Sri Lanka.[1]

In common with aboriginal peoples everywhere, many of the Indian tribes perceived the Sun as a goddess and the Moon as a male god. Sometimes both Sun and Moon are goddesses. Even in the same tribe, one group may have a Sun-goddess and Moon-god, while a neighbouring group sees things the other way round. This is typical of tribal religions, and a similar situation obtains among the Australian aborigines with regard to Sun and Moon.

The Village Ammas

In the villages of the south, goddesses predominate both in number and status; where gods appear, they frequently take a subordinate role. *Amma*, meaning "mother," "woman," or "goddess" is the habitual title of every female *grami-devi*, or village deity. It is totally incorrect to classify the Ammas as "Earth-mothers" or "Moon-mothers." They preside over a vast range of natural phenomena. Indeed, they defy all attempts at classification, and even a comprehensive listing is impossible because women who have died in an heroic, unusual or tragic way are continually added to the list. There are patron Ammas of weavers, potters, hereditary crafts, families, localities and so forth. Some Ammas are worshipped despite the fact that none of the villagers know who they are, or what their names mean.

Worship of unknown Ammas is sufficiently explained by the fact that all Ammas have one function in common—they inflict disease, especially smallpox and cholera. In theory an Amma may have a special "department" and will provide the relevant blessings, but in practice she is worshipped with the idea of avoiding her displeasure. Epidemic, flood or drought means that one or other of the Ammas is offended or discontented. Thus the Ammas closely resemble the nature spirits of Eskimo culture, to whom all misfortunes are attributed, or the "mothers" of the Finno-Ugric spiritual world.

The Sunshine Ammas

In Mysore city an Amma called *Bisal-Mari* is worshipped along with her six sisters. *Bisal* means "sunlight" and *Mari* means "feminine spiritual power." Her shrines are commonly roofless so that the Sun can shine in to enspirit her image or vehicle—a round brass pot against which a circular mirror, the *kunna-kannadi* or "eye mirror", is propped. When Bisal-Mari is worshipped, the mirror is treated as if it were the goddess herself, a practice strikingly reminiscent of Amaterasu's words, "Regard this mirror as if it were my own august self."[2] Here too, as in Japan, we find the ritual association of *Sun-goddess, eye and mirror.*[3]

Another way in which Bisal-Mari is represented is in the form of a mother-daughter pair of conical baetyls, one slightly smaller than the other, each carved with a crude face.[4] This suggests a "Sun's daughter" concept. Sometimes the goddess is represented at festivals in the form of a temporary clay image, made by the village goldsmith, but her real presence is thought to reside in the flame of the *arati*, a lamp waved sunwise in front of the statue by women worshippers. It is moulded from rice-flour and bears the simple pattern of a face, marked out with silver leaf and vermilion. Incense-sticks protrude all round, beneath a crown of leaves and flowers. The fire of the lamp is the divine feminine power of the Sun.[5]

Bisal-Mari is intensely dangerous and vindictive. If offended she will strike the unfortunate person down with smallpox or fever, but if appealed to in the right way, she will also remove these diseases. The belief that a Sun-goddess can cause fever has a primitive logic to it—the sufferer is burning hot, therefore she is possessed by a fiery deity. It is also Sun-goddesses who are considered to heal diseases of the skin. While this belief may derive from practical observation—exposure to sunlight is an effective cure for several skin complaints—there may be a direct connection with another aspect of Sun-goddess cult, the incest myth.

The Sun-sister/Moon-brother story turns up in India, too, often with the motif of the Sun throwing ashes at her brother to mark his face. Ash-throwing is a feature of South American versions of the myth, but there we also find the idea that the Moon's face is disfigured by scars, scratches and bruises inflicted by the Sun as she resists the rape. The Hindu Moon-god *Chandra-mas* also has a scarred face, but his problem is lupus, a tubercular disease which eats him away every month, in punishment for his involvement with a sister-in-law.[6] The tribal Sun-Amma may originally have cursed her Moon-brother with *smallpox*. Indeed, the lunar craters do recall the characteristic pock-marks left by this disease.

When the Hindu priests attempted to make their religion more acceptable to the common people, a move necessitated by the threat Buddhism posed to their domination, they incorporated native goddesses into their theology. Vedic Hinduism had very few female deities, so this vacuum was readily filled by the huge selection of native goddesses ready to hand. In the process, the type of religion called *Shaktism*, centred upon the feminine creative power, or *shakti*, was to evolve. Goddesses of the Sun such as Bisal-Mari contributed to the concept of the shaktic Great Mother as *active* feminine power, in contrast to the passive, receptive feminine principle found for example in Taoism.[7]

SHRINE and BAETYLS OF BISAL-MARI

Other Tribal Sun-Goddesses

Here we find many parallels with Siberian and North American traditions, including shamanistic practices of various kinds.[8] The Kolarian tribes worship a Sun-goddess whose husband is the Moon and whose children are the stars. Among the *Hos* tribe of Chota Nagpur, Sun and Moon are two sisters who made a pact to devour their children, the stars, but the Moon changed her mind on seeing Sun-sister perform the grisly act. The Sun was so enraged by her sister's betrayal that she ran after her with an axe, every now and again hacking a piece of her body away, so that Moon was progressively dismembered. This chase goes on eternally, causing the Moon's cycle of phases.[9]

The *Bondo* of Orissa say that *Tansirjo* the Sun and *Jonmati* the Moon were two sisters, who lived together and shared the care of their children. Each day they would take turns to go to the jungle and collect food, which all would share. But one day Jonmati began to feel resentful. She had collected a lot of food that day, and wanted her own children to have it all. So she hid her children in her hair, fastening it up into a bun, and when Tansirjo came home she lied to her. "I have eaten my children," she said, "because they were so much trouble." Tansirjo thought about this and decided that she too could not be bothered with her children's noise, and the nuisance of feeding them. So the Sun ate up her children. This was exactly the result Jonmati had hoped for. She undid her hair and revealed her children, still alive, at which the Sun flew into a violent rage. She refused to live with the Moon any longer, and this is why we see them separately. But Jonmati came to regret the absence of her sister, which made her very pale, and every now and again she becomes sad and quiet, which accounts for the Moon's phases.[10]

The *Kuttia Kond* of Orissa say that the Sun-goddess and Moon-goddess lived together, but the Sun ate her sister's children. At this the creator-god decreed they should separate. To console the Moon-goddess he tossed grain up in a winnow to form the stars, and now the Moon cares for them.[11]

Another Kond tradition says that the Sun and Moon are both female. The Sun-goddess takes the form of a cow who is brilliant during the day, but turns black at night and crosses the sky invisibly, travelling from west to east to get back to her starting point. Once the Sun-cow was stolen by a thief and hidden, plunging the world into darkness, so he was obliged to let her go again.[12]

In some traditions we find the Sun-goddess represented with seven sister-goddesses, making up what *Shaktism* calls "the eight powers of the universe." She is sometimes the chief among the seven, being the great source of light and heat in the universe, or again she may preside over the other seven as the light from which the seven principles or colours derive. Thus the seven sisters are really all solar, as the *Sherdukpen* of North East India believe. This tribe has seven Sun-goddesses, who all live together but take turns to be on duty in the sky, exactly like the suns of Chinese mythology. This is why the Sun always looks fresh and vigorous, and never ages or declines like the Moon.

The Khasis, A Matriarchal People

The Khasi tribe of the Assam hill country are unusual in preserving many features of the matriarchate, both religious and social. The high creator is with them an almighty Goddess, *Ka-Blei*, who is worshipped but rarely appealed to directly for intervention in human affairs. Families are named after the clan mothers, marriage is matrilocal, and all inheritance comes down in the female line, being passed to the youngest daughter, who is the high priestess of each individual family. Her house is a temple for that branch of the clan, where all will assemble to witness her performing the rites. The Khasis say *ka bat ka niam*, "the youngest daughter holds the religion."[13]

Khasi religion involves the worship of an immense range of nature-spirits both male and female, along with deified ancestresses and clan grandmothers who are commemorated by great megalithic monuments.[14] The importance of women is expressed in a traditional saying, *long jaid na ka kynthei*, "from the woman sprang the clan." A household usually consists of the grandmother (who is a matriarch), her daughters, and her daughter's children, while the husband is not considered to be a member of his wife's family but remains a part of his mother's.[15]

The Khasi Creation Story

According to the Khasi creation story, the creatress Ka Blei made Mother Earth. In the time before humans appeared, Earth had four children, a son and three daughters; they were the Moon, who was male, and the Sun, Fire and Water, who were female. In turn these children helped to make the universe, Sun-sister and Moon-brother creating the stars, while Fire-sister and Water-sister made plants, animals, rivers and all the things which cover the Earth.[16] Khasi cosmology assigns to the female principle the Sun, rivers, lakes and abstract ideas, while the masculine principle includes the Moon, mountains, stones and the vegetable world. These beliefs are reflected in the grammatical gender of words. [17]

When all was complete, Mother Earth asked Ka Blei to send someone who could care for the newly-made world. In response the creatress made humans, who were the Khasi people. At this time everything was happy; Earth and heaven were in harmony. But it was not to last. The great world-tree, *ka dingiei*, which grew on the highest mountain top, linking Earth to heaven, gradually became so huge that it obscured the sky and cut out the light of Sun and Moon. An evil spirit dwelling in the sea heard of the people's discontent. Emerging from the waters he made mischief by encouraging their grumbling, and before long he prevailed upon them to cut down the tree; thus the world was filled with light again and Sun and Moon moved freely. But the link between Earth and heaven was broken, separating all humankind from the creatress, and this is how unhappiness entered the world.

While the Khasi were cursed for cutting down the tree, the animal creation was innocent. The cockerel, who had the kindest of hearts, went to Ka Blei to plead on behalf of the humans, praying that she would not destroy them. She was won over by his words and spared her earthly children. As a reward she bestowed on the cockerel the gift of crowing, by which to announce the appearance of the Sun-goddess each day.[18]

Sun-Sister and Moon-Brother

Disharmony also came about in heaven itself at the beginning of time. *Ka-sngi*, the Sun-goddess, was very beautiful, so much so that the Moon-god, her brother, *U-Bynai*, began to lust after her. While Ka-Sngi was well-behaved, helpful and kind to all, U-Bynai was a wicked young man, selfish and irresponsible. Their respective characters very much resemble those of Amaterasu and Susanawo, even in the details of U-Bynai yearning to go down to the underworld, and refusing to fulfil his duties. Thus the Moon-god spent his time in the caverns under the earth and was absent for days together. Then, missing the comforts of home, he would decide to saunter back and make a nuisance of himself. When Ka-sngi became aware of his bad intentions, she was enraged. She took ashes in her hand and berated him thus:

"Do you harbour such an incestuous and wicked intention against me, your elder sister, who has taken care of you and held you in her arms, and carried you on her back like a mother does; now I will cover your brow with ashes, you wicked and shameless one; begone from the house!"

At this she flung the ashes in his face, and the Moon-god, who had once shone as brightly as his sister, was dimmed to a pale, dusty light. The ashes stuck to his face, making the shadows we now see on the full moon. U-Bynai was deeply ashamed, and fled from his sister, so that they were never again seen together. When he vanishes from the sky he is called *U-Bynai-iong*, "the black Moon."[19]

The Sun and Moon are not especially important in Khasi religion over and above the other native spirits. Rites are concerned chiefly with restoring the broken link between heaven and earth (for which purpose the high priestess conducts her rites at the central post of the house, which is made of sacred oak and symbolizes the world-tree) or with honouring the divine ancestresses. The creatress is not in any way an Earth-goddess or Moon-goddess.[20]

The Ancestral Priestess

Traditional female costume includes a gold or silver crown, made of upstanding rays, which is worn for ceremonial dances, such as that celebrating the divine ancestral priestess, *Ka Pah Syntiew*, "The Flower-Lured One." This solar coronet is called *Pa-Sngi-At*, *Sngi* being the Sun.[21] Interestingly, the myth of Ka Pah Syntiew resembles that of Amaterasu, for the priestess dwells in a cave into which she withdraws further and further. She is only coaxed out by the man who has fallen in love with her, who lures her with a beautiful flower.[22] As we have already seen, the flower can be a solar image, an "imitation sun." This is not the only resemblance between Khasi and Japanese tradition, for both are related to tribal religions of South-East Asia and South China, in which the feminine Sun and masculine Moon are regularly found.

Chapter 20
She Who Maintains the World
Hindu India

"I shall never forget her who is the giver of happiness...
She it is, O Mother, who in the form of the Moon,
Creates the world full of sounds and meaning,
And, again, by her Power in the form of the Sun,
She it is who maintains the world."

—Hymn to Bhairavi

When the Indo-European tribespeople, patriarchal nomads and herders related to the Scythians and Iranians, first entered India in about 1800 B.C., they met the settled Dravidian world with its highly-stratified town life and peaceful villages, and a completely alien religious viewpoint. Most of the deities of the invading people were masculine, the violent yet beneficent forces of rain, storm, wind and Sun, while those of the Dravidians were nature-spirits, concerned with the fruitful earth. Goddesses were very much in evidence, and gods who were lords of the beasts, or deities in animal form.[1]

From the earliest times the Indo-European and native Indian religions began to influence each other, eventually forming the blend we call *Hinduism*. The Indo-Europeans who settled in India, displacing the Dravidians (not necessarily violently)[2] are known as *Vedic* Hindus, after the language in which their scriptures, the *Vedas*, were written. They were not (as is sometimes wrongly stated) "Sun-god worshippers"—the Sun, *Surya*, was a significant deity, but he was not the principal god—that place belonged to *Indra*, god of rain and storm. It was not until much later in history that the Sun-god rose to prominence, and then as the deity of compassion, not war.

When the Vedic Hindus arrived in India they were fully patriarchal in social organization and religion, but they retained some traces of an earlier matriarchate. The *Rig Veda* speaks favourably of matriarchy and the role of priestesses at the same time as it exalts the domineering gods of father-right. The later *Mahabharata* contains matriarchal themes and itself admits that monogamy and female subjection were established late. The Vedic woman was not se-cluded. She could enjoy material and social freedom as well as complete liberty in her choice of lovers and husbands. "It is beyond doubt that the position of women among the Indian Aryans has progressively changed from one of freedom and influence to one of comparative subjection and effacement."[3] There is very good reason to believe that female subjection, along with the caste system, was learnt by the Vedic priests from the *Dravidians*, whose society was so highly ordered and stratified.[4] In the last century a controversial revivalist movement, *Arya Samaj*, attempted to purify Hinduism and restore the original Aryan faith as brought by the prehistoric tribes. One of the reasons Arya Samaj met with hostility was its active involvement in *feminist* causes and the dis-mantling of the caste system. The movement promoted women's rights and social and religious equality precisely because female subjection and caste oppression received no support from Vedic authorities, and were not original practices.[5]

The Vedic Sun and Moon

In the Vedas the deities of both Sun and Moon are masculine, *Surya* and *Mas*, the direct equivalents both in name and function of *Kvare* and *Mah*, the Sun and Moon—again, both male gods—of the Iranians.[6]

Neither Sun-god nor Moon-god play a very important part in Vedic religion. Much more active in Vedic cult than the Sun-god was a feminine Sun, *Suryā* (usually called the Sun-maiden by mythologists), who appears as the radiant golden bride in the *Suryasakta*, the Wedding-Hymn-of-the-Sun-Goddess, still used as liturgy at Hindu weddings.[7] Suryā's bridegroom is *Soma*, the Moon, while the groomsmen are the twin "sons of god," or *Asvins*, stellar horse-gods, exactly paralleling the Baltic mythology.[8] There, when the Sun-goddess marries the Moon, the *Dieva-deli* are the groomsmen. Mythologists opposed to the concept of a feminine Sun are fond of pointing out that the Suryasakta is "late," but its contents point to a very archaic, proto-Indo-European tradition which has been overlaid by the masculist Vedic religion. Suryā is a typical Sun's daughter or young Sun-goddess character, and it is highly probably that Surya-the-god was, in previous times, Suryā-the-mother, the Sun-goddess, whose daughter (or Spring aspect) was given in marriage to the Moon.[9] The *Vedas* call her "the youthful daughter of the Sun with all her glory," who ascends her golden bridal car, "stepping from the clouds with face refulgent." She is extolled as "not fierce of eye, no slayer of thy husband... radiant, gentle-hearted, delightful," praises which rather suggest that, under some unspecified conditions, she *might* be a fierce husband-slayer, like Saule who hacks her husband the Moon to pieces with a sword.

Just as in Baltic myth, which shared the same proto-Indo-European sources as the *Vedas*, the husband of the Sun-maiden is sometimes the Moon, and sometimes the stellar god[s]. In another version of Surya's myth, the Moon competes with the Asvin twins in a race to reach the brilliant Sun-goddess. It is the Asvins who win and take Suryā to wife, providing her with a splendid three-wheeled chariot.[10] The race in which the twins compete to reach the Spring Sun-goddess, or "Sun-maiden," reiterates the theme of the European maze-games, in which two men dance or run the maze to liberate the young Sun-goddess from winter's grip.[11]

The Cult of Surya

The Sun-god Surya did not develop an extensive cult until the sixth century A.D., when East European and Persian Mithraists came to live in India. Surya had already absorbed features of the late Roman Sun-god, becoming as a result a kind of majestic heavenly king. These influences combined with the Vedic Sun-tradition to create a solar cult of great beauty and gentleness which flourished for seven hundred years and gave India some of its most splendid temples.[12]

It is important to realize that, contrary to spiritual-feminist assertions, the masculine Sun-god of Iran and India had nothing to do with violence, hatred, rape, racism or the subjugation of women. Indeed, quite the opposite—although majestic and kingly, Surya is the personification of compassion, healing and friendliness. His cult legends emphasize again and again his kindly healing force which restores crippled limbs, brings relief to sufferers from illness and affliction, and nurtures the world with warmth. He is especially the protector of the orphaned, the downtrodden and the childless, restoring justice for those who are ill-used.[13]

In all of these roles he closely resembles the Baltic Sun-goddess Saule, with whom he shares a common origin in the remote Indo-European past. Far from being the stereotypical killing, life-hating, transcendent Aryan Sun-god of spiritual-feminist demonology, he is actually considered by the Hindus to be one of the deities *least* concerned with the transcendent realm. He is essentially a deity of this-worldly matters, fostering life and correcting wrongs. As the all-seeing eye, he represents *wholeness of thought and vision*, the ability to see things in their entirety—in other words, holistically.[14]

The Sun-god also appears under other names. As Savitar or Savitri he is the generative, stimulating power of the Sun, represented as his innumerable arms and hands which are his life-giving rays.[15] This is the god invoked daily by millions of Hindus, as they make a beautiful obeisance to the rising Sun and recite the *Gayatri* mantra:

> "Resplendent Sun, inspiring us to reverence!
> May we gaze on the splendour of your guiding power
> That charges us with light."

For some Hindus this invocation is made to the Sun as a feminine power.[16] Savitri is also a goddess; in legend, a princess who descends to the underworld and succeeds in bringing back her dead husband, rather like the Ugarit Sun-goddess who goes to the realm of the dead for the sake of Ba'al Hadad.[17] But Savitar is primarily a male god, "the nourisher," whose rays put life into food grains and living beings (according to the *Mahabharata*)—a thoroughly ecological concept![18]

The various Hindu scriptures are full of the most lovely references and invocations to Surya. According to the *Chandogya Upanishad*, "those who worship the Sun as the Absolute ever hear beautiful sounds and are filled with joy"[19]—hardly the description of a life-denying religion. We must bear in mind that the Hindu Sun-tradition may ultimately derive from that of a Sun-goddess.[20]

The Dawn Goddess and Sun Mare

The most important goddess of Vedic India is *Ushas*, the dawn, the only female deity to approach the status of the chief Vedic gods. She is described in terms so like those applied to the Sun that it is hardly sometimes difficult to distinguish them, which is hardly surprising, when one realizes that she is the same goddess as Baltic *Auzrine*, in other words, the Sun's daughter aspect. Her name is etymologically identical to that of the Baltic goddess as well as to Greek *Eos*, Germanic *Eostre* (*Ostara*), and other Indo-European goddesses of Dawn, Spring and the Morning Star. Ushas is a gorgeously dressed woman in a crimson sari and a golden veil, leading the white horse of the Sun through the gates of the sky. Evil spirits who have taken advantage of darkness to work mischief are sent fleeing away by her light, as she recalls the sleeping world to life, consciousness and joy. The poets of the *Vedas* used the most lovely and affectionate imagery for this goddess, calling her the ever-young, and yet at the same time the ancient one, who is reborn day after day, eternally.[21] At one time this goddess of sunlight accompanied the Sun across the whole sky, riding in her own chariot drawn by red horses or red cows—her name can mean not only "dawn," but also "evening light." It is apparent that Ushas has absorbed many features of a previous feminine Sun, or rather, as a typical Sun's daughter, like Baltic *Auzrine*—whose name is the same word—she was already almost a replica of her mother. In one myth Indra, the storm-god, is at loggerheads with her, just as Perun is with Saule, and hurling a thunderbolt smashes her chariot,[22] perhaps a mythic way of describing the struggle between storm and sunshine which is expressed in faraway Japan as the opposition between Susanowo and Amaterasu. Wherever we find this battle between the deities of the dark cloudy sky and bright sunny sky, we should suspect a Sun-goddess hiding somewhere!

Ushas also appears in the *Vedas* as *Asva*, a mare-goddess who is the dawn. To think of the solar light as a mare rather than a stallion is, as we have seen, nothing unusual. In Tantric writings the Sun is sometimes a mare and the Moon her stallion, whose tumescence and detumescence is the waxing and waning of the Moon. It is also in the Tantras, this time the *Siva Samhita*, that menstrual blood is called the "red Sun" and semen the "white Moon." Tantric sexual rites based on this symbology envisage the male partner as absorbing the female red Sun "energy" into himself, and uniting it with the male lunar principal by a process of *coitus reservatus*, thus achieving a spiritual unity, a mystical marriage of Sun-goddess and Moon-god.[23] In such a rite the menstruating woman is herself the Sun-goddess, her blood being considered a form of *Agni*, the fire-god.[24] In Hindu thought the Sun is the fiery principle of life, its active initiating force— here represented by *Shakti*, the female divine power—while the Moon is the primaeval cold, watery and passive element[25]—represented in this Tantric rite as *Shiva*, the masculine divine power. Women may now find it easier to see why the goddess Kali, the violent and destructive shakti-power, dances upon the corpse of her husband under her feet, for he is the lunar partner who is constantly destroyed and regenerated by the terrible aspect of the feminine Sun—just as the phallus itself, like the Moon, is "destroyed" and "regenerated" by the power of feminine "heat." This is a new way of looking at sexual symbolism—new, at any rate, for Westerners who are so used to thinking of the supposedly hot, active, solar masculine and the cold, passive lunar feminine.

The Hindu Moon-God

Hinduism works out the archaic Moon-god idea quite explicitly and naturally. The reader will note that in the Tantric rite mentioned above, the man is the Moon and the woman the Sun *when she is menstruating* (Tantra is almost unique in recognizing woman's increased libido at this time). Indeed, the woman *will* be menstruating; in mythic terms she is in sexual connection with the Moon-god, which is the cause of women's monthly bleeding. *Mas* or *Chandra-mas* is the Vedic Moon-god of the usual primitive kind. The Vedic Hindus said that he was "the first husband of all women," the real influence which impregnated them—their earthly husbands were surrogates who took possession of their wives after Chandra-mas had made love to them (i.e. after their first menstruation).[26] The Moon contains rain (or in some accounts, semen, an idea also found in Iran where the Moon contains the semen of the primordial bull)[27] and when it rains, souls come down to earth in the rainwater, enter the wombs of women, and become reincarnated.[28] For this reason the Moon is the dwelling of the migrating souls as well as the abode of the ancestors. The *Upanishads* say, "All who depart this world go to the Moon."[29] Thus it is thought that the influx of souls arriving at the Moon causes its waxing, while their dispersal unto a new life causes it to wane, a concept also found among the Australian aborigines.

Another explanation of the Moon's changes takes the form of a rather familiar story. The Moon-god was once upon a time a pious, well-behaved man, but he grew arrogant and licentious, eventually seducing the star-goddess *Tara*, a wife of the teacher of the gods. As a punishment, Siva took a sword and hewed the Moon in two."[30] Readers will recognize the similarity to Baltic myth. Yet another story gives the Moon-god *Soma* twenty-seven stars as wives—he shares out his attentions by spending one night with each in turn, but his real love is for their sister, the star-goddess *Rohini*, whom Daksha (father of all twenty-eight) will not let him marry. The pair hide away (the dark of the Moon) to make love in secret, but Daksha discovers them. He curses Soma with lupus, a consumption which eats him away. Fortunately the star-wives intervene, so that Soma gradually recovers—and then the story starts all over again.[31]

Siva, who does not appear in the *Vedas* but certainly seems to be present among the urban Dravidian deities, is in many of his aspects a typical, primitive Moon-god. Despite mythological variations his temples are still distinguished by spires bearing the crescent Moon[32]; he rides a bull, carries a trident, has three eyes, and wears a crescent in his hair; his most sacred emblem is the *lingam*, representative of life and fertility, yet he haunts graveyards and is the god of destruction and death. He is explicitly stated to bring about *cyclic renewal*.

The Cow of Light

Just as the bull in Hindu and Iranian thought expresses in animal form the virility of the masculine Moon, so does the cow have solar associations. In the legend of the *Panis*, demons steal the "cows of light" belonging to the gods and hide them in a mountain cave. It is Indra and his helpers, or in some versions the *Asvins*, who pronounce the sacred formula which releases the cows, whereupon dawn once again lights the world.[33] This is yet another version of the imprisoned Sun-goddess myth, with the cave, the mountain, the twins, the "inspired utterance,"[34] and the reappearance of the Sun in Spring, after the winter darkness when she has been imprisoned in a mountain, or beneath the earth. The word for cow is *go*, which also means "ray of dawn" or "ray of spiritual illumination." Another cow-goddess, *Aditi*, "not-divided," began as a generalized divinity of infinite light or space, and later through influences from Surya's cult was imagined to be the Sun itself, whose nourishing light was her milk. The Mogul royal survey, *Ayin-I-Akbari*, expressly describes Aditi as the Sun.[35]

The idea of the Sun as nourisher and cow-of-light or food-giving cow (*dhenu*) is also used to explain the Moon's phases. The Moon as *Soma* is the cup of nectar which sustains the gods, but it is not its source, for that is the Sun. As the gods finish up their monthly supply, the Moon is replenished from the Sun, an idea suggesting that the Hindus understood the reflective nature of the Moon. This is very possible—classical influences reached India during the Gupta period,[36] Arab scholars versed in astronomy shared their knowledge with Hindus, and the Tantric philosophers took a religious interest in science, even developing a kind of atomic theory.[37]

Indeed, the Hindu deities and religion have been formed by many diverse influences and contain a multiplicity of contrasting elements. It is therefore not surprising that, alongside several versions of the male Sun-god, we should also find traces of earlier Sun-goddesses, including the proto-Indo-European Sun-maiden and her twin brothers, who in Lithuania and Latvia became *Saule* and the *Dieva deli*.[38]

Eclipse of the Sun

Chapter 21
Fiery Needles
Armenia and Georgia

"Hearing the cause of her anger, hope restored me to senses,
Gave power to my eyes to see her and gaze on the glow of her radiance...
...I rose, praised God and then said to the maiden:
'O sun, you have burnt me to ashes. My sun is set and extinguished.
Since I still live let me venture to give you, O sun, an answer.'"
—Shota Rustaveli, *Vepkhistqaosani*.[1]

The people of Armenia, the country which lies between north Turkey and
south-west Russia, speak a language which is the last remaining example of a
separate Indo-European branch. The land itself, however, has seen many
different influences—Hurrian, Phrygian, Roman and others—and hence there
are traces of several distinct religious traditions.

Armenian Cosmology

According to ancient tradition, the sky is made of frozen water, and the Sun
and Moon float through the upper atmosphere supported by air. The Sun is a
young woman of exquisite beauty, while the Moon, her brother, is a handsome
youth; they are the children of mother Earth, and when the Sun sets, the
Armenians say that she blushes with joy as she approaches her mother to
embrace her. This accounts for the Sun's red glow. Mother Earth is sometimes
identified with the Virgin Mary, so that just as in the Basque country, Sun and
Moon are the offspring of Mary and hence sister and brother of Christ.[2]
Otherwise the Blessed Virgin is identified with the Sun-goddess and given the
epithets sun-eyed and fiery-haired, ancient titles of the war-god Vahagn.[3]

Fiery Needles

The Sun-goddess walks across the sky during the daytime because it is safer; nevertheless she is a formidable woman, equipped with an array of needles to transfix anyone who looks at her. She has a bashful, proud and quick-tempered disposition. The Moon-god, who is sick with love for her, walks the sky at night, because the darkness is more dangerous.[4] Tradition represents Sun-goddess and Moon-god as separated lovers (since they are sister and brother, this introduces the motif of incest), who continually seek each other through the skies. The Moon (A*mins*) misses the Sun[5] so much that he forgets to eat, and as he pines away he grows thinner until the two lovers manage to meet (in the three moonless nights when Sun and Moon are absent together under the earth). After this joyous reunion the pair are fated to suffer the pains of separation once again, but the Moon-god feels so much better after his meeting with his sweetheart that, for a while, he regains his health and fullness. Mardiros Ananikian calls the feminine Sun tradition "very transparent and poetical myths [which] have little in them that might be called ancient." Yet, far from being mere modern poetry, the Sun-sister/Moon-brother myth has features in common with Sun-goddess traditions of a very archaic kind, such as those of the Eskimo and native Australians.[6]

Other aspects of Armenian solar lore show evidence of several different influences, particularly Slavic and Anatolian. Horses are sacred to the Sun. Her aniconic form is a great wheel, like one of the giant water-wheels of the Middle East. At the end of her daily journey she is received and bathed by a "mother of the Sun," who is closely similar to Slavic *Perperuna*.[7] When the Sun-goddess is replaced in folklore by the Sun-god, she becomes the "mother" or "sister" of this masculine god, as in the altered Slavic myths.[8]

The combination of the feminine solar element (fire) and the male lunar element (water) was as important to the Armenians as to the other Indo-European cultures. At an ancient sacred site, a spring at the foot of a mountain, they celebrated the cult of "Sister Fire and Brother Spring," in which the embers of the sacred fire were quenched by the spring-water, "wiped with the brother's tears." This is an older, more primitive conception than that which makes the woman the cold, passive element and man the fiery, hot, active one.[9] In the Armenian folktale "Of the Sun and the Moon," water in which the Sun-goddess and Moon-god have washed restores a petrified girl to life,[10]

The Sun-Goddess in Folk Tale

Leon Surmelian's collection of Armenian folktales gives many examples of solar imagery applied to heroines. A woman can be "as fair as the Sun," or "like

SCYTHIAN GOLD PLAQUE WITH
MIRROR-GODDESS AND WARRIOR

a fragment of the Sun itself," or her beauty may seem to say to the Sun, "let me shine instead of you."[11] *Arevhat*, the Sun-maiden, is both the Sun and the Sun's daughter, sometimes appearing alongside the later masculine Sun. Among her adventures she drops a spindle into a cave (in a mountain, of course!) and is trapped there when she tries to retrieve it, only being released by a gift-giving crone who turns her hair golden. I need not labour the point over these motifs— by this stage in the book readers will be well able to interpret for themselves! In another story Arevhat is imprisoned in a cave as an offering to a dragon, who, under the influence of her gentleness, is transformed into a prince. Later he becomes her lover, but he is under an enchantment "to rise when the Sun sets, and set when the Sun rises," which suggests that he is the morning and evening star (compare *Auseklis*, who courts Sun's Daughter in the Baltic myth) or perhaps even the Moon himself.[12] Seklemian's collection also provides much solar feminine imagery. In one story a man dreams of two suns and a star. This turns out to be prophetic—the two suns are two princesses, whom he later marries, and the star is the child of one of these Sun-wives.[13]

The Sun-Goddess of Georgia

Ancient feminine Sun traditions are also found in the neighbouring republic of Georgia. The Georgians were converted to Christianity quite early, in the fourth century, accepting the new religion without coercion, because of their tolerant attitude towards other people's deities. To the pagan Georgians, Christ was just one more god, or son of a god.

At the time Christianity arrived in Georgia, the people worshipped *Morige*, the Moon—a masculine god—as chief divinity. This, however, had not always been the case, for previous to this lunar religion they had worshipped the feminine Sun, known by various names according to locality, like the Sun and the Moon deities of the Arab tribes. For example, in the east of the country, in *Khaketia*—Georgia's best wine-growing region—the Sun-goddess was called *Mtsekale*. She presided over the vines as the deity who ripened the grapes. Evidently she was similar to the Ugaritic Sun-goddess *Shapash*, who also made the grape-vines flourish and blossom with her nurturing warmth.

Elsewhere the Sun-goddess was simply called *Nana*, or "mother." There exists an old lullaby which invokes her and expresses connotations of fertility, again recalling Shapash, and the hymn which asks her to make the sons of El grow from babies to strong young men, in the same way as she fosters the growth of the vine.[14]

The Knight in the Panther's Skin

According to Georgian ancient history specialists, the most archaic stratum of religion in this area knew Sun-goddesses and Moon-gods, with the Sun-goddess having precedence from the beginning. The ancient texts and inscriptions express no doubt or surprise at the idea of the Sun being feminine, and indeed, famous women of Georgian history, like the redoubtable Queen Tamara, were symbolized as the Sun, or even believed to be the Sun-goddess herself.[15]

The great glory of Georgian literature is the epic *Vepkhistqaosani*, "The Knight in the Panther's Skin," written by Tamara's treasurer, Shota Rustaveli. He fell deeply in love with his queen and wrote Vepkhistqaosani to honour her, giving succeeding ages a glimpse of the splendour of Tamara's queendom (1184-1213) when Georgia reached the height of its political and cultural power. But the epic is not merely dead history. In it Rustaveli enshrined the folk-wisdom of traditional Georgia; only the Orthodox Church was hostile to the book, burning it whenever it had the opportunity. To this day Vepkhistqaosani is living tradition and living philosophy for the Georgian people.

One of the most striking features of the poem, for the Western reader, is the profusion of solar metaphors applied to *women*. While both men and women are spoken of as "suns" and "moons," the overwhelming majority of Sun expressions are used of heroines, page after page comparing woman to the Sun. The Queen of the story, *Tinatin* (who is really Tamara), is introduced as "bright as the sun in its glory, shedding radiant beams... She who outshines the sun... bright as the sun's rays at noontide... sunlike, omniscient, her gaze shed light in the farthest places... like the sun in heaven," and so forth. Her lover, the warrior *Avtandil*, addresses her as "O sun! Who dazzles the eyes with your splendour...

O bright one!... God has created in your being a sun which is brighter than the sun that reigns in the heavens... " and so on through the book until the wedding of Avtandil and Tinatin, he "the lion" and she "the sun of the heavens."[16] Even today, Georgians think of the feminine and women as solar. The goddess-name *Medea* is still given to girls, and Georgians believe that this deity was a Sun-goddess.[17]

The Scythian Diana

Georgia lies on the east of the Black Sea, which means that we are in *Scythian* territory. Archaeology and textual studies have confirmed the existence of warrior-women among the *Sarmatians*, a related Indo-European tribal people, although not among the Scythians themselves.[18] A young Sarmatian woman was obliged to train and ride with the young men until such time as she managed to kill an enemy in battle. Not until then was she allowed to marry, after which she put her weapons away and led a considerably more enclosed life.[19] From such tribal practices the Greek and Roman legends of Amazon queendoms arose. Whether or not such exclusive matriarchates ever existed is debatable, but evidence suggests that women played an active role in the clan hierarchy. The Scythians were patriarchal, but their principal deity was a great Goddess, the so-called *Scythian Diana*. Of her Jean Markale says:

> "Artemis and her Indo-European counterpart Arvi are very obscure in origin, but both derive from some older, probably pre-Indo-European word. They are generally taken to be forms of the cruel and ancient Scythian Diana, the sun goddess of the people of the Steppes, who was worshipped throughout the periphery of the Mediterranean at the time of the Hellenistic migrations... the sun goddess of early times who relinquished her solar position to a male god."[20]

Markale also suggests that, with the coming of the Hellenic Greeks, Artemis was changed into the Moon while Apollo usurped her solar character.[21] Therefore she and her Amazonian queens may represent a very ancient, feminine Sun-tradition which was still alive in Tamara's reign.[22]

Eclipse of the Sun

Chapter 22
She Who Dwells in the Spacious Disc
Egypt

In the earliest times the Nile valley peoples practised many different religions, archaic tribal cults each tied to a locality or clan. The deities were nature-spirits appearing in animal form, living expressions of the vital forces of nature. It was not only the beneficent forces which received worship—the Sun, Moon and stars, the Nile with its fecundating powers—but also the destructive forces of the desert wastes and the burning skies of the wilderness. Even after new rulers and cults were introduced and strange priests tried to formalize theology, the intensely conservative Egyptians kept on going back to the old shrines and practising the old cults. Religion was not a matter of theology, but of carrying out those rites essential for all of life. It probably mattered little to the ordinary Egyptian that the priesthood of Re, with its sophisticated theological ideas, had recycled their deities in all kinds of unusual ways. The priests of Horus and Re had both a religious and political interest in including all gods and goddesses in one great, glorious, connected system, and the result can look like hopeless confusion to the modern reader. Nevertheless, the characters of the different deities can be clearly traced, and evidence of the primitive ideas they incorporate is often very striking.

Hathor of Dendera

One of the most important early deities was the sky-goddess *Hathor*, local deity of Dendera in Southern Egypt. She was incorporated into the cults of Re and Horus as Re's mother, or daughter, or Horus' mother, but details of her myths reveal an older, conflicting motif—that of the feminine Sun. Since the cults of Horus and Re were essentially patriarchal, legitimizing the rule of the king as the Sun-god on Earth, a Sun-goddess could not be tolerated—she would be a spiritual rival and a political threat. Such a goddess could be incorporated into the cult of the Sun-god himself, becoming a "feminine personification" of the Sun's power, subservient to him. Hathor's personality absorbed other local sky-goddesses, such as *Nut* and *Isis*, as well as many other lesser deities until in time nearly every goddess was given some of her attributes, or imagined to be a particular version of her.

The House of the Sky

Hathor is the goddess's Greek name. Originally she was *Het-hert*, "Sky-house," "House of the Sky," or even "My house is the Sky." Later, when the Horus-worshippers came from the north, they renamed her *Het-heru*, "House of Horus," saying that she was the sky through which the falcon-god flew, and therefore (by analogy with *Nut*) his mother. It was through identification with Nut that Hathor became the sky-cow whose right eye is the Sun and her left the Moon. But Hathor is first and foremost the *solar eye* of the heavens. Re's cult made her into the Sun-god's eye, but her solar associations predate the supremacy of this god.

As the Sun-Eye she is a fierce and dangerous goddess, the burning power of the Sun in the terrible desert. Thus shrines to her were found in the sun-baked wilderness. At the same time her personality can be mild and beneficent. Every sort of beauty, delight, joy and ornament was hers; her festivals were a riot of colourful display, feasting, drinking, dance, ritual exposure, games and music; her temples called "home-of-intoxication" and "place-of-enjoyment." In consequence of her role as goddess of pleasure, the Greeks identified her with Aphrodite. But readers will recognize again the dual nature of the Sun-goddess, lady of warmth and pleasure, lady of fire and destruction. In her mild aspect she was identified with the cat-goddess *Bast*, who personified the warm, nurturing sunshine of spring and early summer.[2]

The Jealous Eye

Hathor's myths contain details which bear a striking resemblance to Sun-goddess mythology in other parts of the world. As the solar Eye she had a life and will independent of her "master," the official Sun-god, and was inclined at times to give him trouble. We may see in this the difficulty which the Re priests had in keeping the Hathor-worshippers in line, and forcing her to adopt a subservient role in the patriarchal Sun-god mythos. One story tells how, during Hathor's absence as a lioness in the depths of Nubia, Re replaced her with a substitute eye.

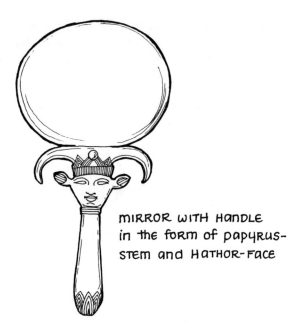

MIRROR WITH HANDLE
in the form of papyrus-
stem and HATHOR-FACE

On her return Hathor became furious and dangerous, so Re pacified her by placing her on his brow as the sacred cobra, the *uraeus*, which is another goddess, *Uadjit*. As this goddess, Hathor spits streams of flame at Re's enemies, scorching and consuming them for a distance of "millions of cubits" ahead—a sort of reptilian flame-thrower. The replacement of the eye by a rival, and the goddess's angry reaction, clearly symbolize the replacement of the Sun-goddess by the new male god. Re was not native to Egypt. He was imported round about 2,500 B.C.E. from the north-east, that is, from Western Asia. This may account for the residual lunar motifs which writers such as Briffault detect in Re's myths.

The eye-replacement motif also occurs in the myths of *Atum*, chief god of *On* (*Heliopolis*). He was at first an earth-god like Geb, representing the hill which first arose from the waters of chaos. (The Egyptians believed the earth to be a masculine god, while the sky was feminine. Nut and Geb were "Mother Sky" and "Father Earth.") Later Atum became assimilated to Re, taking on versions of his myths. He had only one eye, which was the goddess Hathor, the Sun. One day Atum sent his Eye to look for the divine pair Shu and Tefnut, his children, who had become lost in the cosmic waters. When she came back she was enraged to find that Atum had replaced her with another eye, and so she seized her master and carried him off into the depths of Nubia. As a result of the Eye's disappearance, darkness and cold prevailed. Rather like the Shinto *kami* laying a plan to lure Amaterasu from her hideout, the gods conferred and sent *Anhur* ("he-who-leads-what-has-gone-away") to bring back the Sun-goddess. Anhur spent some considerable time softening her up with promises and sweet talk, until he could get in close enough to lasso her with a magic rope and haul her back to her "proper place." For this reason he is shown in art holding a cord by which he leads the Sun.[3]

In this legend the presence of Atum is clearly superfluous; the eye-replacement motif is taken from the Re theology, and in another version Atum simply "insults" Hathor. His trip to Nubia serves no useful purpose, for it is the Sun-goddess whose absence results in darkness and it is the Eye, not Atum, which has to be brought back. There is no suggestion here of rescuing the Sun-god from the grip of an angry goddess, but of persuading *the Sun herself* to come back and restore light to the world.

The Mirror of Hathor

Many details of Hathor's mythos resemble those of Amaterasu, and like the Japanese Sun-goddess, Hathor is closely connected with the *mirror*. Hand-mirrors are very frequently cast in the form of Hathor, with the goddess's face crowned by the circular mirror which represents the Sun's disc. These are assumed to be looking-glasses, for cosmetic purposes, but they may have been used in personal devotions like the large cult mirrors which were dedicated in offering to this goddess. We do not know in what way these were used in Hathor's rites, but they were very probably employed as in Japan, India and elsewhere, to bring the brilliant goddess "down to earth," so that her worshippers might safely be near her. It is thought that some tombs were illuminated by mirrors which reflected the Sun's light deep into the interior. (In this way the wall-paintings could be executed without damage from the soot of oil-lamps.)

Hathor's myth also contains the water-mirror motif, in which fascination with her own reflection puts an end to her life-threatening attitude. In this story her violent and murderous temperament resembles that of the Cherokee Sun-goddess, who purified the earth by fire.

Once people on earth grew corrupt and dedicated to evil, eventually daring to rebel against Re himself. At this, his Eye took the form of Hathor as a female warrior (or the goddess *Sekhmet*, as a lioness) and flew against the human race in a terrifying and inexorable rage. She slaughtered without mercy, so that by and by it began to look as if no-one would survive. To the dismay of the gods, Hathor would not listen to pleas from deities or men, nor would she pause for one instant from her killing. So, to distract her, the gods shallowly flooded the earth with red beer brewed from pomegranates, or in another version, set it out in great vats. The goddess, believing it to be blood, drank and drank until she was too drunk to stand—and so a remnant of humankind was saved.

Another account tells how she saw her own reflection in the beer. Distracted by her own beauty, she fell to gazing raptly at herself, and forgot all about her murderous rage. In celebration of this event, Re decreed that each year there should be brewed in Hathor's honour "as many jugs of beer as there are priestesses of the Sun." Presumably it was the priestesses who drank the beer, but at least in later times all who celebrated Hathor's festival indulged in ritual drunkenness.

Hathor's Iconography

Hathor is represented in many ways, but chiefly as a sleek and beautiful woman, crowned with the red Sun-disc set between cow-horns. This disc is *not* the Moon, nor are the horns meant to represent the Moon. This is a modern idea based on an *a priori* judgement that all goddesses "must be" the Moon. Egyptological sources and records give no support to this notion. The Moon was always a *masculine* deity in Egyptian religion, represented quite differently to the Sun-deities and solar orb. There is no universal law of iconography which allows us to make *all* cows, horns and circular objects into feminine Moons.[4]

In the huge pantheon of Egyptian deities, only Hathor and the fire-god *Bes*, protectress of women, are represented full-face. The connection with the Sun is plain from the expression:

"face of the disc," i.e. the *aten*, the Sun itself. Hathor is also called "she who dwells in the *aten*," and "Hathor, who dwelleth in the spacious disc." Another common title was *Nubt*, that is, the "Golden One," and she was also associated with the star Sept, or Sirius (from the Greek, meaning "sun-like") as well as the morning star, giving us the Sun/Morning Star dyad, which is so frequent in Sun-goddess cult.

Sekhmet the Mighty

Closely identified with Hathor, indeed, considered to be that goddess in her angry form, is another solar goddess, *Sekhmet*, whose name comes from *sekhem*, meaning "to be powerful, strong, mighty, violent." Budge says that she and Bast are "forms of the Sun-god [*sic*]." The ancient texts show that she was imagined to be the fierce, scorching and destroying heat of the summer Sun, identified with the solar eye of Re, the lioness who slaughters rebellious humankind, and the fire-spitting cobra-goddess *Uadjit*, who destroys evil beings. Sekhmet is sometimes called *Nesert*, that is, "Flame." expressly that purifying flame which, annihilating evil, protects and preserves all that is good. In this role she resembles Arabic *Shams* in her positive aspect of beneficent, cleansing solar force.[5]

Sekhmet appears in art as a powerfully-built woman with the head of a lioness, crowned by the red disc of the Sun (red being the colour of the Sun and fire in Egyptian symbolism). Her home was thought to be Mount Manu, "the Mountain of the Setting Sun," located in Libya. This is a particularly interesting association since Libya was the mythic homeland of Amazons and Gorgons, and even today preserves traditions of the Sun-goddess in tribal belief.

Bast, Lady of Flame

Bast is most popularly known in her domestic cat form, although she too adopts the guise of a lioness when identified with Sekhmet or Hathor. Egyptian writings show her to be the Sun's heat of spring and early summer, nurturing life which comes forth from the moist earth, after the Nilotic inundation has receded. Hence she is a goddess of teeming fertility, and often appears with her kittens around her. So close was she to Hathor in her mild, joyous character that the two goddesses and their festivals were almost indistinguishable. Hathor's own holy city, Dendera, was even called "Per-Bast of the South," after Bast's own city, and contained an important temple of the cat-goddess.

Bast appears as a cat, or a cat-headed woman, dressed in an unusual patterned robe which Egyptologists believe indicates her foreign origins. The red colour of her dress recalls other Sun-goddesses who wear red garments, such as Baltic *Saule* and the Australian aboriginal Sun-woman. In both these examples the red garment symbolizes the rising Sun. Since Bast is "Lady of the East" (like Hathor) and personifies the gentle warmth of the Sun, we may regard her also as the power of the morning sunrays, as opposed to Sekhmet who is the fierce heat of noon, and who declines to her home in the Mountain of the Setting Sun.

Many representations of Bast were destroyed in the reaction following *Akhenaten*'s spiritual revolution. The so-called "Heretical Pharaoh" seems not only to have tried to force his own, personal religious vision—a simplified, monotheistic cult of the Sun-disc—onto the whole country, but also in ways which are not clear, seems to have introduced or revived matriarchal ideas. Letters between Egyptian and Hittite politicians mention the Sun as feminine (at the time, the Hittite chief deity was the *Sun-goddess* of Arinna) while

Akhenaten's famous hymn to the Aten invokes the Sun as "Father and Mother of all that thou hast made."[6] He associated the mother-aspect of Aten with Bast herself, in consequence of which her images were later destroyed by conservative priests of Amun-Ra. This was a brief episode, and shortly after, Bast's cult was resumed as before. But the idea of a Sun-goddess, made doubly hateful to Amun's priests by its now radical, political taint, was further weakened in the mythic traditions.

This prepared the way for Greek misinterpretation of Bast's nature. The Greeks ruled Egypt from about the fourth century B.C., introducing their own ideas via Greeks who became priests to the Egyptian deities, and vice-versa. Goddesses who in Egyptian tradition retained vestiges of the feminine Sun, such as Bast, Hathor and Isis, were described as "Moon-goddesses." Such a concept had nothing whatever to do with Egyptian beliefs, in which the Moon was a male god *Aah* (identified with *Thoth, Osiris* and other gods). It was long after the birth of Christ that Plutarch, presenting his own mystical speculation as fact, in the manner of a modern occultist, wrongly identified Isis and Bast with the Moon. It cannot be too much emphasized that this is a *late, classical* imposition on Egyptian religion.

Rat-Taui

Rat-Taui is a precise feminine equivalent of the Sun-god Re. In earlier times she was called *Uert-Hekeu*, a gyandrous deity, "the-Great-of-Magic," who may be the same as *Sekhet-Bast-Ra*, a goddess in the Book of the Dead. Budge says "the attributes of the goddess are unknown, but it is not likely that she was considered to be any more important than any other great goddess." Nevertheless, she had her own cult which continued late into Egyptian history. Perhaps she represents an interim stage between the primitive feminine Sun and the later masculine deity.

The Egyptian Moon-God

Like the Babylonians, the Egyptians worshipped the Moon as a male divinity in his local forms Aah, Thoth, Khons and Osiris.[7] Briffault provides copious details about this masculine Moon which show him to have been everything we might expect. The Egyptian texts simply call *Khons* ("wanderer") the Moon. He is "the Moon, the Full Moon, that becomes an old man when he pleases and a child when he pleases." The god Horus, too, was addressed as "the Old Child... the Circulating One... the Moon is thy name." At Horus's cult centre of Edfu, his identification as the Moon itself was completely unambiguous.

The bull and male fertility both belonged to the Moon-god. Khons was believed to impregnate women during his waxing phase, and an inscription on his temple at Thebes states, "Through his agency women conceived." It was through a ray of moonlight resting on the flank of a cow that the sacred Apis-bull was conceived, the god Osiris himself taking flesh in this way. Numerous inscribed figures name "Osiris, the Moon," but not a single one calls him the Sun. (The account by Plutarch of the "Sun-god" Osiris and "Moon-goddess" Isis is not supported by the Egyptians themselves.) Like other Moon-gods, Osiris was dismembered into fourteen pieces—the lunar phases—he lived twenty-eight years, and his death was celebrated during the waning and dark Moon. His wife and sister Isis (who is winged and wears a sun-disc and cow's horns, often taking on Hathor's attributes) puts him back together again. The resurrected Osiris is the source of the Nile waters, the god of resurrection and rebirth, of souls in the underworld, and cyclic renewal. Since Osiris is the quintessentially masculine Moon of primitive kind, it is then a rewarding exercise to try looking at Isis as perhaps hiding an old Sun-goddess of tribal days.[8]

Chapter 23
Lady Sun, Light of the Gods
Canaan/ Syria

"In all Semitic languages the moon is masculine and the sun feminine."

—Robert Briffault[1]

The land of Canaan, claimed long ago by the nomadic Hebrews in the name of their god El, or *Yahweh*, now forms most of the modern state of Israel. Speakers of a Semitic language had settled here more than two thousand years before the Old Testament stories were composed, but they were not monotheistic descendants of the mythic Adam. Far from it—these one-time nomads, who took up a settled, agricultural lifestyle in the fertile valleys, practised an exuberant polytheism. Their principal deity was the Moon—a *masculine* god, worshipped by each tribe or town under a local name. To the inhabitants of the Sinai territory he was *Sin*, to the people of Jericho and many other places he was *Yarikh* or *Jerah*, while in the city of Ur of the Chaldees he was *Nannar*.

The hostility of polytheists to Abraham's heretical monotheistic cult of the Moon-god drove him to seek the nomadic desert life, at a time when most people were migrating in the opposite direction.[2] Inter-tribal rivalry of this kind seems almost to have been a traditional pastime among Semitic peoples. There were always plenty of excuses for murderous raids and feuds, backed up by oracles from the tribal god. The rape of Canaan was merely the same thing writ large. According to the Hebrew oracles, their god was upset by the religious rites of other tribes' deities, particularly those of other Moon-gods and the Morning Star deities. (The latter were usually male, but the later Morning Star goddess was called "Queen of Heaven." Yahweh was made jealous and angry at the offerings of cakes she received.[3]) The Sun was also worshipped in Semitic lands, in some cases as a goddess, in others as a god. The Bible itself preserves a trace of the old Hebrew Sun-goddess in that the word for Sun, *shemesh* (connected with Arabic *shams* as well as Hebrew *esh*, or *ash*, to burn[4]) appears there in both masculine and feminine terms.[5] In Genesis the setting Sun is feminine [6] but in the Psalms it becomes masculine.[7] The goddess Shemesh gave her name in earlier times to localities or natural features—*Beth Shemesh*, "House (or abode or stone) of the Sun," *En-Shemesh*, "Well of the Sun"[8]—where her worshippers settled, or her rites took place.

A Sample of Canaanite Religion

The record of Canaanite archaeology was seriously damaged by iconoclastic Hebrews, who burned artefacts of wood and ivory, smashed stones and carvings, pots and tablets, and lined the pockets of the Yahwist clergy with looted gold and silver. Women who had been initiated into the rituals of gods and goddesses were murdered, while the uninitiated girls were kept alive as booty for the Israelite soldiers.[9] In these and other ways the invaders tried to expunge all other religions from the land. Their successes mean that we now have many difficulties in reconstructing Canaanite religion, but their failures left us with at least one treasure—the sacred stories or liturgies of Ugarit.

On the north coast of Syria, at its closest point to Cyprus, lies the modern town of Ras-Shamra. In 1928 excavations there brought to light a hoard of clay tablets, now famous as the Ugarit texts. Some were diplomatic letters from Mycenae, Anatolia and Egypt, bearing witness to Ugarit's great days as an international trading port. Others recorded an extraordinary cycle of myths, revealing a little of the strange and complex world of Canaanite religion, a small sample of the numerous deities and local cults which preceded Yahweh's totalitarianism.

Light of the Gods

In the Ugaritic pantheon the Sun is a goddess, *Shapash*, "Sun," or *Shapash-Elat*, "Lady Sun." She is the *baalath*, "owner," the local deity of Ugarit, that is, the form of the Sun-goddess which was native to that city. The terms *baal* and *baalath* have given rise to much confusion. It is important to realize that *there was no such thing as a god named "Baal"*. The word is a general term meaning owner or possessor, that is, the god of a particular locality. The idea that there was a personal name "Baal," and that it means the Sun, is a misconception derived from Christian ideas about Biblical paganism. It was not until classical times that some of the *baalim*, "the Baals" of the Bible, were identified as the Sun. The baalim of Ur, Harran, Palmyra and Sinai were all local forms of the masculine Moon, while those of Larsa, Sippar and Baalbek were local versions of the masculine Sun.[10] The Sun-goddess under different names was the baalath of several places or regions, and consequently some inscriptions speak of Sun-goddesses in the plural.[11]

The Baal of Ugarit (*Baal Hadad*) was in no sense a "Sun-god" (as the texts themselves amply prove). He was the divine personification of rain, deity of the stormy clouds which shed their fertilising bounty over the earth.[12] In his battles with his rival *Mot*, the god of dryness and sterility, Baal Hadad is aided by other important deities, *Anat* (not a Moon-goddess) and the Sun-goddess Shapash, her friend and companion, the Light of the Gods.

The Poem of Aleyin Baal

Many scholars believe that this poem may have been enacted as a dramatic liturgy, a sort of miracle-play, with the actors appearing with typical props— Hadad with his bucket, in which he carries wind, cloud and rain,[13] Shapash with her torch held aloft and her spiny crown of Sun-rays, Anat in her armour, with her bows and weapons. Shapash is not only the Light of the Gods, the Sun of Eternity,[14] but she also plays an important role as emissary, taking messages from the high-god *El* to the other deities.[15]

Hadad is challenged by his rival, Mot. The god of sterility sends the god of rain a sinister invitation, to share a meal of mud with him, in his own kingdom beneath the earth. Baal Hadad accepts, but is forthwith murdered by his host. Without the lifegiving rain, plants wilt and die, so the Baal's place is taken in heaven by *Athtar*, deity of irrigation[16]

When the news of her husband's death reaches her, Anath, the wife and sister of Hadad, is frenzied by grief, yet unable to mourn him properly for no one knows the whereabouts of his corpse. She enlists the help of Shapash. Together the goddesses discover the dead lord of storms; the Sun-goddess loads him onto her friend's shoulders, and they set off for *Saphon*, the holy mountain, there to set Aleyin Baal ("powerful Baal") to rest in "the recesses of the North."[17]

His tomb is a deep grave pit. There Anath descends, accompanied by the Sun-goddess, to grieve out her grief, sating herself with weeping.[18] But now Shapash is under the evil spell of Mot's rule. Her heat and light contribute to the drought which rules in Nature:

> "The lamp of the gods, Shapash,
> The glowing orb of sky

Is in the power of divine Mot."[19]

The thirsty Sun-goddess drinks up Anat's tears just as if they were wine, and in the upper world the baked ground cracks. The hot season has come.

Now that Anat has put her dead to rest, she goes in search of Mot to take violent and merciless revenge, hacking and grinding him like ripe grain, strewing his remains over the land. But this is not the end of the story, for meanwhile El (or Anat) has beheld Baal's return in a prophetic dream. The only problem is that no-one quite knows where the resurrected god is, so once again Shapash, the all-seeing eye and ideal detective of missing persons, is told to keep a look-out for him as she crosses the sky each day. El says to her,

> "Dried up are the fields, O Shapash, dried up are the vast
> fields. Baal is neglecting the furrows of the ploughland. Oh,
> where is Aleyin Baal?"[20]

The Sun-goddess then, it seems, makes her *primordial* journey beneath the earth—the myth seems to explain how it was that the Sun first came to go through the underworld at night. Evidently, she is taking a great risk. She promises Anat that she will attempt this journey in search of the god, and Anat in her turn must promise to drink to her health and give her a garland of leaves, should she come back:

> "Spill sparkling wine from thy vat
> Bring a chaplet of leaves from thy native stock
> And I will seek the victor Baal."[21]

The Hymn to the Sun-Goddess

Not only does Shapash find Hadad, but she also returns safely from the underworld, to the joy of the gods. According to one translation, El praises her for fulfilling her mission, for eating the bread of corruption and drinking the wine of decay, for companying with ghosts.[22] Another gives a somewhat different reading:

> "Bread of aggrandizement shalt thou eat
> Wine of favour shalt thou drink
> O Shapash, over the shades shalt thou have dominion.
> O Shapash, thou shalt have dominion over the upper gods,
> Lo, gods shall be thy witnesses and mortals too.
> Verily Koshar shall be thy escort,
> Khasis thy companion."[23]

(Koshar and Khasis are gods who protect the Sun against the eclipse-demon.)

This eulogy is thought to be part of a seasonal hymn to the Sun-goddess.[24] The bread and wine were perhaps common offerings to this goddess, an allusion easily recognized by those watching the sacred drama.

Another Ugarit text, the *Poem of the Gracious Gods*, telling of the birth of El's twin sons, gives Shapash an important place, honouring her with words of adoration; she makes the limbs of the twin gods grow and flourish, as she does the tendrils and flowers of the vine.[25]

The Fertile Heat of Summer

Later, when Hadad has taken his place again in heaven, Mot insolently presents himself before his throne (having himself also been resurrected). The pair are soon rolling on the ground in a tremendous fight. Shapash, the emissary of El, descends to separate the pair and tick off the presumptuous Mot, like a divine type of boxing referee. She effects a temporary reconciliation. The story is due to start again, whenever there is a drought, or seasonally, although as Cyrus H. Gordon remarks, "The widespread notion that the year in Canaan is divided into a fertile and a sterile season is false. No part of the year is sterile." He goes on to say that the heat of summer was regarded as an especially fertile time, for it was then that figs, grapes and other food-plants came to maturity. [26] As the Ugarit texts indicate, the Sun-goddess presided over this season of fruits and plenty. The grape-vines seem to have been her special concern, like the Sun-goddess of ancient Georgia.

The Ugaritic Moon was masculine, the god *Yarikh* or *Jerakh*,[27] "Illuminator of Heaven" and "Lord of the Sickle," a deity whose cult was very ancient and widespread, but about whom we have few details. [28] He and his bride *Nikkal* have a chapter of the Ugarit texts all to themselves, a romantic story, of how Yarikh's tender courtship won the goddess's heart, and the joy with which their wedding was celebrated. The main role of Yarikh was as provider of rain, by which he turned the wilderness into orchards for his sweetheart; this and his amorous disposition suggest that he was the usual primitive Moon-god, divine lover, fecundator and source of wet weather. Nikkal, on the other hand, seems to have been the original Sun-goddess of Sumeria, better known as *Ninagal*, the consort of *Sin*, the Assyro-Babylonian Moon-god. Her name simply means "Great Lady." *Nikkal* formed part of the name of several Anatolian priestess-queens, the high priestesses of Sun-goddess *Wurusemu* (*Arinitti*). After death such queens were spoken of as if they were each the Sun herself. Undoubtedly the wedding of Yarikh and Nikkal preserves a very archaic theme, the primordial marriage of Sun-goddess and Moon-god.[29]

The Town of Lady Sun

Shapash was not only worshipped in Ugarit itself. Just as classical ideas reached the Near East in early times through trade connections, so too were oriental deities and religions popularized among Greeks and Romans.[30] Eastern travellers settled as immigrants in the great classical cities, rather like the Sikh community which developed in Victorian Bradford, or the Chinese in London's Soho. They even founded their own settlements. One of these was *Sapyselaton*, literally "the town of Shapash-Elat," or "Lady Sun," near Epidaurus in Greece. [31]

Mythologists would like us to believe that Sapys was of no importance. Why then should people name a place after her? Why should she be the messenger of the high-god? Why should she be trusted by the war-goddess with a dangerous mission to the underworld? Why should the high-god tell us that she *rules* above and below? Why is she invited to help his sons grow strong? Why are hymns sung to her? Why do mythologists attempt to put Baal Hadad or Mot or El in her place as "Sun-god"? Shapash's important role makes her undesirable, and that is why her "unimportance" is manufactured.[32]

Chapter 24
Mistress of the Righteous Judgement
Anatolia

"Then the King goes to the mountain, he raises the Great
Sun Goddess, he chants spells and invocations to her... May
the Sun Goddess and the Storm God take to the King's
friendship!"

—A Hittite Ritual Text

The national deity of the Hittites, their Queen of Heaven and Earth, was the
Sun-goddess of Arinna, or *Arinitti*. The Hittites took her over from the earlier
Anatolian people, the *Hattians*, who called her *Wurusemu*. We do not know
what name (if any) the Hittites themselves gave her; to them she was the lady
of Arinna, the city which grew up around her temple, which suggests that she
was a local form of the Sun-goddess. Although Arinna lay only a day's journey
from the capital *Hattusas* (modern Bogazhkoy in Turkey) archaeologists have
so far failed to locate it, and the state of Turkish archaeology does not bode well
for its discovery in the foreseeable future. In any case, the motivation to uncover
the city of a Sun-goddess cult is likely to be extremely small. This city hides the
foundations of Arinna's temple, and most certainly, inscriptions and reliefs,
perhaps even cult statues representing the goddess, and the Sun-discs which
were used in Hittite ritual.[1] (Try to imagine another civilization, say, Egypt, or
that of the Incas, where the city of the national Sun-deity was left unsought-for
and unexcavated!)

An Inclusive Religion

The Hittites, an Indo-European people, arrived in Anatolia just as the third millenium B.C. was closing. (Their civilization reached its height between 1,400 and 1,200 B.C.) Religion was no big theological deal to the Hittites— they already worshipped several masculine Sun-gods, such as Babylonian *Shamash* and Hurrian *Shimegi*,[2] but these were borrowed deities, for Hittite religion was cheerfully tolerant and eclectic. Foreign gods and goddesses of conquered peoples and neighbours were incorporated into the pantheon, but allowing them to keep their own names and attributes. Add to this the fact that the Hittites liked localised cults (as the Arabs, Celts and Egyptians did) and the result is a sort of stamp-collection of deities. Quite why the Hittites took to the Hattian Sun-goddess in the way they did is not clear. The Sun-gods played quite a minor role in Hittite theology, although the Yuzgat Tablet tells a beautiful story of the loss and finding of the Sun-god, which suggests that the Sun played an important part in the seasonal cycle.[3]

Blessed Mistress of Judgement

A clay tablet from Hattusas invokes the Sun-goddess as sovereign over all:

> "Thou, Sun Goddess of Arinna art an honoured deity, thy name is held high among names; thy divinity is held high among the deities; Nay, among the deities, thou alone O Sun-goddess art honoured; great art thou alone O Sun-goddess of Arinna; Nay, compared to thee no other deity is as honoured or as great... Thou controllest kingship in heaven and on earth."[4]

This long prayer to the goddess goes on to address her as a goddess of justice, a role which was specific to the Sun-deities of the ancient Near East, whether male or female. In Mesopotamia the Sun-god (formerly Sun-goddess) *Shamash* was everywhere the personification of right judgement:

> "...the judging god is simply Shamash... he surveys everything, knows everything, reaches everything... 'Illuminator of the earth, judge of the heavens, illuminator of the darkness above and below'."[5]

This is why Shamash presides over the famous *Law Code of Hammurabi*, an Akkadian inscription summarizing Babylonian laws; his function in Babylonian religion was almost exclusively as divine judge, and not as supreme god of a patriarchal system. The hymn to Arinitti amplifies this idea of a deity who sees all and ensures that wrong does not prevail:

> "Thou art mistress of the righteous judgement... Thou dost mark out the borders of the lands. Thou dost hearken to complaints. Thou, O Sun-goddess of Arinna, art a merciful deity.... Blessed mistress of judgement art thou. Thou art unwearying at the seat of judgement."[6]

In an honorific title common in the Near East of that time, Arinitti was invoked as "Father and Mother of every land." This does not mean she was "really a Sun-god." The term was used of gods and goddesses alike, a kind of hyperbole meant to express the extent of a deity's divine powers, his or her all-sufficiency, not really the same thing as any mystic idea of androgyny, more a kind of flattery.

The hymn tells us that Arinitti shines in the worlds of gods and humans:

> "The blessed man is dear to thee, O Sun goddess of Arinna. To him dost thou, O Sun-goddess of Arinna, grant for-giveness. Within the compass of heaven and earth art thou, O Sun-goddess of Arinna, the light. In the lands art thou the honoured deity... Thou art honoured among the age-old and eternal gods."

Evidently, too, the Sun-goddess was a sort of priestess of the gods:

> "For the gods, dost thou, O Sun-goddess of Arinna, prepare the rites of sacrifice. Thou dost mete out the portion of the age-old and eternal gods."

Apart from this, what is known of Arinitti makes her very much like other Sun-deities. The hymn goes on

> "Thou dost open the doors of heaven. And thou dost smite the gate of heaven and stride through."[7]

The sky of the ancient Near Eastern cosmologies was a solid vault provided with gates, doors and windows. Representations of Ishtar (the planet Venus) show her peeping through a window, and the Storm-god was imagined to let the rain out by opening little windows in the firmament—an idea which passed into Hebrew tradition, and is found in the Bible.[8]

Goddess of Battles

In her role as deity of the state, Arinitti was expected to take a personal hand in battles on behalf of the Hittite king and nation. Whenever a political crisis loomed, when military campaigns were mounted or enemies threatened the land, Arinitti was invoked as divine protectress. In the Annals of Mursilis II, the king invites her to descend to earth and strike the king's enemies with her own hand. There then follows the official record of her help obtained in this particular battle, with the king's vow that he would always record her blessings in the annals, and set them before her. Another Hittite king, Hattusilis, describes in his autobiography the ways in which Arinitti favoured him, how she always "held him by the hand," and how in consequence he was preserved from committing any evil deeds.

The Queens and the Sun-Goddess

Many other texts indicate the special relationship existing between the Hattian queens, who took an active political role alongside their husbands. Each queen had her own state seal, that of Queen Puduhepa showing her in the embrace of the Sun-goddess. The correspondence between Puduhepa and the Egyptian queen, which has been preserved, shows that the Hittite queen was effectively an autonomous ruler.

As well as sharing government in this way, the queen acted as High Priestess of the nation, just as the Sun herself was High Priestess of the gods. After death each queen was named in ritual as if she was the Sun-goddess, perhaps reflecting Egyptian practice where the dead pharaoh in a sense "became" the Sun-god. The names of the queen-priestesses reveal the identification which the Hittites made between Arinitti and two other deities, *Hepat* and *Ningal*, both mother-goddesses who appear to have already had a solar character in their own myths. (For example, Ningal's story as told at Ugarit makes her the wife of the Moon-god.) *Kupapa*, another version of Hepat, was also identified with the Sun-goddess. A Hittite relief in the British Museum depicts her in traditional style, a plump matron in a stiff robe, carrying a mirror and pomegranate. The arch above her head is formed by the winged Sun-disc.[9] A similar but better-known and more elaborate representation of the Sun-goddess appears at Yazilikaya, near Bogazhkoy, where the mountain wall is figured with giant reliefs. There Arinitti faces her husband, the storm-god *Teshub* or *Taru* (his Hattian name). She is a formal, regal figure. She balances on the back of a snarling lioness, followed by her son *Sharruma* and other deities, while her husband, mace in hand, stands on the shoulders of two oppressed-looking little gods. Both Arinitti and Teshub hold curious symbols which have never been satisfactorily identified. Their son is the agriculture god *Telepinu*; he is the subject of a myth which resembles that of Demeter and Persephone, but the text depicts him as a diligent

sun-goddess of Arinna

farmer who looks after the soil and *irrigates* it. In his absence the land *dries up* and people starve, so Telepinu is clearly a Hittite equivalent of Baal Hadad, the rain-god.[10]

Sun-Goddess of the Earth

Hittite burial customs made reference to *the Sun-goddess of the Earth*, that is, the Sun as she passed through the underworld during the night. Like Babylonian Shamash, and so many of the other Sun-goddesses we have already met in this study, Arinitti gave warmth and light to the dead, caring for them on her nightly journey. The Hittite ritual for the building of a new palace describes a scene in the underworld; the king's reign is being predicted by "Istustaya and Papaya, the primaeval Netherworld goddesses [who] are sitting there bowing down...one holds a spindle, they both hold filled mirrors."[11] These two goddesses accompany Arinitti as she passes through the underworld. In the palace ritual they are busy divining the years allotted to the king by spinning a thread and scrying in "filled mirrors" that is, basins of water. Both the spun thread and the water-mirror, however, are important in several cultures as part of the female Sun-cult; compare the Swedish tradition in which Mistress Sun spins the golden sunrays before she rises, and the Slavic and Armenian traditions of the Sun-goddess washing herself in water, deep under the earth.

Sun's Daughters

Arinitti, like so many other Sun-goddesses, appears with two daughters, *Hulla* and *Mezulla*, perhaps the goddesses of morning and evening. She also has a grand-daughter, the child *Zintuhi*. These goddesses are pre-Indo-European and conceivably represent the same matriarchal stratum of belief which appears to have shaped religion at *Çatal Hüyük*, one of the earliest Neolithic towns, located in southern Turkey about 125 miles from Hattusas. There a bas-relief of a red-decorated goddess, giving birth to a horned child and flanked by two leopards, may very well represent a *Sun*-goddess, instead of the Earth or Moon-goddess she is usually claimed to be, and the cult of the bull which takes principal place in the shrines is much more likely to have been that of a Moon-god, not goddess. Just as in the rest of the Near East, the most ancient Moon-deity was always male for Hattians and Hittites alike. To the Hittites he was *Arma* (the same as Hurrian *Khushukh*), represented as a winged man with a pointed horned cap, on which sits the crescent Moon.[12] The Hittites also knew *Agu*, the name of the male Moon among the Akkadians, from whom the Hittites borrowed Shamash.

Dictionaries and histories of religion usually deal with Arinitti by leaving her out, and talking instead about her husband the storm-god as if he were supreme national deity.[13] Another way of disposing of her is to speak only of *Hepat* when referring to the storm-god's "consort." Although Arinitti was referred to as the Sun, and worshipped as the Sun by the Hittites themselves, Robert Graves calls Teshub "the Sun-god," likewise Jean Cooper and several other authors; a wholly false identification based on the fallacy "storm-god = Sun-god".[15] Eliade, *Pears' Encyclopaedia* and Reader's Digest *Vanished Civilizations* all go in for the subliminal message, *viz:*

"The most important temple was sacred to the great god of
the empire, the Weather God. His consort was the sun-
goddess of Arinna."

E.O. James opts for "must-have-been-an-Earth-goddess," excluding Arinitti
from being the "real" Sun on the basis of her underworld aspect—yet withholding
the information that male Sun-gods of the Near East also have this aspect.
Arinitti's hymn, he says, describes the Sun-goddess in "masculine terms." It
seems not to have occurred to him that the ancients may not have shared his
preconceptions about what is "feminine," and that the concept of a woman as
the Sun, judge, chief deity, etc., might have seemed quite normal in another age
and culture. Indeed, as Near Eastern texts and prayers show, it was perfectly
usual to speak of goddesses in terms radically different from those which most
modern men would prefer.[16]

It is not only misogynists who don't want to admit that Arinitti is the Sun.
Judy Chicago's *The Dinner Party*, detailing the goddesses who appear in the
beautiful art exhibition of that name, gives thirty-one lines of text to Arinitti
without revealing her solar nature. All the goddess's titles are listed, with the
single exception of "Sun-goddess of Arinna."[17] As this title is used repeatedly in
the Hittite references to this goddess, it could hardly have been missed by
accident—so we are forced to conclude that it was deliberately left out. Why?
This impressive artwork claims in some sense to celebrate or be representative
of all women, especially the unconventional kind, yet it celebrates no Sun-
goddesses. Even Amaterasu is missing. Barbara G. Walker's *Women's Dictionary* also refuses to acknowledge the facts about Arinitti:

"Arinna—Hittite name of the Great Goddess as 'Mother
of the Sun.' In Mesopotamia and Egypt, the sun-god was
generally considered a child of the moon-, earth-, sea-, or
heaven-goddess."[18]

Arinna was the name of the city, not the goddess, Anatolia is neither in
Mesopotamia nor Egypt, Arinitti was never called the mother of the Sun-god,
Egypt did not have either a moon, sea or Earth-goddess, and Mesopotamians
habitually saw the Moon as a masculine god. The idea that the Moon-goddess
gives birth to the Sun-god is also a modern fallacy, a constructive interpretation
made by arbitrarily identifying *all* mother-goddesses as the Moon. As the Sun-
god generally has a mother somewhere, it's a simple matter to label her "the
Moon-mother" and so "prove" that the Sun was thought to come from the
Moon. (Except that it is no proof at all, merely more question-begging.)

What matters here is, not what we think Arinitti "originally" was, or what (according to some esoteric formula or other) we think she ought to be, but what the Hittites themselves thought of her, as evidenced by her prayers, hymns, titles and ceremonies. And for them she was, quite simply and clearly, the Sun-goddess.

Chapter 25
Far-Seeing Mother of the Eyes
Rome and Greece

"...the Mother Sun... the maternal Sun Goddess... {is} a notable phenomenon in a primal orientation to the world... We want to take both 'sunlikeness' and 'woman' with equal seriousness...We would be stepping outside of my-thology, which is an intelligible language to be heard, and we would be encountering it as something alien, if we were to explain the Sun-women as merely an accidental feminine expression for the sun."

—*Goddesses of Sun and Moon.* Karl Kerenyi[1]

Juno Lucina of Rome

Traces of the primitive feminine Sun are to be found even in Rome and Greece, whose masculine Sun-cults still shape our Western inheritance of symbolism and literature.

The Sun-god *Sol*, patron of charioteers, was (as we have seen) a minor Roman deity until the late Empire. While the Romans doubtless enjoyed the pleasures of the Italian sunshine, they seem to have taken it for granted, and worshipped rather those deities, such as lightning-wielding Jupiter, who were risky to deal with and needed regular appeasement. Early Roman deities were paired—*Lunus* and *Luna*, god and goddess of the Moon, *Cacus* and *Caca*, god and goddess of fire, *Dianus* and *Diana*, god and goddess of the woods, and so on. The basis of this was, presumably, that it was not good for a deity to be alone, and a family pair implied fecundity, but at present we may only speculate. The idea of paired deities came from the Romans' predecessors, the *Etruscans*, whose language and inscriptions remain undeciphered, but the names of whose deities, oddly enough, outlasted those of Roman gods and goddesses, coming right down to our own time. Somewhat like Baltic folklore, the Etruscan lore has proved extremely resilient. Charles Godfrey Leland's study showed that the Etruscan gods and goddesses were active spirits in folklore. A woman told him:

> "Losna is a spirit of the Sun and Moon—of *both*, not of the moon alone. When a brother debauches a sister it is her doing."[2]

Losna is the Etruscan *Lusna*, the later Roman goddess *Lucina*, who appeared both as *Diana Lucina*, the Moon, and *Juno Lucina*, the Sun. As her name seems to mean just "light," she is the deity of both celestial bodies. This is a rare motif in mythology. Some South American Indians believe that the god who shines as the Sun by day becomes the Moon by night, while Mithraists believed the same of Mithras,[3] and Celtic and English poems speak of the Virgin Mary in the same way:

> "Heyle vyrgyn mother of god, thow arte the sonne of the day above and the mone of the nighte of the world."[4]

Leland's report also indicates that Losna was associated with brother-sister incest (and even remarks on the similar connection in Eskimo myth). Moreover, Losna is a *mirror*-goddess.[5] According to Philostratus, a thunderstorm or heavy rain may be stopped by holding a mirror before a sleeping man, a superstition which Leland associates rather unclearly with Losna—but, since the Sun-goddess commonly battles with the storm-god for possession of the sky, Losna's mirror is a solar, rather than a lunar symbol.

Juno Lucina was the midwife of the gods, the goddess who brought the light of day to the eyes of the newborn. Her annual festival, or her birthday, was celebrated on the twenty-first of December, the day of the Midwinter Solstice. Otherwise not a great deal is known about her, but her popularity may be gauged from the fact that the Church had to canonize her as "Saint Lucia," presumably because people persisted in worshipping her. Saint Lucy was supposed to be a pagan maiden who, upon conversion to Christianity, vowed her virginity to Christ. A noble pagan, wishing to marry her, flattered her with praise about the incomparable beauty of her eyes—whereupon Lucia, true to the Bible's recommendation, plucked them out[6] and had a servant deliver them to him on a dish. Iconography shows Lucia holding her two eyes on a platter, or on a leafy stalk like two strange cherries. This association of *eye* and *Sun-goddess* is so common that it hardly seems necessary to draw the reader's attention

SAINT LUCY,
CHATEAU FORT,
LOURDES

to it at this late stage! An old wooden statue of St. Lucy in the chapel of the Château Fort, at Lourdes in the High Pyrenees, shows her holding a large golden plate, upright towards the observer like the Sun's disc, with two eyes— complete with eyebrows!—inscribed on it, like the traditional Sun's face. (Pyrenean tradition depicts the Sun as feminine.)

St. Lucy's festival is celebrated in Scandinavia on the thirteenth of December, whence it was moved from Winter Solstice day, to avoid competition between the Scandinavian Sun-rites (Lucia being a replacement for the old Sun-goddess) and the Christian Christmas. In Sicily, an island which the ancient Romans believed to be the Sun's own home,[7] it continues to be celebrated on the old date of the twenty-first of December, with much ado about candle-lighting, once thought to strengthen the Sun's light by sympathetic magic.[8] The delightful Scandinavian customs of Lucia's day are well known and often feature on T.V. during the run-up to Christmas. In Sweden, the youngest daughter of the family gets up before dawn, puts on a white dress and a rather dangerous-looking candle-bearing crown, and wakens the family with refreshments. She is *Lussibruden*, "Lucy-bride" or "Lucy-Queen," and her day is called "Little Yule" (i.e. Christ the Sun-god's day is the bigger Yule). Another old practice was for the maiden-goddess to go around the village on the back of a white horse, with attendants called "star-boys" (*cf. Dieva deli*) and a retinue of mummers dressed as demons and trolls, who would be conquered by the reviving Sun.[9] A traditional song from this day says

> Now Lucia's day is come
> Darkness cannot linger.
> Winter, banished by the Sun
> Lifts his icy finger.[10]

The processional rite is clearly the same kind of ceremony as that of the Sun-goddess Kolyada in Slavic tradition. E.O. James is only willing to see Lucy as a "harbinger" of the Sun's return, but she is the returning Sun itself, "the maiden who'll ride on her mother's paths," the reborn Sun of Winter Solstice.

The old Roman goddess Lucina turns up in an even more unlikely context than Swedish Yuletide customs. Antique sculptures of Juno Lucina were the inspiration for Bartholdi's "Statue of Liberty." Lucina wears the sun-ray crown (which is ultimately derived from Syria and appeared late in Roman art) and holds up the blazing torch of the Sun, like Syrian *Shapash*. The gift of the statue symbolized friendship between America and France, but Lucina herself was meant to signify a "new dawn" of liberty for immigrants who would see her on the horizon, as they approached the New World.

Theia of Greece

Karl Kerenyi is one of the few authors who swims against the tide of opinion and actually *wants* to take seriously the solar feminine element in Greek religion. In *The Gods of the Greeks* he calls attention to Pindar's ode addressing the goddess *Theia*. The Greeks did not regard her as the Sun or Moon, but as the universal mother of all light-divinities. In Pindar's verses she is poetically depicted as the Sun itself:

> "Thou beam of the Sun,
> Far-seeing mother of the eyes...
> ...Star supreme, reft from us in the daytime,
> ...Swift driver-divine of steeds... "

...and other solar terminology. The occasion of this ode was the solar eclipse in 463 B.C., when spectators at Thebes saw almost the whole disc obscured. Pindar seems to have been unnerved by the omen. He pleads passionately with the Sun to reveal her divine intentions, assuming that she is angry and means to visit the earth with typhoons, plagues and political unrest. This Sun is a dangerous weather-goddess who leaves off warming and drying the earth—the deadly chill which suddenly falls during totality suggests to Pindar that she means to bring frost and snow.[11]

Kerenyi comments, "It was not *a priori* impossible to regard the sun as a maternal divinity." In *Goddesses of Sun and Moon* he discusses the nymphs called *Heliades*, the sisters of Phaethon (who took a fatal joyride in his father's chariot) and daughters of the Sun-god Helios. *Heliades* literally means *Sun-maidens*, so it comes as no surprise to find that their individual names are those appropriate to the Sun-goddess—*Helia*, "Sun" (the feminine equivalent of *Helios*), *Lampetia*, "the illuminating," *Phaethousa*,"the shining," *Aegle*, "brightness, lustre, sunshine," and so on. When their brother dies in his attempt to ride the Sun-chariot, these seven goddesses become poplar trees which eternally weep drops of *amber*, the golden resin sacred to the Baltic Sun-goddess.[12] (Baltic solar songs describe the sky as being made of amber, and Freya, whom Briffault theorizes to be a Sun-goddess, weeps tears of gold and amber, while the Slavic Sun-maiden sits on an amber stone.)

The Greek western paradise is the home of more Sun-women, the three *Hesperides*, who seem once to have been the same as the Heliades. The original seven Hesperides were reduced to three in later times: *Aegle* (whom we have already met), *Erythraea*, "the red one," and *Hespera*, "evening light" (who turned herself into a poplar at the approach of the Argonauts). These goddesses, aspects of solar light, or of the old Indo-European Sun-goddess herself, are responsible for guarding the golden apples of the west, which grow on an orchard-island very similar to Baltic *dausos*. Mother Earth grew these magical fruits as a wedding-gift for the goddess *Hera* (whose name Mueller derived from *Svara*, "Sun"). Triple and septuple goddesses are by no means obliged to be lunar. *Eos*, the goddess of dawn (mythically and etymologically identical to Baltic *Auzrine*, Vedic *Ushas*, Teutonic *Eostre*, Roman *Aurora* and other Indo-European dawn goddesses[13]) is a typical Sun-maiden, who once accompanied the Sun during the whole of his course across the sky, like the Hindu Ushas.[14] The Hesperides as a threesome may once have done the same, personifying the red glow of sunrise, the brightness of noon, and the mild evening light.

The Mysterious Femininity of the Sun

Kerenyi speaks of "that mysterious femininity which the Greeks perceived in the Sun in addition to Helios' fatherhood."[15] The femininity gets a little less obscure when we stop routinely identifying all Greek goddesses as versions of the Moon, and start comparing elements of their myth and cult with those of known female Suns. The primitive Sun-goddess can be traced in Greek myth via her one-time partner, the masculine Moon, or as he was known in Anatolia,

Men. Briffault remarks

> "In Anatolia and the north Aegean the son of the Great
> Mother bears the name which in all languages of the Aryan
> family is the name of the moon, Men."

This god, the same as Baltic *Meness*, had an important cult among Phrygians and Anatolians.[16] In Greece, he became the Moon-goddess *Mene* or *Selene*. *Mene* is still the proper Greek word for the Moon, and Briffault goes on to say that Greek peasants persist in viewing the Moon as a masculine being.[17] Alongside this we find solar traditions associated with peasant women, in the form of the Sun-design which was formerly painted on the cheeks of a bride, and solar identifications of the Blessed Virgin. Churches are dedicated to her in her special aspect *Beautiful-as-the-Sun.* Greek folktales and folk-songs also contain the Baltic-like theme of the maiden who boasts that she is more lovely than the Sun itself.[18]

Selene as Moon-goddess is a late idea, which is why she lacks any real lunar mythology.[19] On the contrary, she has several solar attributes proper to the Sun-goddess of the North. She wears a radiant golden crown, her chariot is drawn by two white horses, and the *Sel* element of her name appears to be cognate with the *Hel* of *Helen* and *Sul* of *Sol* or *Sulis*. Rather like the Sun-goddess of the Australian myth, she pays a night-visit to her lover *Endymion*, down below on earth. The two bulls who draw her chariot in some iconography are not really hers at all, but belonged to the former Moon-god, "bull-faced Men."[20] There has quite clearly been some reshuffling of material here. In respect of Graeco-Roman mystery religion, Spartianus reported that the mystics regard the Moon as male, which leaves us to wonder whether the same mystics regarded the Sun as female in their seemingly-alternative tradition.[21]

Helen as Sun-Maiden

The relationship between the mythological *Helen* and her brothers, the twin *Dioscuroi*, has been the subject of much discussion among serious mythologists. These deities are known to be the same characters as Baltic Sun's Daughter (*Saules mieta*, or the Sun-goddess in her young, maiden aspect) and the Sons of Dievs (*Dieva deli*), as well as the Hindu Sun-maiden *Suryā* and the twin sons of Dyaus, the *Asvins*. Helen is undoubtedly a Sun-maiden, and that of a very important kind. The topic is too involved to discuss within the short compass of this book, but interested readers are recommended to consult Jack Lindsay's excellent *Helen of Troy* and Miriam Robbins Dexter's essay *Proto-Indo-European Sun-Maidens and Gods of the Moon.* Donald Ward's *Solar Mythology and Baltic Folksongs* also discusses the Twins and their Sun-sister. He summarizes:

> "Elements of the theme occur in Vedic, Greek, Germanic, as well as Baltic mythological traditions. The complex of motifs constituting the theme can be roughly summarized as follows. The Sun Maiden is promised in marriage to her brothers, the Divine Twins, but is given to (or abducted by) the Moon. She is then delivered to the mother or wife of the Moon [i.e. the Sun-goddess] for safekeeping. The twin gods then liberate the maiden... The various treatments of the theme share so many details that it is evident that the theme belonged to the original stratum of Indo-European mythology."[22]

And if other mythologies are anything to go by, it comes from a yet-more-primitive stratum than that. The theme of the young Sun-goddess and the Twins is one of the best-attested in mythology. Why then is it so little known?

Well, apart from the fact that it deals with the taboo subject of female Suns, the misinterpreted rehash of this myth is one of the essential supports of the Sun-is-always-male belief. A good example of this Sun-goddess-eclipsing technique is to be found in John Kraft's *The Goddess in the Labyrinth*, based on Ernest Krause's work on the maze-games of old Europe. In these labyrinth games Krause discovered that the female figure was the Sun-goddess *Saule* or *Sol*, and that the spring game involved the release of this goddess by two men. This actually re-enacts, in the form of the Sun-maiden myth, the release of the Sun from winter imprisonment, by her lovers the twin star-gods (compare myths where the reappearance of the Arctic Sun is announced by the reappearance of the morning/evening star—which is what the twin gods sometimes are).

Kraft simply dismisses this, calling it "weak." What does he opt for? Yes, of course—the goddess in the labyrinth must be *Mother Earth* and the twins must be the *Sun-god* who comes in spring to rescue Mother Earth from imprisonment—it seems she has gone down inside herself (like a hibernating earthworm?) by some amazing process (maybe the labyrinth represents ever-decreasing circles?) and has to be released from herself by the Sun-god—after which he fertilizes her with his ray-penises.[23]

This constructive interpretation has no basis in mythology and helps us understand and connect nothing at all. Yet it is very popular, because it is so facile and can be effortlessly used to explain any encounter between any god and goddess, ensuring that the Sun in each and every case will always be the male god. (It rather recalls the early Church's objection to the Holy Spirit being feminine—"Whoever heard of a woman getting another woman pregnant?") *The idea that the Sun fertilizes Mother Earth ensures that the Sun is kept securely male*, even though it isn't true, and the gods who fertilize Mother Earth are not Sun-gods, and they don't fertilize her with Sun-rays, but with *rain*.[24]

En route, Selene/Helene, the Moon-god and the Twins and one of the most rich and enduring mythic themes left to us from very ancient, pre-literary traditions, have to be erased and ignored, to the detriment of the study of Greek, as of other mythologies. Our understanding of Graeco-Roman and all myth would be improved by some *lateral thinking*, by including solar feminine themes as interpretative possibilities, trying them out, seeing where they lead, being more flexible and explorative in our attitudes to the goddesses and our reasoned speculations about them. It was the Graeco-Roman world and the Christianity of that world which taught us to be inflexible towards Sun and Moon myths. Now it is time to put that right.

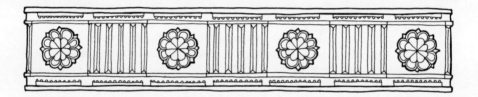

Chapter 26
Releasing the Sun

"Constant change is here to stay."

—Anon.

"Sceptical scrutiny is the means, in both science and religion, by which deep thoughts can be winnowed from deep nonsense."

—Carl Sagan [1]

Once we have faced up to the fact that the concept 'Sun-goddess' is a part of human religious thought just like any other, and in no sense extraordinary or alien, our thinking on the whole of myth and religion is automatically affected. To accept Sun-goddesses in this way does not mean adopting a religious belief in them, or agreeing that they are beneficial, or anything like that. (Much less am I proposing that all goddesses are really solar, or denying the occurrence of male suns—to do that would be every bit as absurd as claiming that all goddesses are lunar.) But this acceptance will, I know, be impossible for some. It requires considerable redrawing of our mental map of reality. The cognitive dissonance brought about by female suns will be too much for some to cope with; their only option will be to anathematize the author as "Sun-obsessed" or just plain "unspiritual," or set about "proving" that all Sun-goddesses are "really" or "originally" Moon-goddesses.[2] A vast amount of human security and meaning is vested in the belief in a sacred, everlasting order of the cosmos, the solar masculine and lunar feminine principles (or, if you prefer, *yang* and *yin*)—and

I am not just talking about people who are religious or even think about such things. Western patriarchal society has put a great deal of energy into making sure that everyone thinks of things 'the right way round'. It is only natural that anxiety should be generated when this paradigm is questioned—or, as some see it, attacked.

Something is going on here which recalls the anxiety generated among Christians by the idea of women priests. It is an actual threat to God. One of the stock objections to female priesthood is that *it will change the nature of the Godhead*—almost as if Ultimate Reality had sprung a leak. It will admit into the pure, transcendent masculine-self-same, solar and Absolute, a disruptive, chaotic, contaminating, alien element—*the feminine*—just as a cracked water-main would be contaminated by impurities seeping in from the surrounding soil. As we have already seen, solar symbolism is a vital part of the Christian conception of godhead. (The priest at the altar represents Christ, and so by extension he is solar too.) And, despite lip-service paid to the idea that God transcends or includes both male and female, in all practical and philosophical terms the Christian god is purely masculine—pure Masculinity, distilled off, volatilized, 101 per cent proof spirit, free of all feminine impurities or additives. (In the words of C.S. Lewis, "What is above is so masculine that we are all feminine in relation to it.") Women priests are the female suns of Christianity; a spiritual perversion.

Just as Christians do themselves a disservice by rejecting female priests, so also do Western scholars, thinkers, alternative religionists and indeed everyone else by rejecting female suns, by trying to dismiss them, to explain them away or treat them as heresy. All this is wasted, redundant effort, for female suns pose no threat to us; in fact we disadvantage ourselves by denying them validity. When we loosen our rigid and narrow ideas about myth to admit female suns and male moons, we expand possibilities for ourselves. Our thinking thereby is made more flexible and creative in respect of other issues, not just those of myth and religion, but in many, many areas—the most obvious being the relationship between men and women, and how both sexes can live most fully, widely, bravely, freely. To say that the Sun is most "authentically" male and the Moon most "authentically" female might give certain temperaments meaning and security, but at the expense of closing off all kinds of avenues of thought and being. It is linear thinking; 'halfistic', not holistic; two-dimensional, not multi-dimensional; when proffered as the only true way of thinking about things and the only true model for actual men and women, it makes both myth and life mean and small.

The Authority of Myth

Let's get back to basics. It will help us to clear away the clutter of associations from Sun and Moon by describing them in natural terms. The Sun is a blazing ball of gases, a quite minor star among the unbelievable number of stars in the universe, yet it is the star whose energy sustains our planet, driving its living and non-living systems. The Moon is a barren rock which circles our Earth, and although its gravity draws our seas into tides, in itself it is almost inert. Neither Sun or Moon is a thing with a thinking mind. They are as inane as two house-bricks; they are not persons, they are less than persons. They only have divine or human qualities insofar as humans choose to give such qualities to them—and in doing so, humans create Sun-deities and Moon-deities.

Now, some people will say that I've got this the wrong way round. They would say that such a view of Sun and Moon is "merely materialistic"—that these bodies express on a *material* level certain *spiritual* realities. Whereas scientists know what they know about Sun and Moon by reason, they themselves know about the deeper realities by means of a higher faculty, *intuition*. Therefore the idea that the Sun is male and the Moon female is not accessible to reason (or "solar thinking") but only to intuition (or "lunar thinking") which the *OED* defines as "direct apprehension without the use of reason."

Intuition, therefore, is a faculty which allows us to tell whether myth is true or false, without applying thought to it. Indeed, myth itself, is said to be the product of intuition—it was created by wise men or women who saw into the inner realities of e.g. Sun and Moon, giving form to those true intuitions in myth. Particularly in the new alternative religious movements, and very especially in feminist spirituality, intuition alone is said to be the surest guide to truth. (Reason belongs to men and the Sun. Intuition belongs to women and the Moon.)

But there's a great big problem here. People's intuitions obviously conflict. When I used to talk to other spiritual-feminists about my intuition that the Sun is a goddess and the Moon a god, I was not infrequently told that my intuition was *false*.[3] Clearly, people who believe in the primacy of intuition recognize that one can have a true intuition or a mistaken one. Spiritual-feminists believe the intuitions of Christians and Muslims about the masculinity of God are not just wrong but actually bad.[4] But how do intuitionists tell the difference between true and false intuitions?

When I asked this question in respect of Sun-goddesses, I was invariably answered with an argument from number:

"Certainly, one does find both moon *gods* and sun *goddesses*. Yet the following generalizations hold. There are more moon-goddesses than moon-gods, and there are many more sun gods than sun goddesses."[5]

And, one might add, there are many more mythologies in which the Earth is flat, than ones in which it is round. Mythic truth cannot be decided by majority vote like this, any more than any other kind. A lot of people can be very wrong for a very long time (including the author of the foregoing, incorrect statement). Indeed, this applies more to myth and religion than to any other area of life, for by nature these are closed systems and can't afford scepticism and close examination of their claims.

More importantly, arguments like the one just quoted are really tacit admissions that intuition on its own is not a sure guide to truth. When one person says that another person's intuition is "wrong," what test are they using to evaluate the rightness or wrongness of *their own* as well as other people's intuitions?

When asked this, intuitionists automatically present evidence (or at any rate, what they consider to be evidence) in support of their case, or against someone else's, as with the example I have just given, which calls on number as proof. But what the intuitionist has been doing here, without actually realizing it, is *to subject intuition to the test of reason.* This is the only way to check whether your intuition is true or false. You can intuit as much as you like, but the very moment you pause to think about your intuitions, you are applying rational processes to them—the moment you start in any way to examine them, to find out the difference between a true perception and mere self-delusion, then you subject intuition to reason.

It really is not good enough to say that we know the everlasting truth of Sun-male/Moon-female by intuition. This is like the Christian who says he knows that the Bible is infallible "by faith." Modern pagan revivalists are really arguing for the *authority* of certain myths in the same kind of way that Christians argue for the authority of the Bible. "The Sun is masculine" and "the Moon is feminine" thereby become truths to be received no matter what one's personal feelings might be on the matter. The ancient wisdom guides and overrides personal intuitions—we know if our intuitions are true by matching them up against the testimony of myth. Thus Sun-male/Moon-female becomes a truth to be preserved and protected, which means suppressing, erasing, dismissing, discrediting and tampering with evidence which would controvert it. And when reason is given a low value, or attempts even made to exclude it, then doubt, free inquiry, questioning, thought and intellectual honesty are also devalued, with disastrous results. Take away reason, and leave only intuition, and we deprive ourselves of the means whereby to evaluate critically our own ideas. Moreover we are unable to dialogue, to communicate rationally with those who disagree with us—all that is left is to anathematize them as patriarchal or Satanic; and this is the way holy wars over true religion and false religion begin.

Freeze-Frame Mythology

There are very good reasons why myth cannot and must not be religiously authoritative for us "post-modern" Westerners. Past myth is for us not social but personal—the context in which it lived has gone forever, and the myths have become like the material artefacts which those dead cultures left behind. They are poetry and art, and always, *always* nostalgic—you can no more detach the nostalgia from them than you can remove the miaow from the cat.

I know that some women and men, having read about the Sun-goddesses, will be delighted with them, and will already see in them the outlines of a new, revived, Sun-goddess cult, with beautiful stories and rituals. Indeed, I could have spent this chapter in constructing a synthetic Sun-goddess mythos, using such recurrent motifs as the Sun-mirror, the goddess's winter withdrawal into the cave, the conflict between Sun-goddess and Storm-god, the Sun-maiden, the incest myth, and so on. Such a mythos would certainly be appealing both in its loveliness and its satisfying coherence. But beware. It would also be in a very real sense a distortion, no matter how factually true in terms of actual ancient or tribal beliefs. Sun-goddess and Moon-god are not fixed entities—they have no existence in any abstract or spiritual sense—they are or were *verbs* whose full meaning was only actualized, in context, by the people of a particular era and society.

The stories I have told you of the Sun-goddesses are freeze-frame images, snapshots of mythology, silent and still. We cannot re-enter those worlds, no matter how deeply they move us; we are like people in an art-gallery beholding the Venus of Willendorf, or the Icon of Our Lady of Vladimir; we bring to that beholding everything that we are as twentieth-century people. While we share our humanity with the people who created myth, legend and sacred art, that is not the same thing as *being in* the myth, experiencing it in the way that the people of a particular social context actually experienced it. Things are further complicated by the fact that the world and human development chugs on, under its own steam, and in even the most traditional and conservative societies, beliefs, practices and meanings continually and imperceptibly shift and change. The static quality of traditional societies is the same sort of illusion as the flatness of the earth. It only seems like that because we cannot take in the wider view. Myth flows; we fail to perceive it.

We read myths of other cultures through the filter of our Western minds and particularly through language. Using a language shapes the world and experience in a certain way, so that as soon as we even start to describe or record another culture's myths in our own language, we begin to alter them, often very radically. Merely to use the word *goddess* is to bring the full weight of Western inheritance about deity, being, religion, sex-roles (patriarchal or feminist) and a whole lot of other things to bear on issues of divine femininity where they are not appropriate. This is not to say that we can't understand anything about myth. Obviously-enough, we are able to discover and record many things intelligibly—we know, for example, that the Cherokee Sun-deity is female, because real flesh-and-blood Cherokees tell us so, and we know that the Hittites called the Sun a goddess, because they left clay tablets addressing her as that in prayers. But if we believe that we can have a myth raw and organic, so to speak, then we delude ourselves. We *process* myth the moment we look at it or touch it, like a reverse Midas turning gold to some baser metal. Paradoxically, this is the very reason why we must make every effort to respect myth as it was (or is) for the people who believed in it. There is no room for the explaining-away of Sun-goddesses as not really the Sun, or as second-class suns.

Modern Sacred Myth

Some readers will say, "Surely myth changes anyhow by its passage from one culture to another—isn't that a natural process? What's wrong with our changing it from *our* cultural viewpoint?" And following on from this, they might point out that we can and do create our own religious myths—for example, in the Goddess-movement.

This, however, is something different. Whether we create myth consciously or base it on dreams and ecstatic experience, it is not at all the same thing as myth in ancient and tribal societies, just as our art is not the same kind of thing as the cave-art of Altamira, or Cycladic sculpture—art which expresses a shared social vision, a lived myth, where people were unable even to conceive of such a thing as a non-sacred world. Religion then was *all*, it was existence itself, the matrix in which everything moved. There was no possible way of standing back from it. But for us to even name "*myth*," even to think of it as a "something," means we have become conscious of it as a separate entity. We have lost our metaphysical innocence. Once having become aware of myth, we've woken from the spell of enchantment, left the Garden of Eden. Having become conscious of myth, we cannot just 'unknow' that knowledge and climb back into a dreamtime, any more than an audience shown the secret of a conjurer's trick can see it as an illusion again.

Once broken like this, the old integrated world can't be scotch-taped back together again, no matter how much we desire or need such a world. (Facile remedies, such as glibly saying spirit and matter are just the same, achieve precisely nothing.[6]) Efforts to do so have issued in recent years in fanatical, strident fundamentalisms, with their hostility to change, their reaction against science, free inquiry and the rational mind; their deeply paranoid anxieties about doctrinal purity, and their efforts to reinstate the fantasy of the Golden Age (whether first-century Christianity or Palaeolithic Moon-mother religion). These attempts to hold the whole metaphysical world-view together despite of change require huge exertion, vast wastage of our mental resources, and a deliberate turning-away from our responsibility to ourselves to be intellectually honest and courageous, to accept unpalatable truths about ourselves and the world—they are what one author has summed up as "a diversion of energies not very promising for our survival".[7]

Science or Spirituality?

The fix we now find ourselves in is not going to be solved by supernatural methods. We cannot adopt the childish solution of pulling the metaphysical bedclothes over our heads and pretending the twentieth century will somehow go away. The Earth and the human race itself will not be saved by our anathematizing scientific inquiry from the safety of some One True Religion position, nor by moonbathing, Tarot-card reading, or pretending to be Neolithic woman, but by *breadth of understanding*, by rationally communicating with each other, and by rational solutions.

This does not mean a choice between science and spirituality, or between reason and intuition, any more than our bodies have a choice between food and oxygen, but a matter of understanding both without deceiving ourselves. To derive pleasure, understanding and comfort from myth does not necessarily mean that we must give up scepticism or scrupulous intellectual honesty. The leading of a fully rational life does not exclude all the precious things such as love, art, creative fantasy, joy, myth, but it *does* exclude credulity, mental laziness, self-deception and closed systems of belief. It *does* mean that we must be prepared, quite calmly and bravely, to give up even our most cherished beliefs when faced with evidence that they just aren't true. It means that we must live in an *open* way, without certain defences. Religious systems tell you what's what— they give you things prepacked, cut and dried—they are *closed* systems. The rational and scientific approach is an *open-ended system*, constantly open to new ideas and new evidence, constantly inquiring in fresh fields, and always able in principle to incorporate new knowledge, to revise, improve and redraw the maps of reality. It has no argument with intuition, feeling and emotion in themselves, indeed it affirms them as just a natural part of being human, but it never allows them to lead the individual into the cowardly bypaths of self-delusion.[8]

Science is not primarily a body of knowledge, but a *method*. It generates knowledge, some of which is irreducible—we aren't suddenly going to find that lavatory bleach is a nourishing food for babies, that Pluto is the centre of the solar system, or that the human liver is made of wood. The constancy of Nature allows us to function in the world. But even this irreducible knowledge is constantly improved and refined. New knowledge is generated by impartial, stringent testing, to distinguish what is so from what isn't so. Everything is in principle subject to test, and every scientific idea subject to change, because there is no point whatever in hanging onto something in the face of overwhelming contradictory evidence. To do so is just to delude ourselves, like people who believe that the Earth is flat or that geese grow from barnacles. People who sneer when a long-held scientific theory, found to be wanting, is changed or refuted by scientists themselves, and who say, "There, look, scientists don't know everything, and science can't tell us the truth!" have never even begun to understand what science is all about.

Others say, "Oh, well, objective knowledge is just an illusion!" The standard rationalist answer to this is to invite the person to throw themselves out of an eighth-story window, and thus discover by practical test what is and what is not objective. If this kind of objective knowledge is an illusion, then it's a remarkably reliable and useful one.[9]

Many people who protest against what they misconceive to be "science" are really protesting about the ways in which the results of science are used by governments and commercial interests to dehumanize our lives, to make them loveless, bleak, ugly and unnourishing. Just as we badly need more understanding about science as a method of inquiry, and more understanding about its multiplicity, and what all the different sciences can really tell us; just as we need to develop the skills of rationality that Nature gave us, so too do we need to develop our skills of joy, fantasy, creativity and love. But we now urgently need to find ways of doing this without manufacturing security from old illusions about the supernatural, and without demonizing abstractions such as "patriarchy" or "the solar principle" as the "spiritual" source of planetary problems.

Undoubtedly some readers will say, "Well, yes, of course, she would be arguing for rationality, wouldn't she? She's in the grip of the solar, masculine principle." But they are missing the point. Certainly, in an historical sense, the modern, rational, scientific attitude is connected with the Greek Sun-god Apollo, but only insofar as *that* culture associated the god in a limited sense with the rational faculty. It is taking a very parochial viewpoint to suggest that this is always, necessarily and inevitably the case with Sun-deities—as I hope this book has already shown. The Sun-deity is not the mytho-political package deal which he (or she) is made out to be. But my point about the rational approach has nothing to do with the Sun-cults *as ideologies*. It is every bit as damaging, in my view, to try and reinstate religious cults of Sun-goddesses as of any other deity. My purpose in talking about both Sun-goddesses and rationality is to affirm the essentially human and natural character of our world and universe, to emphasize its diversity and also its unity. There is no part of life or myth that we can select, or cut out, saying, "Well, that bit certainly isn't ours!" Nor is there a supernatural or spiritual or psychic realm, either "within" or "outside" or "the same as" Nature. There just *is* Nature. And no part whatever of mythology is alien to us, because it is all purely human, and *ours*, the nasty bits as well as the nice bits. To assert the human and diverse nature of myth, as opposed to religious factionalism, is the rational approach that I present to you, the reader, to do with what you will. For, to accept Sun-goddesses (and Moon-gods) as a legitimate theme in purely human religious thinking really does point us in that direction. I want the reader to really grasp that pluralist nettle.

While we must face the biological realities of the world we live in—or else that world will perish, and us with it—we are very considerably free and indeterminate in another sense[10]. Nature has made us with a brain that is not absolutely bound to instinct, and which can imagine a future, which can fantasize, explore, extend a thousand miles in every direction. Our manner of living and being is passed not only through our genes, but through our ability to communicate thought-traditions, through speaking, writing and the arts, a non-genetic inheritance passed on to future generations. This faculty gives us our creativity, the ability to make and experience joy and beauty. *This is the one natural resource which has no limits.* And I believe that this is our real "spirituality," which has no need to exorcise or deny either science or sacred story, the rational or the non-rational, but understands them on their own terms. We badly need to recover a sense of wonder, curiosity and child-like openness and joy towards the universe, but at the same time (and I truly believe that we can do both) we need to cultivate an adult, practical, rational, fearless realism which wastes no energy on self-deception and scorns safe, enclosed doctrinal refuges. We need to be more naïve, yet more knowing; more glad, but more courageous.

The inclusion of the feminine Sun as part of human mythic inheritance adds to everyone's comprehension of myth, and by writing about it I do indeed mean to expand both knowledge and joy. When admitted to human status, myth, with all its marvellous, fantastical, absurd, sad, scandalous, happy, lying-and-truthful world of sacred poetry and story, with all its beauty and ugliness, its disclosures of human wisdom and folly, holds no religious threats or frights for us. There is no need any longer to exorcise the Sun-goddess. Our radical security lies, not in an ancient view of a cosmic spiritual world, no matter how sanctioned by time and use, but in wholeheartedly embracing our essential humanity as wholly human, wholly natural.

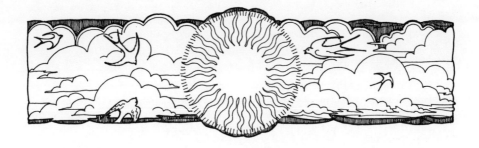

Notes on the Text

Introduction

1. "Goddess" is used throughout this book for convenience and simplicity, even though in its Western sense it is technically incorrect for the divine figures of e.g. certain tribal mythologies. It avoids any sense that a goddess is "not the real Sun."
2. Monaghan (1989).
3. "Synthetic"—many different elements put together to form one whole or system. The modern Wiccan movements date from 1929, all based on Margaret Murray's article "Witchcraft" in the *Encyclopaedia Brittanica* of that year. They are forms of pantheism and Nature-worship, not Satanism. (*En. Brit..* Vol. 25, p. 95)
4. *Yin* and *yang* are concepts in the Chinese philosophy and nature-religion called *Taoism.* Alan Watts' *The Watercourse Way* is an excellent introduction.
5. Starhawk (1988), p. 73.
6. Adler, revised ed. (1983), p. 218.

Chapter I. *The Woman Who Stands on the Moon*

1. *OED* XVII, 184, entry "Sun."
2. Briffault, Vol. II, p. 596.
3. Malachi 3.20. (Jerusalem Bible) In this book "the Sun of righteousness" is the ordinary Sun. Later interpreters took it to refer to Christ.
4. That is, after the Babylonian exile. Books written by Moses were supposed to have been "discovered" in a back room of the temple, but this was a common way in the ancient world of making claims for new religious compositions.
5. The identification of morning-star (planet Venus) goddesses such as Ishtar and Inanna as "Moon-goddesses" is a modern error. See e.g. *ERE* Vol. 2, p. 116.
6. Briffault, Vol. III, p. 106.
7. For details of the development of anti-Semitism in early Christianity, see Maccoby, *The Mythmaker.*
8. John 1.5. For details of the *logos* concept in Judaism, see Asimov (1981), p. 960-965.
9. Ephesians 5.14. (Maccoby suggests St. Paul was in any case not a Pharisee.)
10. Grant, p. 126-129.

11. *En. Brit.* Vol 20, p. 351; Grant, p. 185-187.
12. *En. Brit.* Vol. 24, p. 705; Grant p. 187..
13. Chadwick, p. 126.
14. Dowley (1977), p. 130-131.
15. "The Missionaries." BBC2, 1990.
16. Manichaeism, a third-century Persian movement which also influenced Christianity, said that men contained some particles of solar light, but women contained none at all, and that Christ lived in the Sun. (Durham, p. 116-117).
17. Revelation 12.1. (*The Bible.* Revised Standard Version)
18. Metford, p. 266.
19. Briffault Vol.2 p. 588.
20. Warner, p. 93.
21. The idea of Christ as the Sun and Mary as the Moon was supported by Origen, Ambrose, Augustus and many other saints, and is even today being propagated by the Roman Catholic Church as anti-feminist doctrine. Warner (1978), p. 257-258.
22. Warner (1978), p. 257.
23. Cooper (1982), p. 21.
24. The Neoplatonic tradition is Graeco-Egyptian in origin. Discovery of a mass of such texts in the 1470's led to a neoplatonic revival in the West. "Free Inquiry," Vol. 10, no. 2, p. 19 (Spring 1990).
25. I Corinthians, 11.7.

Chapter 2. Not a Job for a Woman

1. Cirlot, p. 318-319. (The idea that an interpretation of symbols is "*broadest*" and "*most authentic*" when it actually *excludes* is typical patriarchal double-think.)
2. Grimal, in 1972 Larousse, p. 14.
3. Gage, p. 12.
4. Mallory, p. 269; 277, note 38.
5. Even liberal Christian theologians misidentify Baal Hadad as the Sun—see, for example, Cupitt, p. 114-115.
6. E.g. Chetwynd (1986), p. 206, includes El, Mot and Aleyin Baal in his list of "Sun-gods." In the Ugarit tablets from which these names are taken, the Sun (Shapash) is a *goddess*.
7. E.g. Briffault claims that "the Sun plays no part in Australian conceptions of the supernatural" (Vol. 2, p. 694), that the Moon-god was superior to the Sun-goddess among the Balts (Vol. 2, p. 677) and that the Eskimo thought the Sun's heat and light were "derived from "the Moon (Vol. 2, p. 721)—all completely untrue. Indeed, Briffault's attempts to belittle a Sun-goddess are almost invariably clues to her importance.
8. *ERE* Vol. 12, p. 68.
9. Olcott, p. 38.
10. Grimm, p. 703, 705. See also Howitt, p. 427.
11. Al Faruqi, p. 127-128. The author is Joseph Kitagawa, apparently a Japanese Roman Catholic.
12. *Pears Encyclopaedia of Mythology*, "The Ancient Near East," p. 24.
13. Eliade (1978), p. 140-141, 156. The Christian Eliade saw world religion in terms of his own supernatural belief, a highly patriarchal *sophia perennis* which sees world religions as having declined from a solar, monotheistic cult of the High God or All-Father. Eliade and Kitagawa

(see note 11) appear as editors of *The Encyclopaedia of Religion*, a work conspicuous for its erasure of Sun-goddesses.

14. *Funk and Wagnall*, p. 607 ("Latvian Mythology," Jonas Balys).
15. "The Edda speaks of the *sun* and *moon* as brother and sister" (Grimm, p. 703). *Sister and brother*, actually. (See chapter 12)
16. *Funk and Wagnall*, p. 633. ("Lithuanian Mythology," Jonas Balys)
17. Another version of the song (Katzenelenbogen, p. 55) calls her "little Sun, God's daughter."
18. E. Tonnelat, "Germanic Mythology," 1959 *Larousse*.
19. In a similar way Aston (1905) argues that the feminine sex of the Japanese Sun-goddess is of no consequence. He claims that the Japanese attach no meaning to the sex of a kami (untrue); yet, later in the book, we find him postulating a minor *male* kami as the "real" Sun-god!
20. Clodd, p. 27.
21. Jamieson, quoted in Harley's "Moon Lore."
22. Al Faruqi, p. 127-128. Kitagawa argues that Amaterasu "must be" an Earth-goddess because she does "earthly" things like growing crops and living in a cave. It is hard to conceive of *anything* a personified deity could then do which would *not* be "earthly." E.O. James (1967), p. 80, 95, argues that the Hittite Sun-goddess is an Earth-goddess, on the basis of things which *all* the Middle Eastern Sun-gods do, and the title "Sun of the Underworld," which such *male* gods also possessed. See e.g. Gaster (1975), p. 227-228 and Young (1981), p. 161 for examples.
23. Thouless (1958), p. 37. A recommended work for those who want to avoid muddled thinking.
24. Cooper (1978), entry "Sun."
25. Cooper (1978 and 1982) are full of this—see, for example (1982), p. 53, 58.
26. Piercy (1981).
27. Sjöö and Mor, p. 151.
28. Walker (1989), and Sjöö and Mor (1987) are the chief offenders here. See also the blithe assumption in Stein, p. 8.
29. "Faith is the essential root of all knowledge... by faith is meant the assumption that a divine perfection is the everlasting basis of all things," Baggott, p. 118.

Chapter 3. The True Feminine

1. Schuon (1978), p. 54, note 1.
2. E.g. Nor Hall, *The Moon and the Virgin*, Sylvia Perera, *Descent to the Goddess*.
3. *En. Brit.* Vol. 24, p. 715.
4. Jacobi (1963) is a recommended general text on Jungian psychology.
5. See Jung's introduction in Harding (1973) and also p. 11, 20, 67.
6. Harding (1973), p. 31, 35.
7. Harding (1973), p. 16, 18, 65-66.
8. Harding (1973), p. 20, 64-65.
9. Harding (1973), p. 16, 18, 65-66.
10. Stevens (1986), p. 16-17.
11. Stevens (1986), p. 188.
12. Stevens (1986), p. 174.
13. Stevens (1986), p. 176-177.
14. Shuttle and Redgrove, p. 146, 166.
15. Harding (1973), p. 117.

16. Mattoon and Jones, in Nicholson (1989), p. 150.
17. See remarks in Daly, p. 253.
18. Gage, p. 211.
19. Crow (1971), p. 173-175. Farnham declared the reign of science to be over and the spiritual reign of women to be at hand.
20. Weideger, p. 27-28.
21. Ephesians 5.23.
22. For a detailed account, see Faderman's *Surpassing the Love of Men*.
23. Greek symbology showed warriors overcoming Amazons as a representation of culture and spirituality overcoming what was perverted and chaotic. When we consider that Amazons may have worshipped a *Sun-goddess*, the intention becomes even clearer. Cf. Markale, p.240.
25. See for example Goldenberg's *The Changing of the Gods* for detailed explanation of "solar" and "lunar" attributes; also Cooper (1982 and 1979).
26. This phrase is supposed to guard the Church of England's doctrinal statements from heresy or innovation.
27. Rush, p. 48.
28. For a witty review of these two books see M. Harismides in *Harvest* magazine, May 1988, p. 11-12. "Read critically," the reviewer wisely suggests, "Let's not make the mistakes of those who came before who could not see outside the patriarchal paradigm." Quite.
29. In Victorian times when women campaigned for admission to higher education, doctors claimed that intellectual activity in a woman would atrophy her sexual organs. Rush (p. 48) claims that academic discipline destroys Moon-consciousness. The thinking behind each of these is identical. True womanhood and the rational mind are fundamentally opposed.
30. For these and other reasons, Jungian psychology is considered to be a *pseudoscience* by many of the scientific community. See Hines, p. 138-139.
31. Stevens implies that objective information about such matters as archetypes would assist us in making laws. Since he is strongly anti-feminist, this bodes very ill for women's rights. Presumably, legislation would be used to keep us "lunar." (Stevens, p. 25)
32. Jung's hypotheses were formed before modern discoveries in many of these and related areas.

Chapter 4. *The Paths of the Moon and the Sun*

1. Burl (1983), p. 18.
2. A *Sun-cult* is the worship, symbols, myths, etc., of an individual Sun-deity. A *Sun-religion* is one dominated by the Sun-deity (e.g. Ancient Egypt, late Imperial Rome). There are thousands of Sun-*cults*, but very few Sun-*religions*—and, for that matter, very few Moon-religions.
3. See the entry on Rabbinical traditions regarding the Sun in *J.En.*, Vol 15, p. 517-518.
4. Gooch (1979), p. 55.
5. Burl (1983), p.16.
6. See Nigel Pennick's *Solar Patterns and Labyrinths*, an article in *Caerdroia*, No. 12, April 1983, p. 4-5.
7. Burl (1983), p. 17.
8. A good general reference is North's *Mastering Astronomy*.
9. The Antarctic region is uninhabited. People in the Southern Hemisphere have seasonal solar myths but not usually ones about the total absence of the Sun.

10. According to Procopius, the inhabitants of Thule in the far north, after thirty-five sunless days, watched on the mountains for the Sun's return and then celebrated a great festival. *ERE*, Vol. 1, p. 48.

11. The grain-goddesses Ceres and Proserpina, or Demeter and Persephone, hide an old Sun-mother/Sun-daughter dyad. Some writers hint at this without realizing its full import: Newall (p. 29) says, "...we have here the subterranean aspect of the sun. When it descends into the mountain again at dusk, we are reminded of the Graeco-Roman myth explaining the seasons; Proserpina, gathering flowers, is snatched by "gloomy Dis" and winter falls on the land for a six-month's cycle. The sun descends into its mountain and night falls for a period of twelve hours." The fact that the story fits the Greek seasons very oddly, also points to a northern provenance.

12. See for example James (1967), p. 78, on Ishtar as the "Earth-mother"—the explanation theorizing how the Earth goes up and down inside herself is particularly garbled. The same absurdity is adopted by Kraft (1985) and Sayce (1887) who says of Ishtar, "It is the earth, as she passes slowly downward into the palace prison of the infernal goddess," yet soon afterward he notes an inscription which says that Ishtar is not only the planet Venus but also *the Sun!* (p. 251, 253)

13. This is recognized by many northern peoples, e.g., the Lapps and Eskimos. Not all cultures made the mistake of thinking the Moon governs the seasons. See Rush, p. 53.

14. *En. Brit.* Vol. 15, p. 472.

15. Readers are recommended to consult the long article on the Calendar in *En. Brit.* Vol. 15, pp. 460-477

16. de Zoete, p. 9.

17. A beautiful description is to be found in Thomas Hardy's *Far From the Madding Crowd* (Penguin, 1981), p. 61-62.

18. For a vivid account of the night-stages in nomadic life, see Cable and French, p. 105-108.

19. For a good discussion of this and other problems, see Brown (1979).

20. Burl says of Irish and North British megalithic carvings, "Their symbols may have been solar in origin... *although* the eyebrow patterns... have been thought to stand for the watchful gaze of some female deity." (Emphasis mine) In other words, they can be solar *or* female, but not both! Burl's assumptions about the Sun seem quite unconscious. See Burl (1981), p. 171.

21. The definitive text on New Grange is Michael O'Kelly's 1982 account of the excavations.

Chapter 5. Holy Blood, Holy Moon

1. Ralph Estling, *New Scientist*, May 27, 1989, p. 75-76, and Shuttle and Redgrove, p. 145-146.

2. "In accordance with their primary function as 'the real husband of all women'... primitive lunar deities are predominantly masculine; the moon is a man and the sun is commonly his wife." Briffault, Vol III, p. 46.

3. Briffault, Vol. III, p. 48.

4. Ancient and primitive people saw menstruation simply as *bleeding* which came and then dried up, i.e., just as from a wound. With no knowledge of the endometrium and its behaviour, they could not imagine the womb lining in modern terms, as we do, i.e., as *regenerative tissue*. Lunar analogy which implies this is a twentieth-century concept read back into ancient mythology.

5. Shapiro et al (1970).

6. Kelly, Rotton and Culver (1985). This review includes a useful list of research papers on the lunar effect. See also Kelly, Saklofske and Culver (1990) showing that lunar phase has no

effect on disasters, etc.

7. This is known as *cognitive bias*. See Kelly et al (1985), p. 138.
8. Hines, p. 157.
9. Sjöö and Mor, p. 189, from Shuttle and Redgrove, p. 167, who found the idea in a popular occult magazine *Man, Myth and Magic*, No. 67, p. 1876. This belief about the Moon—presented by Sjöö and Mor as a piece of objective science ("biologically accurate") comes from a folk-tale!
10. Shuttle and Redgrove, p. 145.
11. Rush, p. 53.
12. I heard this idea in women's-spirituality meetings around 1985. Other "flat-Earth" type beliefs about the Moon (e.g. that NASA has photographs of ancient civilizations' buildings on the Moon, but has suppressed them—see *Womanspirit* magazine, March 1982, Vol. 8, No. 31, p. 44) seem to be part of a kind of paranoia, concisely expressed in Rush, p. 16-17, who says we should read all patriarchal writings on the Moon as propaganda, instead judging the truth by "our collective female body experience."
13. The biological value for marine animals, of reproductive swarming at certain tides, is to bring a high concentration of them together at once—especially necessary when sperm and ova are liberated directly into the water. No mystical fertilizing virtue is imparted to them from the Moon, and the high tides on which they depend are a *lunisolar* phenomenon, not lunar. See Frazier, p. 239.
14. A simple explanation of lunar phases: North, p. 94-96; and of tides, Asimov, p. 84-85 and Frazier, p. 229-231.
15. Shuttle and Redgrove, p. 156-157, referring to Dewan (1969).
16. *En. Brit.* Vol. 9, p. 643-644.
17. In a recent experiment an Italian woman developed amenorrhoea after spending four months underground. *She* magazine, "Medical Notes," November 1989.
18. Charlotte Brontë, *Villette*, (Chatto and Windus, 1977), p. 294.
19. This is the fundamental error of Lieber and Sherin's book on the lunar effect. See Abell's review in Frazier, p. 228-234.
20. Kelly et al (1985), p. 134-135. If Sun, Moon and all the planets were to line up so as to combine their gravitational pull on Earth, the effect on the individual would be nullified if he or she sat down from a standing position (thus bringing the body 25 inches closer to the Earth's gravitational centre). Randi, p. 57.
21. Recent research on the Mount St. Helen's volcano in the U.S.A. suggests this movement contributes to earthquakes and volcanic events. *Horizon*, BBC2, 14th May, 1990, "Legacy of a Volcano."
22. Kelly et al (1985), p. 134.
23. Any good GCSE biology text will give you a resumé of homeostasis.
24. Sjöö and Mor, p. 153, 191.
25. Osman and McCorry, Vol. 5, p. 105-111, gives an exceptionally clear explanation of this and other aspects of lunar astronomy.
26. Asimov, p. 89-90.
27. Shuttle and Redgrove, p. 143-144. The confused thinking and wild, compounded postulation in this work are remarkable even amongst spiritual-feminist Moon-books. (It is a Jungian book.)
28. Asimov, p. 89.
29. Rush, p. 55.

30. The only other mammal with a 28-day female sexual cycle is the opossum. Unless this species alone of all non-human animals is especially attuned to the Moon, then its 28-day cycle must be a coincidence. So why not a coincidence for humans too? Frazier, p. 233-234.
31. See the lists in Nicholson, p. 101.
32. Asimov, p. 86.
33. Asimov, p. 92.

Chapter 6. *The Sun, the Moon and Mother Earth*

1. Leonard Zusne and Warren H. Jones, *Anomalistic Psychology* (Lawrence Erlbaum Associates, 1982).
2. Briffault, Vol. III, p. 2.
3. Sjöö and Mor, p.282.
4. Barandiaran, p. 102.
5. There are "Earth-energies" responsible to a lesser extent for warming the planet, but there is nothing occult about them, they are the volcanic and radioactive sources within the Earth.
6. Things are more complicated regarding the second stage, the so-called "dark reaction" (so-called because it doesn't use light, not because it requires darkness—it doesn't). For fuller details see Simpkins, *Advanced Biology*.
7. This energy is measured in the dreaded *calories*. If you eat more fuel than your body can burn, it will be stored as fat.
8. See comment on the greenhouse effect in *Pipes of Pan*, No. 34, Spring 1990, p. 11, which associates Sun-worship causally with global warming in a way which clearly "blames" the Sun.
9. See below, Chapter 12.
10. Contrary to popular opinion, the Moon does not influence the weather. Even the "ring around the Moon" rain forecast is not reliable. *En. Brit.* Vol 16, p. 519.
11. Stith Thompson, motif No. A712.1.
12. Dew was imagined to come from the Moon—another mistake. On clear nights the lack of cloud cover means that the temperature drops, condensing moisture in the air and forming dew. On such nights the Moon may shine, but it doesn't drip dew, which is not really surprising as it's a dry rock 250,000 miles away. I only point this out because some people still think dew is distilled from (or by) the Moon. Folklore habitually requires the conjunction of solar fire with "lunar" water before it is fit for magical use. Hence dew and spring or well-rites at *sunrise*.
13. In some barren deserts, the food chain is sustained by scraps of dead vegetation blowing in from plants in distant areas.
14. Known as *phloem* tissue. Trees barked by deer die because this tissue is interrupted.
15. Mrs. Grieve, p. 586.
16. Sjöö and Mor, p. 282: "It was the Sun now who was seen to germinate the seed with his phallic sunbeams. A false notion; the sun is a necessary but not sufficient cause of life. All planets receive sunlight, but only the one with earth and water grows anything." This is total confusion. *Germinate* is an intransitive verb (seeds can't be "germinated *by*" anything). Whether the planets "grow anything" is a completely separate issue from that of germination. And germination is neither a sexual nor a reproductive process!
17. The production of flower buds is timed by many plants using the length of darkness (flower production being inhibited by light). Commercial growers use different proportions of

artificial daylight and darkness to bring flowers into bloom out of season. See e.g. Simpkins and Williams, p. 386-387.
18. Frazier, p. 234.

Chapter 7. Great Female Possessor of Noon

1. The principal source for this chapter is Herbert's *Shinto* (strongly recommended to the reader as the only Western book recounting what Shintoists *themselves* actually do and believe); also Aston(1905), Maraini (1959) and Campbell (1960) Vol. 2.
2. Al Faruqi, p. 127-128.
3. Eliade (see e.g. (1964) p. 504-505) and other scholars believe that women shamans, Sun-goddesses and seeming matriarchal practices are late developments following on from the decline of pure-religion patriarchies with male-only sky deities and shamans.
4. Kidder, p. 44, 51; Murphy, p. 97-102.
5. Peter McGill, "Skeleton in Japan's Cupboard," *Observer*, 9 April, 1989.
6. Aston (1905), p. 1, 58.
7. Gimbutas (1963), p. 38-44; Mallory, p. 182-185.
8. Influences from Korea and North Asia which flowed into Japan also travelled to Northern Europe and America, influencing the Celtic La Tene culture, Ireland, Kamchatka and North-East Canada. Campbell Vol. 2 p. 465.
9. Chamberlain (1981).
10. Aston (1896).
11. However, in China primitive and tribal traditions preserved quite a different cosmology, with a masculine Moon and feminine Sun. Even today some tribal minorities (e.g. the Miao) regard the Sun as female; red in old Chinese tradition is feminine, representing creative ability and sexual power of *woman*, while the old ideogram for *man* is a square plot of earth. Parrinder (1980), p. 77; *The Sun Goddess*, Monaghan.
12. *Kami* = higher, what is above. The name for any *numen*, animate or inanimate.
13. *Dainichi Nyorai* of the Shingon Buddhist sect. Herbert, p. 371.
14. Paradoxically, some shrines rejected Amaterasu because of her association with Roshana, and attempted (unsuccessfully) to replace her with various male kami whom they claimed to be be—you guessed it—the "real" Sun.
15. The definitive study of this and other Japanese shaman-religion is Carmen Blacker's *The Catalpa Bow*.
16. Herbert, p. 372.
17. Herbert, p. 33-34, explains the reasons for this diversity of Shinto and its relaxed attitude towards divergent theological views.
18. Munetada Kurozumi (1780-1850). See Herbert, p. 521. For sayings of Kurozumi, who founded the Sun-goddess sect of early modern Shinto, see Bouquet, p. 320-323.
19. Herbert, p. 465.
20. Herbert, p. 59-60; Aston (1905), p. 26.
21. "An archaic word applied to what is wonderful, miraculous and ineffably worthy of honour, and to the Sun, *par excellence*.....the sun, the fire, the light, the soul, the Deity, etc." Herbert, p. 67.
22. For other examples of ritual ascent, see Eliade (1964) and Czaplicka.
23. Gooch, p. 130. Rush, p. 119, calls Tsuki-yomi "the Moon-goddess."
24. *Larousse* (1968), p. 415; Herbert, p. 466-467.

25. Sun-goddess and Moon-god separated after Tsuki-yomi murdered the food-goddess. Another version makes Susanowo the murderer (Nihongi I, 27). Herbert, p. 500-501.
26. See below, Chapters 17 and 19.
27. Fraser, p. 397.
28. Aston (1905), p. 6.
29. Herbert, p. 151, 412.
30. Herbert, p. 153.
31. Maraini, p. 130.
32. Herbert, p. 239, 503.
33. Herbert, p. 466.
34. Chamberlain (1902), p. 159.
35. Herbert, p. 372.
36. See entry "Sun" in Cooper (1968).
37. Miles, p. 66. After talking about Moon-goddesses, Miles introduces Amaterasu as "supreme" but without revealing that she is the Sun. She goes on to say that Amaterasu "fights" Susanowo (in direct contradiction of all Shinto sources, which unanimously say she withdraws rather than fights!) and that "he steals her light" and so "she may only shine by night." It cannot be too much emphasized that this is pure nonsense. Having thus grossly misinformed the reader, Miles goes on to say that the Sun is universally a male god! This is an excellent example of the way in which the requirements of religious dogma override those of scholarship.

Chapter 8. Dearest Goddess, Mother Sun

1. Katzenelenbogen, p. 55.
2. Ward, p. 234; Katzenelenbogen, p. 1-4.
3. Biezais, *En. Brit.*Vol.18, p. 905; Katzenelenbogen, p. 113.
4. Biezais, p. 665.
5. Balys, *Funk and Wagnall*, p. 633, claims the Moon-god was more important than the Sun-goddess; "In Lithuania the moon was apparently worshipped more than the sun... I have collected sixty prayers to the New Moon." This would sound a lot to the reader who didn't know that thousands of Sun-prayers have been collected!
6. Biezais, p. 906.
7. Katzenelenbogen, p. 55, daina 7.
8. Gold and silver are used indiscriminately as metaphors of light and splendour in Baltic lore.
9. Benjamins, p. viii. Benjamins combines Saule and the happiness-goddess Laime as the "Dearest Goddess" without distinction.
10. Benjamins, p. vii.
11. *En. Rel.*Vol 2, p. 52. Dainas which describe Saule "lifting her skirts" are thought by some scholars to signify ritual exposure, see e.g. daina no. 231, Katzenelenbogen, p. 151 (Saule is "St. John's mother" in this Christianized song).
12. Gimbutas' paper on Baltic Sun-symbols (1958) and Gimbutas (1963), p. 200-210.
13. Gimbutas (1958), p. 10. Unfortunately the author, though calling the Moon "he" and a "god" erases the Sun-goddess by calling Sun "it" and "a deity". In her later work she admits to the Sun's femininity—but grudgingly, putting "Saule, *deity* of the sun" and "Menuo, moon *god*" in the index (1963), p. 284, 282.
14. Gimbutas (1963), p. 199.
15. Katzenelenbogen, p. 89, 131, daina no. 5.

16. Ward (1967), p. 234-235.
17. *ERE* Vol. 12, p. 102.
18. Gimbutas (1963), p. 199-200.
19. The Sun-post is of great importance in Baltic symbology and folk-art. It has a number of striking parallels to the motifs and rites of sacred pole, ladder, roof-tree, etc. in Siberian shamanism (see Eliade 1964, p. 190-191, 375-427). Gimbutas' 1958 paper gives many descriptions and illustrations. See also *En. Rel.* Vol. 2, p. 52 and Gimbutas (1963), p. 195; (1958) includes illustrations of solar motifs on sacred poles.
20. Biezais, p. 906.
21. cf. Roman writer Lasicius on the Balts, "*Ausca* dea est radiorum solis [vel occumbentis vel] supra horizontem ascendis." *ERE* Vol. 1, p. 34.
22. *ERE* Vol. 12, p. 102; Katzenelenbogen, p. 55, daina no. 6.
23. Gimbutas (1963), p. 201.
24. Benjamins, p. 37.
25. Dievs (from the I.E. root *dyeu*) does not mean the day-sky but simply "the heavens." Baltic motifs of Dievs sleeping or vanishing for three days make his lunar character obvious, as also his role in fertility through rain-giving. *En. Rel.* Vol. 2, p. 50; Biezais, p. 665; Coxwell, p. 943 (a Lithuanian folktale in which the devil makes an imitation Sun to burn up the earth while Dievs sleeps for three days. Dievs pours water on it to put it out—it becomes our Moon.)
26. *ERE* Vol. 12, p. 102; Katzenelenbogen, p. 55, daina no. 8.
27. Coxwell, p. 925.
28. Ward, p. 238.
29. Briffault, Vol. 2, p. 67, quotes only the Moon-god's side of one of these arguments, omitting the context, in order to misrepresent the Moon as principal deity. This is shameless misinformation.
30. See below, Chapter 17.
31. Lurker, p. 229; Biezais, p. 665; Ward, p. 238 ("The Moon, a warrior,/Is in his boat day and night.")
32. Balys, p. 633.
33. Menulis is *Dangaus Karalaitis*, "Heavenly Prince" (Lurker, p. 230). See also Gimbutas (1963), p. 201.
34. *En. Rel.* Vol. 2, p. 53.
35. Gimbutas (1963), p. 202-203.
36. Katzenelenbogen, p. 131, daina no. 2.
37. *En. Rel.* Vol 2, p. 52.
38. Balys, p. 633.
39. Benjamins, p. vii.
40. Biezais, p. 906. Davies, p. 233, says Perkunas is the Sun-god despite having pointed out earlier (p. 214) "the Sun is a feminine god."
41. Ralston (1872), p. 242.
42. Gimbutas (1963), p. 201.
43. *ERE* Vol. 12, p. 102.
44. Balys, p. 607; Biezais, p. 664. The round cheese is a Sun-symbol in several areas of Europe. In Gloucestershire cheese-rolling is associated with fire-rites at two solar festivals, 1st May and Midsummer Day: Mary Reed, "Cheese Rolling in Gloucestershire," *Festivals*, Vol. 6, No. 3 (n.d.).
45. *En. Rel.* Vol. 2, p. 53; Gimbutas (1958), p. 10-12.

46. See below, Chapter 10.
47. Gimbutas (1963), p. 203; Ralston (1872), p. 192.
48. *Larousse* (1972), p. 420.
49. Important sources on this topic are Dexter (1986) and Ward (1967 and 1968).
50. This association was first noted by Ernst Krause, in his work on labyrinth folklore. It has been dismissed (for obvious reasons) and re-read as the "Earth-mother" being rescued from the Earth(?) by a duplicated Sun-god! See below, Chapter 25.
51. Lawson (1970), section on Baltic dances.
52. Coxwell, p. 926. (See also the author's pamphlet "Brighde," revised edition 1987, Fieldfare Publications.)
53. D.J. Ball, assistant Curator of reptiles at the London Zoo, informs me that the Zaltys was the common grass snake, *Natrix natrix.*
54. Gimbutas (1963), p. 203.
55. Objections that the dainas are merely modern hey-nonny-no (e.g. see "Baltic Lands" in *Larousse* (1968), have been refuted by Katzenelenbogen, and Ward (1967), p. 235.
56. *En. Rel.*Vol. 2, p. 39.

Chapter 9. Fair Maiden Bright Sun

1. Ralston (1873), p. 176-177.
2. *Larousse* (1968), p. 401-402.
3. Rice (1957), p. 180-181.
4. Ralston, p. 202.
5. *En. Brit.*Vol. 18, p. 9, emphasis mine. (The author goes on to say that only the Moon was worshipped by the Slavs!)
6. Mallory, p. 129.
7. Ralston (1872), p. 171.
8. Warner (1985), p. 57.
9. Ralston, p. 17.
10. Ralston, p. 52.
11. Warner (1985), p. 56.
12. Ralston, p. 319.
13. Warner (1985), p. 52.
14. See Patty Rice, *Amber, Golden Gem of the Ages.*
15. Ralston, p. 368-377.
16. *Larousse* (1968), p. 285.
17. Ralston, p. 91. Perperuna was later identified with the Virgin Mary.
18. *Larousse* (1968), p. 112, 284.
19. Cumont, p. 118.
20. Briffault, Vol. 3, p. 175.
21. Ralston, p. 361.
22. Ralston, p.. 171.
23. Ralston, p. 53.
24. *Larousse* (1968), p. 285.
25. Briffault, Vol 2, p. 589.
26. Ralston (1872), p. 305.
27. See Chapter "Bird Maidens" in Armstrong, *The Folklore of Birds.*

28. *Larousse, Prehistoric and Ancient Art* (1962), p. 173. Both the Hyperborean Apollo and the Irish Sun-woman Grainne had chariots drawn by swans.
29. Gostelow, p. 94-95, 102. This again is based on the misidentification of the Sun-goddess and the Twins, as "Mother Earth" fertilized by a "double Sun-god."
30. Rice (1957), p. 182-183.
31. Ralston (1872), p. 37.
32. *Larousse* (1972), p. 401.
33. Warner (1985), p. 56.
34. Hinnells, p. 299.
35. *Larousse* (1968), p. 285.
36. The egg does *not* always represent the Moon. In particular "in old Aryan [i.e. Indo-European] myth the springtide Sun was typified by a red or golden egg." Cox (1881), p. 31. Round cakes represent the Sun in Lapp and Saxon Sun-goddess tradition.
37. Ralston, p. 221.
38. Lenkiwska, Oresta." Ukrainian Painted Eggs,"*The Lady*, May, 1975.
39. Newall, *An Egg at Easter* illustrates and describes Ukrainian eggs.
40. Coleman, p. 215. Interesting details about the thunder-goddess are given in Ralston (1872), p. 91 and Katzenelenbogen, p. 4.
41. Coxwell, p. 989. (Cf. Siberian Sun and Moon mirrors, also Jewish tradition which says the Sun is too bright to look on because God's holy name is written on it.)
42. Ralston (1872), p. 246, 364-350.
43. Mueller, Vol. 1, p. 40-41.
44. Ralston, p. 186-187.
45. *ERE* Vol. 2, p. 38.
46. Ralston, p. 187-188.
47. *RSOW*, p. 263.
48. Benet, p. 71, 93-94.
49. Coxwell, p. 1016-1018.
50. Ralston, p. 202. The Northern Slavs kept the feminine Sun-tradition longest; further south, classical, Mithraic and other influences resulted in the sex-change.
51. *Larousse* (1972), p. 402-403.
52. Lurker, p. 281. Gimbutas (1963), p. 202, says they are related; Mallory, p. 129, that the comparison between the names is "debatable."
53. *En. Brit.* Vol. 18, p. 909.

Chapter 10. Sun-Woman of Ireland

1. Jackson (1951), p. 91, from original Gaelic collected by Carmichael, Vol. 3, p. 310.
2. Cotterell, p. 123-124.
3. Modern "Druidism" is a fantasy-religion, a product of 17th-18th century romantically-minded antiquarians. For a serious, realistic account of the Druids (and a refutation of the fantasy) see Piggott (1968).
4. Sun and Moon images were used in pagan worship, a practice the Christians had trouble keeping out of their own churches. *ERE* Vol. 12, p. 74.
5. Bonwick, p. 192.
6. Campbell (1893), Vol. 2, p. 372 et seq.
7. Jackson, p. 124.

8. Dineen (1927), entry "*Mor.*"

9. See chapter on fire-bringing birds, Armstrong.

10. This is false etymology, based on the *homonymous theory*, which says that if one word simply sounds like another, the two are the same, or related. Gallic *Bel* is supposed to be Canaanite *Baal*. The absurd theory is devoid of any foundation, yet much used by occultists (e.g. Walker, 1983, 1989). The Celtic deity *Belenos* was not a Sun-god (*ERE* Vol. 12, p. 74). See also Mackenzie, p. 278 and *ERE* Vol. 2, p. 283-285.

11. Beltane is claimed by spiritual-feminists to be a lunar festival (because it is a cross-quarter day) but all the rites associated with it show that it celebrated the *Sun* and the *arrival of summer*. I suggest that, by a comparison of equivalent Baltic and Slavic rites, the May feast once celebrated the bringing of fire/warmth/summer from the Sun to Earth. By the beginning of May the swallows and swifts have arrived, and the trees are nearly in full leaf. Interestingly, on the corresponding date of the next quarter (i.e. September 1st) the Slavs kindled needfire at sunrise saying that the swallows had gone to bury themselves *in wells*. Ralston (1872), p. 254.

12. Mackenzie, p. 279.

13. In 1960, at the Catholic school where my father worked, he was met one fine Easter morning by the Irish nun on duty—she was in a highly excited and exalted state, having just seen (as she believed) the Sun dancing.

14. Campbell, Vol. 4, p. 252-253.

15. Danaher, p. 74-75.

16. Borlase, p. 847-848.

17. Borlase, p. 848-849, describes the pattern at *Kilnagreina*, County Cork. *Tober Ghraine* at Ballycroom in the same country is an eye-well.

18. Beard, p. 126-129.

19. See Anne Ross, *The Folklore of the Scottish Highlands*.

20. Mallory, p. 129.

21. Partridge, *Origins*, entry "Sun." Stewart, p. 80. Stewart's book is based on the tired old fallacy about the male Sun and the female Earth/Moon, therefore he chooses a secondary meaning of *suil*, "hole" (= vagina). This page is worth reading for the way Stewart obfuscates the solar connections and rules out the solar feminine from the start.

22. Markale. p. 240.

23. Rees, p. 149, 184. (Single-pillar grianan, p. 147, 236, 262.)

24. Derry Youth and Community Workshop, *Grianan of Aileach.* (leaflet)

25. Markale, p. 78.

26. Mackenzie, p. 278.

27. Ross (1974), p. 288.

28. Smyth, p. 15, 97.

29. Parrinder (1971), p. 173-174.

30. O'Flaherty (1981), p. 278.

31. In his *On the Reckoning of Time* of 725 A.D., the Venerable Bede remarks that February was *Sol-monath*, "Sun-month," when cakes were offered "to the gods." Compare this Anglo-Saxon practice with that of the Lapps; Collinder (1949), p. 144.

32. *OED* Vol. 16, p. 151. (*Paradise Lost*, VII. 247)

33. *OED* Vol. 16, entry "Sun."

34. And also in art. The *Rainbow Portrait* of Elizabeth I by Marcus Gheeraerts, c. 1600, bears the motto "No rainbow without the Sun". Strong (p. 50) remarks, "The Queen is the Sun."

Maurice Kyffin's "The Blessedness of Brytaine" exalts Elizabeth in these words: "Adore November's sacred Seventeenth Day, Wherein our second sun began her shine." (Strong, p. 123) Such Sun-imagery was not merely due to Elizabeth being a sort of honorary king or male.

35. Blakeborough, p. 75; Morris, p. 224.
36. Blakeborough, p. 486, 305.
37. See Introduction to Morris (1892).

Chapter 11. Grandmother Sun, Good Lady

1. Barandiaran, p. 97, 100.
2. *ERE* Vol 2, p. 435.
3. De Marliave, p. 47 (illustration).
4. Barandiaran, p. 75, 78.
5. Barandiaran, p. 97.
6. De Marliave, p. 47.
7. De Marliave, p. 46.
8. Biezais, *En. Brit.* Vol. 9, p. 664; Katzenelenbogen, Chapter 6.
9. De Marliave, p. 51.
10. De Marliave, p. 51-52.
11. De Marliave, p. 54-58.
12. Barandiaran, p. 99-100.
13. Barandiaran, p. 100-102.
14. Briffault, Vol. 2, p. 597; Vol. III, p. 76.
15. *ERE* Vol. 2, p. 435.
16. De Marliave, p. 48 (genders of Sun and Moon not given).
17. Barandiaran, p. 102.
18. De Marliave, p. 48-49.

Chapter 12. She Who Makes the Day Glad

1. Grimm, p. 741.
2. Ranke, p. 157.
3. Young (1954), p. 12-13.
4. *MOAR*, Vol. 2, p. 196-197.
5. Grimm, p. 705.
6. Hollander, p. 113.
7. Bray, p. 31.
8. Rydberg, p. 177.
9. Bray, p. 279.
10. Rydberg, p. 303.
11. Grimm, p. 1514.
12. Rydberg, p. 478.
13. Rydberg, p. 305.
14. See e.g. Anderson, p. 178.
15. Anderson, p. 177.
16. Bray, p. 17.
17. Young, p, 38; Anderson, p. 178.

18. Anderson, p. 181.
19. Young, p. 86.
20. Bray, p. 55-56; *ERE* Vol. 12, p. 102.
21. Rydberg, p. 679.
22. *Eostre* is only known from the writings of the Venerable Bede. *ERE* Vol. 12, p. 102; *CE* Vol. 5, p. 224, 227. Her continental counterpart was Ostara. Hares or rabbits *dance* to greet this goddess of spring—nothing to do with "lunar" rabbits but with "Mad March hares."
23. Rydberg, p. 304.
24. Wilkins, p. 101, note 30.
25. Gelling and Davidson, p. 179. The association of the twins with the Sun in folk-customs continue into the 19th century and was connected with the kindling of the needfire, i.e., the ritual recreation of the *bringing of fire* was associated with the reappearance of the Sun. However, the authors opt for the twins *being* the Sun who fertilizes Mother Earth (see Chapter 25). As a result of this rejecting of actual northern Sun-tradition, they are puzzled by the "figure with weapon" who stands beside the "mystic marriage" scene in Bronze Age carvings. Deleting the female Sun generates all kinds of spurious "mysteries" like this.
26. Mueller, Vol 2, p. 435.
27. Neumann, p. 229.
28. These elves dwell in the furthest East. Parrinder (1971), p. 16.
29. Gardiner, p. 485 (N5); Grimm, p. 1500.
30. Briffault, Vol 3, p. 67.
31. Rydberg, p. 248.
32. Grimm, p. 1512-1513. Cf. Baltic folktale in which the son of Perkhons, in revenge against the Sun-goddess, forges for her a golden chair from which she cannot rise (Coxwell, p. 926)—an unusual explanation for the Arctic Sun's failure to rise in winter.
33. See below, Chapter 17.
34. Grimm, p. 1501 (he calls the Sun "he.")
35. Grimm, p. 1501-1502.
36. Grimm, p. 705.
37. *ERE* Vol.2 p. 34.
38. Rydberg, p. 468; Grimm, p. 705.
39. Olcott, p. 198.
40. Olcott, p. 38-39.
41. Olcott, p. 42. Cf Rubulis, p. 19. There are many connections between Bavarian and Slavic lore. (Baring-Gould, p. 247-248)
42. Grimm, p. 1500. E.g. *Sunnebrunno* near Dusseldorf.
43. Rydberg, p. 397.
44. Rydberg, p. 428.
45. A similar taboo is thought to account for the lack of English place-names connected with Freya. English Christian tradition taboos the giving of the holy name *Jesus* to mere mortals (whereas some European countries have no such taboo).
46. Tolkien (1968), p. 176 and note, p. 865.
47. Tolkien (1983), Vol. I, p. 186-187. The Moon-ship is male, *Rana*, also the spirit who steers it, *Ilinsor*, while the Man-in-the-Moon is another character.
48. *En. Rel.* Vol. 2, p. 52. (The oars are sunrays.)
49. Tyler, p. 19 (This entry seems to insinuate that the Sun is male.)
50. The Nazis called Frau Sonne "Mother of the Aryan Nation." In the S.S. wedding ceremony

she was represented by a sunburst made from herbs and flowers.

Chapter 13. Mother of the Merciful Rays

1. *Larousse* (1972), p. 423.
2. Spencer, p. 91-98; Vorren and Manker, p. 94-129.
3. The principal source for this Chapter is Harva (Holmberg) (1927) and *MOAR*, Vol. 4.
4. Collinder, p. 144-145.
5. Collinder, p. 144.
6. The fire symbolized the Sun's heat. *En. Rel.* Vol. 12, p. 499.
7. Collinder, p. 144-145.
8. In the Finnish epic, the *Kalevala*, the Sun is called "God's spindle."
9. *En. Rel.* Vol. 12, p. 499.
10. *Larousse* (1968), p. 307. Although Shundi-mumi is the Sun, the following list is given: "Obin-murt, rain-man; Vu-murt, water-man; Shundi-mumi, mother of the sun; Muzem-mumi, earth mother." This is an attempt to make it seem as if Shundi-mumi is the mother "of" some other Sun, by inconsistent and misleading translation. It is not what the Votyak believed.
11. Harva in *MOAR*, Vol. 4, p. 222-223.
12. *Larousse* (1972), p. 435-436.
13. Harva in *MOAR*, Vol. 4, p. 309-422.
14. Eliade (1964), p. 148. This is the main source for details of the shamanic costume and accessories.
15. Most of the peoples of Turkish origin in Siberia have a feminine Sun and masculine Moon. Harva, *MOAR*, Vol. 4, p. 422.
16. *MOAR*, Vol. 4, p. 420.
17. Coxwell, p. 96-97.
18. *MOAR*, Vol. 4, p. 421.
19. *Larousse* (1968), p. 435.

Chapter 14. The Great Warmer

1. Bruemmer, p. 55, 130.
2. Weyer, p. 384. A parhelion is an illusion of two or more suns, caused by certain atmospheric conditions.
3. Weyer, p. 382.
4. Weyer, p. 383.
5. Rasmussen (1908), p. 173.
6. Briffault, Vol. II, p. 627, admits the Moon-god *stokes* her fires, but elsewhere (Vol. II, p. 721) twists the sense of this motif: "The sun, who is the sister of the moon, plays no part in their theology, and the heat and light of the luminary are supposed to be derived from the moon."
7. Herbert (1976), p. 26.
8. Weyer, p. 387.
9. Nansen, p. 277.
10. Alexander, p. 8.
11. Details and illustrations are given in Dorothy Jean Ray's *Eskimo Masks*.
12. Grosvenor, p. 94.
13. Herbert (1976), p. 97.

14. Rasmussen (1908), p. 176-177 and (1921) p. 82.
15. Weyer, p. 386-387.
16. Rasmussen (1908), p. 174.
17. Jeness, p. 179 (and note).
18. Nansen, p. 276.
19. This version given in Savill (1978).
20. *En. Rel.* Vol. 10, p. 88.
21. Herbert (1976), p. 35-36.
22. Very full details of this complex masculine Moon are given in *Larousse* (1965), p. 444, and Weyer, p. 381-385. Claims that the Eskimo worship a "Moon-goddess" are based on misinterpretations of a female character who goes to the Moon after death, or because the Moon-god abducts her. The Sea-mother Sedna is also *not* the Moon; she lives permanently on the sea-bed and never travels through the sky or does anything identifiably lunar. This false idea is due to a facile equation—the Moon affects the sea, therefore all sea-goddesses must be Moon-goddesses, or even all Great Goddesses are Moon-goddesses.

Chapter 15. Great Sun, Six-Killer

1. Briffault, Vol. 2, p. 578.
2. A useful essay on these hybrid religions is to be found in *Fodor's Guide to Indian America.*
3. In a Dene (Tinneh) story two lost travellers meet a radiantly beautiful woman who tells them she is the Sun. Her husband the Moon, patron of travellers, helps them find their way home. Coxwell, p. 92.
4. According to Olcott (p. 37), some Iroquois consider the Sun female. Among some Huron, the Sun is the face of *Ataentsic*, a woman who fell from heaven and who was too bright to look upon. *En. Rel.* Vol. 10, p. 88. Other Indian groups consider Ataentsic to be the Moon, but some of her features suggest that she was once a primitive Sun-goddess.
5. Stirling (1945).
6. However, the Sun of some western tribes is Spider-woman, an important mythic figure. *ERE* Vol. 12, p, 68.
7. Briffault, Vol. II, p. 721-722.
8. Levi-Strauss, Vol. 4, p. 564-565.
9. Levi-Strauss, Vol. 4, p. 235-237.
10. Gifford and Block, p. 158.
11. Gifford and Block, p. 158; Olcott, p. 132.
12. Gifford and Block, p. 158.
13. Gifford and Block, p. 154.
14. The smoke-hole, like the hearthstone, pillar, tent-pole, etc., are in shamanic religions imagined to be the routes to the upper and lower worlds.
15. Olcott, p. 7.
16. Gibbs, p. 32-38.
17. Gibbs, p. 61.
18. Personal communication 22/4/88, Chief Hugh Gibbs.
19. According to Hugh Gibbs, this version (Alexander, p. 56) combines two distinct myths, the bringing of the Sun and the origin of fire.
20. Clarke, p. 207. (She calls the Sun-goddess "he.")
21. Alexander, p. 56, 60.

22. Olcott, p. 5.
23. See below, Chapter 17.
24. Olcott, p. 98-99.
25. Alexander, p. 55-56.
26. Durdin-Robertson, (1982), p. 332.
27. Mooney, p. 252-254.
28. *ERE* Vol. 12, p. 66-67, and general article "Cherokee." The ritual ball-play is associated with the Moon-god, but since it has come to be played in *daylight*, the players are warned that the Sun is watching them and will see if they mishandle the ball (i.e. profane the Moon). *ERE* is incorrect in saying the ball-play is sacred to the Sun. See Culin, p. 574-588.
29. Speck (1909), p. 102-111; Alexander, p. 56.

Chapter 16. Tales of the Sky Women

1. Briffault, Vol. 2, p. 739. *Larousse* (1968), p. 486. Unsourced material in this Chapter came from my early notes made in the British Museum Ethnography Department Library in the '70's. Due to the present economic situation, this library has recently been closed to everyone except Fellows of the Royal Anthropological Institute.
2. *Larousse* (1972), p. 485.
3. Stone (1979), Vol. 1, p. 79-80.
4. Briffault, Vol. 2, p. 284.
5. Stone, Vol. 1, p. 80. See also below, Chapter 19.

Chapter 17. Goddess of Life

1. *Parabola* VIII, p. 59-60 (Berndt, 1979); Briffault, Vol. 2 p. 694.
2. Smith (1930), p. 23-58.
3. Smith (1930), p. 34.
4. Smith (1930), p. 31-58.
5. Smith (1930), p. 44.
6. Smith (1930), p. 69-71.
7. Parker (1905), p. 98.
8. Smith (1930), p. 55, 67-69.
9. Waterman, p. 29, no. 141.
10. Waterman, p. 28, no. 129.
11. Waterman, p. 30, no. 159.
12. Waterman, p. 28, no. 129.
13. Waterman, p. 29, no. 147.
14. Dixon, in *MOAR*, Vol. 9, p. 276. *En. Rel.* Vol. 10, p. 88.
15. Waterman, p. 29, no. 138.
16. Spencer and Gillen (1899), p. 561. Compare the Baltic daina in which the Sun-goddess goes down a "deep rock pit." Benjamins, p. 8.
17. *ERE* entries "Sun" and "Australia."
18. Spencer and Gillen (1899), p. 563-564.
19. Spencer and Gillen (1904), p. 624-625.
20. Spencer and Gillen (1899), p. 566.
21. Waterman, p. 29, no. 135.

22. Howitt, p. 427.
23. Howitt, p. 428.
24. Waterman, p. 64, nos. 1800, 1805.
25. See note 1.
26. Harvey, p. 46-49.
27. Harvey, p. 92-93.
28. Harvey, p. 46, 127.
29. *Larousse, Ancient Art* (1962), p. 79.
30. Notes from book *The Australian Aboriginal*, no author or date.
31. *MOAR*, Vol. 9, p. 275.
32. *MOAR*, Vol. 9, p. 275.
33. E.g. Harvey, p. 138.

Chapter 18. She Who Darts Forth Her Rays

1. Hugo Winckler, in Cheyne and Black, Vol. 4, p. 4821.
2. There are few major sources in English on pre-Islamic religion. The principal ones (and on which this chapter is based) are the articles in *NCE* Vol. 1, p. 716-721, *En. Brit.* Vol. 24, p. 71 *et seq.*, and *ERE* Vol 1, p. 661.
3. The main Islamic source on pagan religion is the *Book of Idols*, c. 800 A.D., by Hisham ibn Al-Kalbi. It deals only with the Meccan deities and contains virtually nothing about astral worship.
4. The state of academic knowledge on pre-Islamic religion is still backward, archaeology likewise. Islamic countries have no motivation to find out about their pagan past.
5. This mistake comes from Huart's *History of the Arabs* and is repeated for example in Walker (1983), entry "Sun."
6. *ERE* Vol. 1, p. 882.
7. The Akkadians (south Mesopotamia, 3rd millenium B.C.) changed the sex of the Sun-goddess, "a change which was latterly imposed on the entire north-west Semitic religions." Langdon, p. 4-5.
8. *RSW*, p. 20.
9. Westermarck, p. 111.
10. *NCE* Vol. 1, p. 719; *ERE* Vol. 1, p. 884; Smith (1927), p. 94, note 6.
11. Westermarck, p. 111-113. Some Central Africans do this too; Olcott, p. 121.
12. *J. En.* Vol. 8, p. 1046; Whitehead, p. 24.
13. In Bulgaria, on St. John's Day (Midsummer) the rising Sun-god loses his way, and the dawn-maiden appears to lead him on the right path. Ralston (1872), p. 171, 42. (The Slav Sun became male in Bulgaria through Mithraic influence.) See also Eddic Sun-goddess, Chapter 12.
14. Legey, p. 43 et seq.
15. Musil, p. 1-2.
16. For similar titles of the Moon-god see Langdon, p. 15.
17. The Moon-god of Ur was called *Sin* (Moon), *Nannar* (bright one) and *Aku* (disc). He was represented as an aged man with bright horns and a crystal beard. *RSW*, p. 19. The Moon was widely honoured under the name Sin. Sinai (Mountain of Sin), where Moses received the Ten Commandments (according to Hebrew mythology) was an important cult site of the Moon/bull god, which is probably why the Israelites made a golden calf, and why Moses came

down wearing "horns" (or with a "shining face.") Exodus 34. 29.

18. See for example Walker (1989), Introduction, ix.

19. There were pagan monotheists of Allah before Islam proper. According to Muslims they called themselves *hunafa*, "orthodox." Lings, p. 16.

20. Monaghan (1981), p. 10: "By the salt, by the fire, and by Allat who is greatest of all," an oath of the pagan Arabs.

21. Allat is still known as the Sun in Arab traditions (Langdon, p. 15). Strabo called Allat "the Sun-god" (*ERE* Vol. 1, p. 661) while Herodotus (I.131) identified her with Mithra. (Bayley, Vol. I, p. 283).

22. Lurker, entry "Allat."

23. Winnet, p. 115.

24. Lings, p. 5, 15, 183, 301.

25. Lings, p. 321.

26. Parrinder (1971), p. 161. The story of these verses was recounted by Ibn Ishaq, Mohammed's biographer.

27. Sura LIII "The Star," v. 19 et seq. (Arberry translation).

28. *En. Rel.* Vol. 10, p. 85.

29. Sura XXVII v. 24.

30. "By the Sun and his glorious splendour, by the Moon as she follows him." (Sura XCI "The Sun" v, 1,2) The Sun is revelation, the Moon the prophets who reflect it.

31. Briffault, Vol. 1, p. 376-377.

32. Lings, p. 320.

33. Schuon (1981), p. 221.

34. Westermarck, p. 111-112.

35. Gaster (1975), p. 249.

Chapter 19. Shakti Power of the Sun's Light

1. Al Faruqi, p. 71-72.

2. Alston (1956), p. 83.

3. Whitehead, p. 37.

4. Whitehead, p. 22, Plate 3.

5. Whitehead, p. 37-38.

6. *Mas*, directly equivalent to Iranian *Mah*, is the Moon-god of the Vedic Hindus. See below, Chapter 20.

7. See e.g. Mookerjee and Khanna, *The Tantric Way*, pp. 93-123.

8. Eliade (1964), p. 421 et seq.

9. This myth is also found among Malayan tribes, e.g. the *Nimtira*, whose Sun-goddess and Moon-goddess plan to eat their children, to save humans from so much brightness and heat. But the Moon hid her children. This myth is enacted every day, when the Sun eats her children at dawn, while her sister hides hers until night, when the angry Sun-goddess is far away. Cox, p. 245.

10. Elwin, p. 57.

11. Elwin, p. 62.

12. Elwin, p. 56.

13. Gurdon, p. 83.

14. Gurdon, p. 144-147.

15. Gurdon, p. 82.
16. Gurdon, p. 209.
17. Gurdon, p. 165; Stone (1979), Vol. II, p. 27.
18. Gurdon, p. 165.
19. Gurdon, p. 172.
20. Gurdon, p. 109.
21. Gurdon, p. 156.
22. Gurdon, p. 70, 167.

Chapter 20. She Who Maintains the World

1. See Sir Mortimer Wheeler's account of the excavations in his *Early India & Pakistan*.
2. Al Faruqi, p. 71.
3. Briffault, Vol. 1, p. 347.
4. Al Faruqi, p. 71; Parrinder (1980), pp. 6-7.
5. See article on Arya Samaj in *ERE* Vol. 2, p. 57-62.
6. See Boyce, p. 6. The Indo-Iranians did not have a Moon-goddess. The Iranian *Anahita* was a dawn-goddess very like Eos or Ushas. She was *imported* from Mesopotamia and amalgamated with the native river-goddess Aredvi-Sura. She has nothing to do with the Moon. (Boyce, p. 61) See also *NCE* 9. 1103.
7. During the ceremony, a *mirror* is placed in the bride's left hand. *ERE* Vol. 8, p. 696.
8. They are *Divo napala*, "Sons of God" (*Dyaus*) Ward (1967), p. 235.
9. A useful compilation of sources on Suryā is to be found in Durdin-Robertson's *Goddesses of India, China and Tibet*.
10. *Suryasakta*: see Griffith (1892), Vol. 4, p. 266-268; O'Flaherty (1981), p. 267.
11. See Kraft, *The Goddess in the Labyrinth*; also Sterne, *The Northern Origin of the Story of Troy*.
12. For example, at Konarak. Surya had an important cult at Benares. There have also been found traces of a *female* Sun-cult, the Sun-goddess being *Chakresvari* (Eck, p. 180-181.)
13. Eck, p. 182-183, 274.
14. *Larousse* (1972), p. 230.
15. *Larousse* (1972), p. 230. For multi-armed Sun-goddess, see Chapter 17.
16. *NCE* Vol. 9, p. 796; "Every Hindu began his day with a prayer and a hymn of praise to the sun (Surya) the giver (feminine) of light, heat and fruitfulness."
17. Parrinder (1980), p. 13: The goddess Savitri is "like a golden statue." Such brilliance comes from her that people are dazzled and cannot approach her.
18. Danielou, p. 93.
19. Danielou, p. 93.
20. Another goddess, *Shri*, lived in the Sun. She was also called *Anushayini*. She descended from the Sun to Earth, and her eyes lit up the room. (Jobes, p. 1443) *Devi*, a complex goddess, also has some very significant solar features—she absorbed many aboriginal goddesses. In Hindu Bali, *Devi Shri* is the Rice Mother, who lives in heaven as well as descending to Earth and being mystically present in the rice-crop. Archaic representations of her often show her with a radiate crown, or in a mother-daughter pair, or as twins. Her daughter is *Devi Melanting*, goddess of gardens. This recalls the relationship between Amaterasu and Toyo-Uke-bime (see above, Chapter 7). Japan and Indonesia share certain aboriginal south-east Asian influences—the resemblance between the architecture of Ise and that of Balinese rice

granaries is not coincidental. See Covarrubias, p. 172-181; Bayley, p. 178.

21. See entry on *Ushas* in Durdin- Robertson; also Ward (1967) and Dexter (1986).

22. See Durdin-Robertson, note 21.

23. O'Flaherty (1980). In Tibetan Tantra, semen is called "moon-fluid." Parrinder (1980), p. 52.

24. Like the Zoroastrians, the Vedic Hindus distinguished fire in a wide number of forms. The flames of Agni are female: O'Flaherty (1981), p. 118. Menstrual blood is a form of Agni. See also *Larousse* (1968), p. 231.

25. Danielou, p. 99.

26. Briffault, Vol. 3, p. 133; Vol.. 2, p. 585 (personified as Soma).

27. Briffault, Vol. 3, p.199.

28. Danielou, p. 99.

29. Danielou, p. 99-101.

30. Danielou, p. 101.

31. Ions, p. 81; *Larousse* (1968), p. 233, 245.

32. Eck, p. 176.

33. O'Flaherty (1981), p. 151-156.

34. Aston (1956), p. 44. The "inspired utterance," a mystic sequence of numbers, spoken by Uzume the shaman-goddess, released Amaterasu from the cave.

35. See compilation "Aditi" in Durdin-Robertson (Note 9).

36. The Greek *Anaxagoras* (500-428 B.C.) devised a theory of lunar phases, based on his idea that the Moon shines by reflected sunlight. Sagan (1981), p. 182.

37. Mookerjee and Khanna, *The Tantric Way*.

38. Dexter (1986).

Chapter 21. Fiery Needles

1. Rustaveli, vv. 523-4, p. 80.

2. Coxwell, p. 1021. The author calls these "curious conceptions," but they are exactly reproduced in Basque Sun-goddess tradition (see above, Chapter 11). Some scholars believe there to have been ancient connections between Basque and Georgian cultures.

3. *En. Rel.* Vol. 1, p. 418; *ERE* Vol. I, p. 798-799.

4. Coxwell, p. 1021.

5. None of the sources on Armenian lore available to me gives the name of the feminine Sun.

6. Ananikian, p. 51.

7. See Chapter 9, note.

8. Ralston (1872), e.g. p. 190.

9. *ERE* Vol. I, p. 796.

10. Coxwell, p. 1016-1018.

11. Seklemian, p. 129.

12. Surmelian, (1968).

13. Seklemian, p. 47-48.

14. Personal communication, Frances Howard-Gordon. (Information directly obtained from ancient history specialists in Georgia itself, 1989.) See also below, Chapter 24.

15. See note 14.

16. See the translation by Urushadze (1979).

17. Personal communication, Frances Howard-Gordon. The solar identity of Medea is analyzed in Monaghan, *The Sun Goddess*.

18. Rice (1957), p. 48. See also Rothery, *The Amazons in Antiquity and Modern Times*.
19. Armed women have been found in Sarmatian but not Scythian cemeteries (Rice, p. 48). See also Rolle pp. 86-91.
20. Markale, p. 105, 109.
21. See Markale, p. 109, 240.
22. The amputation of the breast by Amazons ought to be compared with Eskimo myth (Chapter 14). The Artemis of Ephesus, whose appendages are supposed to be breasts, is in fact dressed (as recent research as shown) in the testicles of castrated bulls. This Artemis was closely associated with the Phrygian Moon-deity, a masculine god, *Men*, later identified with Attis— who castrated himself. Artemis may be wearing the testicles of her castrated lunar husband, "Bull-faced" Men.

Chapter 22. She Who Dwells in the Spacious Disc

1. Smith (1927), p. 517.
2. The principal sources for this chapter are Budge, *The Gods of the Egyptians*, Vol. 2; the compilations on the various goddesses in Durdin-Robertson's *The Goddesses of Syria, Chaldea and Egypt*, and Ames' *Egyptian Mythology*.
3. See above, Chapter 18, note 13, on the Sun-leading motif. Among some aboriginal tribes of India the Sun is led along a string by her husband. A rope also figures in Amaterasu's myth (see above, Chapter 7) where it is used, although somewhat differently, to keep the Sun where she ought to be.
4. See Briffault, Vol. 2, p. 681, for his confused (and erroneous) argument that all Egyptian Sun-discs are really the Moon. Also compare Rush (p. 83): "Most musical instruments are made in lunar forms." Since crescent-shaped instruments are somewhat rare items, what is meant here are *round* instruments. This is a facile assumption that anything round must be lunar, as if there was no other round object in the universe but the Moon!
5. See above, Chapter 18.
6. Smith (1927), p. 516-517. The term "Father and Mother" is often found in Near Eastern hymns, etc., as a term of praise (see below, Chapter 23) but does not necessarily mean that culture believed the deity to be androgynous, nor that they were "confused" as to its sex.
7. *NCE*, Vol. 9, p. 1103.
8. Briffault, Vol. II, p. 763-789; Ames, p.27, 99.

Chapter 23. Lady Sun, Light of the Gods

1. Briffault, Vol 2, p. 596.
2. i.e., into the fertile irrigated valleys. Al Faruqi, p. 5.
3. Jeremiah 44. 17, 25. This is misinterpreted as referring to a "Moon-goddess" by spiritual-feminists and others. The Moon was a *king*, not a queen, to the Canaanites.
4. See compilations "Shams" and "Shapash" in Durdin-Robertson (1975).
5. *J. En.* Vol. 15, p. 516-518.
6. Genesis 15. 17.
7. Psalms 104.19.
8. Cheyne and Black, Vol. IV, p. 4821; Oesterley and Robinson, p. 32.
9. See e.g. Numbers 31. 17, 18; Judges 21. 11, 12.
10. *ERE* Vol.2, p. 283-285.

11. Smith (1927), p. 94 (and note 6).
12. Driver (1956), p. 16-18.
13. Driver (1956), p. 17.
14. Gordon (1965), p. 493-494.
15. Driver, p. 13, 19.
16. The replacement of Hadad by Athtar—essentially deity of irrigation (see Gaster (1975), p. 133, note 6) is the replacement of rain by artificial watering in the dry season.
17. Driver (1956), p. 109.
18. Gaster (1975), p. 94.
19. Young (1981), p. 168. "Shapash the lamp of the gods [was burning hot] without [rain of] heaven on account of Mot,: Driver (1956), p. 91, 103.
20. Gaster (1975), p. 94.
21. Driver, p. 113.
22. Driver (1956), p. 19.
23. Gaster (1975), p. 100-101.
24. Gaster (1975), p. 230.
25. Driver (1956), p. 22. Observant readers will notice that here again we have the association of the morning/evening *twins*, sons of the sky-god, with the Sun-goddess. The text says "They [Shahar and Shalim] are set down beside the Lady Sun and the fixed stars." Gaster (1975), p. 431.
26. Gordon (1949), p. 4-5.
27. For alternative spellings, see Sykes' Dictionary, entry *El* and *Jerah*.
28. *En. Brit.* Vol., 24, p. 73-76.
29. Gordon's *Ugaritic Literature* contains the Yarikh hymn. He identifies Nikkal as "a" Moon-goddess, but see above, Chapter 23.
30. Reinach, p. 89.
31. Lindsay, p. 70-71.
32. Only Gaster (1975), p. 47, gives her full credit for her "particularly important role."

Chapter 24. Mistress of the Righteous Judgement

1. Gaster (1975), p. 269. Title page from Schwarz, *A Hittite Ritual Text.*
2. The Hurrians were a non-Indo-European, non-Semitic people from the Armenian mountains. They lived in Anatolia and Mesopotamia during the second millenium B.C. Their language had some affinities with Georgian.
3. Gaster (1975), p. 88-89, 96.
4. Stone (1979), preface.
5. Keel, p. 207.
6. Lehmann, p. 264-265.
7. Cf. Psalm 19, v. 4-6.
8. Cf. Genesis 7.11, 2 Kings 7.2, 19. In Rabbinical tradition the Sun is provided with 366 windows in the sky, through which it successively appears and vanishes during the course of the year. *J. En.* Vol. 15, p. 517.
9. British Museum catalogue number WA 125012.
10. Cotterell, p. 49-51.
11. Kramer, p. 149.
12. Lurker, p. 36.

13. *En. Rel.*, entry "Hittites" refres to Puduhepa, for example, but Arinniti is not even mentioned.
14. Cooper (1978), p. 16.
15. Also on p. 52 "Sun God" (Hittite) but on p. 60 "sun-goddess" (Ugarit). Examples like these show how entrenched and perhaps unconscious is the prejuduce against the feminine Sun.
16. James (1967), p. 95. James argues that *every* goddess who goes underground is the Earth-goddess, even Inanna and Ishtar (p. 78). But Canaanite and Arabic terms for "setting of the sun" are connected with the words "to go underground" and in an stronomical tablet Ishtar is described as the *Sun* and as the *evening star* (i.e. at sunset) Gordon (1965), p. 451 and Sayce (1887), p. 253.
17. Chicago, p. 104.
18. Walker (1983), p. 57.

Chapter 25. Far-Seeing Mother of the Eyes

1. Kerenyi (1979), p. 2.
2. Leland, p. 90.
3. Durham, p. 110.
4. *OED*, entry "Sun," 3a (the poem is dated 1450).
5. Leland, p. 93.
6. Matthew 18. 9.
7. Frothingham, p. 352.
8. Compilation Lucia/Lucina/Lucy in Durdin-Robertson (1975).
9. James (1961), p. 293.
10. A slightly different version is given by Cooper (1982), p. 96.
11. Sandys, p. 547-551.
12. The Japanese also believed the solar feminine principle, *hi*, to be present in trees. See above, Chapter 7.
13. Robert Graves dismissed Eos as nothing but a "Hellenic fancy," which could hardly be further from the truth!
14. She had her own chariot drawn by *twin horses*, "Shining" and "Bright."
15. Kereny (1979), p. 2.
16. *Men* was represented as a young man in floppy trousers and a Phrygian bonnet, wearing the crescent Moon, or carrying the orb of the full Moon in his hand. He ruled over both the sky and the underworld, produced rain, and encouraged the growth of plants in his waxing phase. The fact that he was, unusually for such a god, worshipped separately from the Great Goddess in his principal shrines,, may indicate a Sun-goddess/Moon-god divorce theme.
17. Briffault, Vol. 3, p. 120.
18. Olcott, p. 255.
19. A fact admitted by Briffault, Vol. 3, p. 48.
20. Briffault, Vol. 3, p. 193.
21. Briffault, Vol. 3, p. 120.
22. Ward (1967), p. 238.
23. The penis symbolized as a Sun-ray is an invented motif which is *not*, as is claimed, general and universally-true in mythology. Quite the contrary—it is nowhere to be found, except perhaps in connection with Dionysos who was in any case not the Sun, but the Moon (Briffault, Vol. 3, p. 130-143), solar ideas being added to his cult in late times. Sky-gods shed *rain* into the Earth, not sunlight.

24. Whole books and theories are built on this false idea, resulting in a gross distortion of mythology—see e.g. Branston *The Lost Gods of England*, which ignores and deletes Sunna (even erasing her name from Snorri's list of goddesses) and other information in order to preserve the solar sky-father dogma.

Chapter 26. Releasing the Sun

1. Cited in "Another Look at Christianity," *Freethought Today* (Freedom from Religion Foundation, P.O. Box 750, Madison, WI 53701, USA), April 1990, p. 11.
2. The idea that if something is *original* it is therefore *true* is based on extremely conservative and reactionary ideas of religious truth. It's a false idea, just like the idea that because something *comes* from something else, it *is* that thing itself. On this basis, humans are amoebae and oak trees are plankton!
3. For a clear discussion of the reason/intuition issue, see Richards, Chapter 1. The popular fallacy that reason is located in the left, "solar" hemisphere of the brain and intuition in the right, "lunar" hemisphere, is refuted in Hines, p. 297-301.
4. See Budapest, p. 232-235. Patriarchal beliefs are "incredibly bad mythology" from which people need to be exorcised and their intuition retrained.
5. Gooch, p. 52.
6. See for example "Bride's Day," Monica Sjöö, *Wood and Water*, Spring 1990, Vol. 2, No. 31, part II, p. 12. This is Neoplatonism slightly rehashed.
7. Sagan (1977), p. 237-238.
8. Creative ways in which we can explore a life-affirming yet rational approach are found in Larue's *The Way of Positive Humanism* (1989).
9. On the issue of "faith in" science and objectivity, see George H. Smith's clear exposition in *Atheism, the Case Against God*, p. 145 et seq.
10. A lucid discussion of what exactly is *natural* and how far we are bound by it is to be found in Richards, Chapter 2.

Bibliography

Abbreviations

CE   *Catholic Encyclopaedia.* Caxton, London, 1907-1918.
En. Brit.   *Encyclopaedia Britannica.* 1989 edition.
En. Rel.   *The Encyclopaedia of Religion.* Ed. Mircea Eliade, Collier Macmillan, London, 1987.
ERE   *Encyclopaedia of Religion and Ethics.* Ed. J. Hastings, T.&T. Clark, Edinburgh, 1908-1921.
Funk and Wagnall.
            Funk and Wagnall's Dictionary of Folklore and Mythology. Ed. Maria Leach, New York, 1949.
J. En.   *Jewish Encyclopaedia.* Keter Publishing, Jerusalem, 1972.
Larousse   *Larousse Encyclopaedia of Mythology,* 1959 and 1968 editions.
MOAR   *Mythology of All Races.* Ed. J.A. MacCulloch, 1916, 1931, Ed. Louis H. Gray, 1964.
NCE   *New Catholic Encyclopaedia.* McGraw-Hill, New York and London, 1967.
RSW   *Religious Systems of the World.* George Allen and Unwin, 1889, 10th edn. 1911.

Journals and Magazines

Caerdroia (Mazes and Labyrinths) 53, Thundersley Grove, Thundersley, Benfleet, Essex, U.K.
Free Inquiry (Quarterly Journal of the Council for Democratic and Secular Humanism) 10, Crescent View, Loughton, Essex, U.K; 3159, Bailey Avenue, Buffalo, NY 14215, U.S.A.
Freethought Today (Monthly newspaper) Freedom from Religion Foundation, P.O. Box 750, Madison, Wisconsin WI 53701, U.S.A.
Harvest (Eight times yearly newsletter, modern Wiccan and neopaganism) P.O. Box 228, South Framingham, MA 01701, U.S.A.
Pipes of Pan (Quarterly, anti-nuclear, neopagan) Pagans Against Nukes, Blaenberem, Mynyddcernig, Nr Llanelli, Dyfed, Wales.
Skeptical Inquirer (Journal of the Committee for the Scientific Investigation of Claims of the Paranormal) 10, Crescent View, Loughton, Essex, U.K; Box 229, Buffalo, NY 14215-0229, U.S.A.

Womanspirit. Published between 1975-1984, forty issues. Ed. Ruth and Jean Mountaingrove, Wolf Creek, Oregon, U.S.A.

Wood and Water (Goddess movement, ecopaganism) 4, High Tor Close, Babbacombe Rd., Bromley, Kent, U.K.

Bibliography

Adler, Margot. *Drawing Down the Moon*. Beacon Press, Boston, 1979, 1986.

Alexander, Hartley Burr. "North American Mythology". *MOAR* 1964, Vol. 4.

Al-Faruqi, I.R. and Sopher, D.E. *Historical Atlas of the Religions of the World*. Macmillan, New York, 1974.

Ames, Delano (Trans.) *Egyptian Mythology*. Hamlyn, 1965.

Ananikian, Mardiros H. "Armenian Mythology," *MOAR* 1964, Vol. 7.

Anderson, Rasmus B. *Norse Mythology*. Foresman and Co., Chicago, 1898.

Anesaki, Masaharu. *History of Japanese Religion*. London, 1930.

Arberry, Arthur J. *The Koran Interpreted*. Oxford University Press, n.d.

Armstrong, E.A. *The Folklore of Birds*. Collins, 1958.

Asimov, Isaac. (1) *Asimov's Guide to the Bible*. Avenel Books, NY, 1981.

Asimov, Isaac. (2) *The Relativity of Wrong*. Oxford Paperbacks, 1989.

Aston, W.G. (1) *Nihongi, Chronicles of Japan*. George Allen and Unwin, 1956 (1896).

Aston, W.G. (2) *Shinto, The Way of the Gods*. Longmans, Green and Co., London, 1905.

Bachofen, J.J. *Myth, Religion and Mother Right*, 3 Vols. Princeton University Press, 1861.

Baggott, Rev. l. J. *Spiritual Priorities*, SPCK, London, 1963.

Balys, Jonas, *Latvian Mythology* and *Lithuanian Mythology*, *Funk & Wagnall*, 1949.

Barandiaran, Jose Miguel de, *Mythologie Basque*. Annales Pyrenees, ESPER, Toulouse, 1989.

Baring-Gould, S. *Strange Survivals*. Methuen, 1892.

Batchelor, John. *The Ainu and their Folk Lore*. Religious Tract Society, London, 1901.

Bayley, Harold. *The Lost Language of Symbolism*. Benn, 1968 (reprint).

Beard, Charles R. *Lucks and Talismans, A Chapter of Popular Superstition*. Sampson, Low and Marston, 1934.

Benet, Sula. *Song, Dance and Customs of Peasant Poland*. Dennis Dobson, London, 1951.

Benjamins, Eso. *Dearest Goddess: Translations from Latvian Folk Poetry*. Current Nine Publishing, Arlington, 1985.

Berndt, Catherine H. *Land of the Rainbow Snake*. Collins, 1979.

Biezais, Haralds. "Baltic Religion," *Encyclopaedia Britannica*, Vol. 18, p. 905-909.

Blacker, Carmen. *The Catalpa Bow—A Study of Shamanistic Practices in Japan*. George Allen and Unwin, 1975.

Blakeborough, Richard. *Yorkshire Wit; Character, Folklore and Customs of the North Riding of Yorkshire*. W. Rapp and Sons, Saltburn, 1911.

Bonwick, James. (1) *Daily Life and Orighin of the Tasmanians*. Sampson, Low and Marston, 1870.

Bonwick, James. (2) *Irish Druids and Old Irish Religions*. Dorset Press, U.S.A. (1986 reprint)

Borlase, William Copeland. *The Dolmens of Ireland*. 3 Vols. Chapman and Hall, London, 1897.

Bouquet, A.C. *Sacred Books of the World*. Cassell, 1962.

Boyce, Mary. *Zoroastrians, Their Religious Beliefs and Practices*. Routledge and Kegan Paul, 1979.

Branston, Brian. (1) *The Lost Gods of England*. Thames and Hudson, 1974.

Branston, Brian. (2) *The Gods of the North*. Thames and Hudson, 1964.

Bray, Olive, ed. and trans. *The Elder or Poetic Edda*. Viking Club, 1908.

Breasted, James H. *The Development of Religion and and Thought in Ancient Egypt*. London, 1912.

Brennan, Martin. (1) *The Boyne Valley Vision*. Dolmen Press, Eire, 1980.

Brennan, Martin. (2) *The Stars and the Stones, Ancient Art and Astronomy in Ireland*. Thames and Hudson, 1983.

Briffault, Robert. *The Mothers*. 3 Vols. George Allen and Unwin, 1927.

Brown, Peter Lancaster. *Megaliths and Masterminds*. Robert Hale, 1979.

Bruemmer, Fred. *Seasons of the Eskimo*. McClelland and Stewart, Toronto, 1971.

Budapest, Zsuzsanna. *The Holy Book of Women's Mysteries*. Wingbow Press, Berkeley, 1989.

Budge, Wallis E. *The Gods of the Egyptians*. 2 Vols. Methuen, 1904.

Burl, Aubrey. (1) *The Rites of the Gods*. Dent, 1981.

Burl, Aubrey. (2) *Prehistoric Astronomy and Ritual*. Shire, 1983.

Burland, Cottie. *North American Indian Mythology*. Hamlyn, 1968.

Cable, Mildred and French, Francesca. *The Gobi Desert*. Hodder and Stoughton, 1942.

Cadogan, Alan and Green, Nigel. *Biology*. Heinemann Educational, 1985.

Campbell, Joseph. *The Masks of God*. 4 Vols: *Primitive Mythology (1960), Oriental Mythology (1960), Occidental Mythology (1965), Creative Mythology (1968)*. Secker and Warburg, U.S.A.

Campbell, J.F. *Popular Tales of the West Highlands*. 4 Vols. Alexander Gardner, 1893.

Carmichael, A. *Carmina Gaedelica*. 4 Vols. Oliver and Boyd, 1928.

Cavendish, R. ed. *Man, Myth and Magic. An Encyclopaedia of Myth, Religion and the Unknown*. Marshall Cavendish (partwork), 1983.

Ceram, C.W. *Narrow Pass, Black Mountain; the Discovery of the Hittite Empire*. London, n.d.

Chadwick. Henry. *The Early Church*. Hodder and Stoughton, 1967.

Chamberlain, Basil Hall. (1) *The Kojiki, Records of Ancient Matters*. Tuttle/ Prentice Hall, London, 1981. (reprint)

Chamberlain, Basil Hall. (2) *Things Japanese*. 4th edn., John Murray, 1902.

Chattopadhyay, Kalamadevi. *Tribalism in India*. Vikas Publishing, India, 1978.

Chetwynd, Tom. (1) *A Dictionary of Symbols*. Paladin/ Grafton, 1982.

Chetwynd, Tom. (2) *A Dictionary of Sacred Myth*. Unwin, 1986.

Cheyne, T.K. and Black, J.S., ed. *Encyclopaedia Biblica*. Adam and Charles Black, London, 1907.

Chicago, Judy. *The Dinner Party*. Anchor/Doubleday, NY, 1979.

Cirlot, J.E. *A Dictionary of Symbols*. Routledge and Kegan Paul, 1962.

Clarke, Helen A. *ABC Guide to Mythology*. London, 1919.

Clodd, Edward. *Myths and Dreams*. Chatto and Windus, 1885.

Coleman, Marion Moore. *A World Remembered—Tales and Lore of the Polish Land*. Cherry Hill Books, Cheshire, U.S.A., 1965.

Collinder, Bjorn. *The Lapps*. Princeton University Press, 1949.

Cooper, J.C. (1) *An Illustrated Encyclopaedia of Traditional Symbols*. Thames and Hudson, 1978.

Cooper, J.C. (2) *Symbolism, The Universal Language*. Aquarian Press, 1982.

Cotterell, Arthur. *A Dictionary of World Mythology*. Guild/Book Club Associates, 1979.

Covarrubias, Miguel. *Island of Bali*. London, 1936.

Cox, Sir George W. *An Introduction to the Science of Mythology and Folklore*. Kegan Paul, 1881.

Cox, Marion Roalfe. *An Introduction to Folklore.* David Nutt, 1895.

Coxwell, C. Fillingham. *Siberian and Other Folk Tales.* C.W. Daniel Co., London, 1925.

Crow, Duncan. *The Victorian Woman.* G.A. Unwin, 1971.

Culin, Stewart. *Games of the North American Indians. 24th Annual Report of The American Bureau of Ethnology,* 1902-3. Reprinted, Dover Paperbacks, 1975.

Cumont, Franz. *The Mysteries of Mithra.* Kegan Paul, Trench and Co., 1903.

Cupitt, Don. *The Sea of Faith.* BBC Publications, 1984.

Czaplicka, M.A. *Aboriginal Siberia.* Clarendon Press, 1914.

Daly, Mary. *Gyn/Ecology—The Metaethics of Radical Feminism.* The Women's Press, 1978.

Dames, Michael. *The Silbury Treasure.* Thames and Hudson, 1976.

Danaher, K. *The Year in Ireland, A Calendar.* Mercier Press, Eire, 1972.

Danielou, Alain. *The Gods of India.* Inner Traditions, NY, 1985.

Davidson, Hilda R. Ellis. *Myths and Symbols in Pagan Europe.* Penguin, 1964.

Davies, E.C. *A Wayfarer in Estonia, Latvia and Lithuania.* Methuen, 1937.

Dawson, James. *Australian Aborigines.* George Robertson, Melbourne, 1881.

Denning, Esler. *Japan.* Ernest Benn, 1960.

Dewan, E.M. "On the possibility of a perfect rhythm method of birth control by periodic light stimulation," *American Journal of Obstetrics and Gynaecology,* Vol. 99, Issue 7, Dec. 1967.

Dexter, Miriam Roberts. (1) "Proto-Indo-European Sun-Maidens and Gods of the Moon," *Mankind Quarterly,* 1986, p. 137-141.

Dexter, Miriam Roberts. (2) *Whence the Goddesses, A Sourcebook.* Pergamon Press, 1980.

Diner, Helen. *Mothers and Amazons.* Anchor Books, Garden City, 1973 (1929).

Dinneen, Rev. Patrick S. *Irish-English Dictionary.* Irish Text Society,, Dublin, 1927.

Dixon, Roland B. "Australian Mythology," *MOAR,* Vol. 9.

Douglas, Mary. *Purity and Danger.* Penguin, 1970.

Dowley, Tim. *Handbook of the History of Christianity.* Lion, 1977.

Dowson, John. A Classical Dictionary of Hindu Mythology. Routledge and Kegan Paul, 1968.

Driver, G.R. *Canaanite Myths and Legends.* T and T Clark, Edinburgh, 1956.

Durdin-Robertson, L. (1) *The Goddesses of Chaldea, Syria and Egypt.* 1975.

Durdin-Robertson, L. (2) *The Goddesses of India, China, Tibet and Japan.* 1976.

Durdin-Robertson, L. (3) *Juno Covella, A Perpetual Calendar.* 1982, Cesara Press, Donegal, Eire.

Durham, M.E. *Some Tribal Origins, Laws and Customs of the Balkans.* George Allen and Unwin, 1928.

Dwelly, E. *Illustrated Gaelic-English Dictionary.* 1901-1911.

Eck, Diana L. *Banaras, City of Light.* Routledge and Kegan Paul, 1983.

Eliade, Mircea. (1) *A History of Religious Ideas.* 2 Vols. Chicago University Press, 1978.

Eliade, Mircea. (2) *Shamanism, Archaic Techniques of Ecstasy.* Princeton University Press, 1964.

Elwin, Verner. *Tribal Myths of Orissa.* Oxford University Press, 1954.

Faderman, Lillian. *Surpassing the Love of Men.* Junction Books, 1980.

Faris, Nabih Amin, ed. *The Arab Heritage.* Princeton University Press, 1944.

O'Flaherty, Wendy Doniger. (1) *The Rig Veda—An Anthology.* Penguin, 1982.

O'Flaherty, Wendy Doniger. (2) *Women, Androgynes and Other Mythical Beasts.* University of Chicago Press, 1980.

The Fodor Guide to Indian America. Hodder & Stoughton, 1976.

Fraser, Mrs. Hugh. *A Diplomat's Wife in Japan.* 2 Vols. Hutchinson, 1899.

Frazer, James. *The Golden Bough, A Study in Magic and Religion.* 12 Vols., 1911-1919.

Frazier, Kendrick, ed. *Science Confronts the Paranormal*. Prometheus Books, 1986.

Frothingham, A.L. "Medusa, Apollo and the Great Mother." *American Journal of Archaeology*, Macmillan, NY, Vol. 15., 1911, p. 349-37.

Gaer, Joseph. *What the Great Religions Believe*. Signet/New American Library, 1963.

Gage, Matilda Joslyn. *Woman, Church and State (1893)*. Persephone Press, Massachusetts, 1980 reprint.

Gardiner, Alan. *Egyptian Grammar*. Oxford University Press. 3rd Edition, 1966.

Gasparini, E. "Slavic Religion,".*Encyclopaedia Britannica*, Vol. 18, p. 909-911.

Gaster, Theodore H. (1) *The Oldest Stories in the World*. Viking Press, NY, 1952.

Gaster, Theodore H. (2) *Thespis, Ritual Myth and Drama in the Ancient Near East*. Gordian Press, NY, 1975 reprint.

Gelling, Peter and Davidson, Hilda Ellis. *The Chariot of the Sun, and Other Rites and Symbols of the Northern Bronze Age*. J.M. Dent, 1969.

Gibbs, Chief Hugh W. *My People the Cherokee*. Hugh Gibbs, U.S.A., 1988.

Gifford, Edward W. and Block, Gwendoline Harris. *California Indian Nights Entertainment*. Arthur H. Clark, Glendale, U.S.A., 1930.

Gimbutas, Marija. (1) "Ancient Symbolism in Baltic Folk Art", *Memoirs of the American Folklore Society*, Vol. 49, 1958.

Gimbutas, Marija. (2) *The Balts*. Thames and Hudson, 1963.

Gimbutas, Marija. (3) *The Slavs*. Thames and Hudson, 1971.

Glasse, Cyril. *The Concise Encyclopaedia of Islam*. Stacey International, London, 1989.

Goldenberg, Naomi. *The Changing of the Gods: Feminism and the end of traditional religions*. Beacon Press, Boston, 1979.

Gooch, Stan. *Guardians of the Ancient Wisdom*. Wildwood House, 1979.

Gordon, C.H. (1) *Ugaritic Literature*. Pontifical Biblical Institute, Rome, 1949.

Gordon, C.H. (2) *Ugarit Textbook*. Rome, 1965.

Gostelow, Mary. *Embroidery of All Russia*. Mills and Boon, 1977.

Grant, Michael. *The Roman Emperors*. Weidenfeld and Nicholson, 1985.

Graves, Robert. (1) *The Greek Myths*. Cassell, 1969.

Graves, Robert. (2) *The White Goddess*. Faber and Faber, 1959.

Grieve, Mrs. M. *A Modern Herbal*. Jonathon Cape, 1977.

Griffith, Ralph T. *The Hymns of the Rigveda*. 4 Vols. Benares, 1892.

Grimm, Jacob. *Teutonic Mythology*. Trans. by James Stephen Stallybrass, Bell and Sons, 1888.

Grosvenor, Gilbert M. *The World of the American Indian*. National Geographic Society, 2nd edn., 1979.

Hall, John Whitney. *Japan from Prehistory to Modern Times*. Weidenfeld and Nicholson, 1968.

Hall, Nor. *The Moon and the Virgin. Reflections on the Archetypal Feminine*. Harper, NY, 1980.

Hammer, R. *Japan's Religious Ferment*. SCM Press, 1961.

Harding, M. Esther. *Women's Mysteries*. Rider, 1971 (1955).

Harley, Rev. Timothy. *Moon Lore*. (London, 1885) Reprint, EP Publishing, 1973. (Swan Sonnenschein.)

Harney, W.E. *Tales from the Aborigines*. Robert Hale, London, 1959.

Harris, J. Rendell. *The Cult of the Heavenly Twins*. Cambridge, 1906.

Harshananda, Swami. *Hindu Gods and Goddesses*. Sri Ramakrishna Math, Madras, 1987.

Harva (Holmberg), Uno. *Finno-Ugric and Siberian Mythology*. Stockholm, 1927.

Herbert, Jean. *Shinto, The Fountainhead of Japan*. George Allen & Unwin, 1967.

Herbert, Wally. *Eskimos*. Collins International Library, 1976.

Hines, Terence. *Pseudoscience and the Paranormal, A Critical Examination of the Evidence.* Prometheus, NY, 1988.

Hinnells, John R., ed. *Penguin Dictionary of Religions.* Penguin, 1984.

Hoddinott, R. F. *The Thracians,* Thames & Hudson, 1981.

Hollander, Lee M. *The Poetic Edda.* University of Texas Press, 1962.

Homet, Marcel F. *On the Trail of the Sun Gods.* London, 1965.

Howitt, A.W. *The Native Tribes of South East Australia.* Macmillan, London, 1904.

Ions, Veronica. *Indian Mythology.* Hamlyn, 1967.

Jackson, Kenneth H., ed. *A Celtic Miscellany.* Routledge and Kegan Paul, 1951.

Jacobi, J. *Psychology of C.J. Jung.* London, 1963.

James, E.O. (1) *The Ancient Gods.* Weidenfeld and Nicholson, 1967.

James, E.O. (2) *The Cult of the Mother Goddess.* Thames and Hudson, 1959.

James, E.O. (3) *Seasonal Feasts and Festivals.* Jarrold, 1961.

Jenness, D. "The Life of the Copper Eskimos," *Report of the Canadian Arctic Expedition,* 1913-1918, Vol. XII. Ottawa, 1922.

Jobes, Gertrude. *A Dictionary of Mythology, Folklore and Symbols.* The Scarecrow Press Inc., NY, 1962.

Jones, Arthur A. *An Illustrated Dictionary of World Religions.* The Religious Education Press, 1982.

Katzenelenbogen, U. *The Daina: An Anthology of Lithuanian and Latvian Folk Songs.* Lithuanian News Publishing Company, Chicago, 1935.

Keel, Othmar. *The Symbolism of the Biblical World.* SPCK, 1878.

Kelly, I.W., Rotton, James and Culver, Roger. "The Moon Was Full and Nothing Happened: A Review of Studies on the Moon and Human Behaviour and Lunar Beliefs," *The Skeptical Inquirer.* Vol. 10, No. 2, Winter 1985-86, p. 129-143 (includes complete list of sources on lunar studies.)

Kelly, I.W., Saklofske, D.H. and Culver, Roger. "Worldwide Disasters and Moon Phase," *The Skeptical Inquirer.* Vol. 14, No. 3, Spring 1990, p. 298-301.

O'Kelly, Michael. *Newgrange; Archaeology, Art and Legend.* Thames and Hudson, 1982.

Kerenyi, Carl. (1) *Eleusis, Archetypal Image of Mother and Daughter.* Routledge and Kegan Paul, 1967.

Kerenyi, Carl. (2) *The Gods of the Greeks.* Thames and Hudson, 1976.

Kerenyi, Carl. (3) *Goddesses of Sun and Moon.* Spring Publications, Dallas, 1979.

Kidder, Edward. *Ancient Japan.* Elsevier/ Phaidon, 1977.

Kirby, W.F., trans. *Kalevala.* J.M. Dent, 1907.

Kraft, John. *The Goddess in the Labyrinth.* Abô Akademi, Sweden, 1987 (1985).

Kramer, Samuel Noah. *Mythologies of the Ancient World.* Doubleday, 1961.

Kurtz, Paul. *The Transcendental Temptation—A Critique of Religion and the Paranormal.* Prometheus, NY, 1986.

Lang, Andrew. *Custom and Myth.* Longmans, Green and Co., 1885.

Langdon, S. "Semitic Mythology," *MOAR,* Vol. 5, 1931, 1964.

Lamont, Corliss. *The Philosophy of Humanism.* Continuum Publishing, NY, 6 edn., 1988.

Larue, Gerald A. (1) *Ancient Myth and Modern Life.* Centerline Press, California, 1988.

Larue, Gerald A. (2) *The Way of Positive Humanism.* Centerline Press, California, 1989.

Lawson, Joan. *European Folk Dance.* Pitman, 1970.

Legey, Francoise. *The Folklore of Morocco.* George Allen and Unwin, 1936.

Lehmann, Johannes. *The Hittites, People of A Thousand Gods.* Collins, 1977.

Leland, Charles Godfrey. *Etruscan Roman Remains in Popular Tradition*. T. Fisher Unwin, London, 1892.

Levi-Strauss, Claude. *Introduction to the Science of Mythology*. 4 Vols. Jonathan Cape, 1981.

Levin, M.G. and Potapov, L.P. *The Peoples of Siberia*. University of Chicago Press, 1964.

Lieber, Arnold. *The Lunar Effect; Biological Tides and Human Emotions*. Anchor Press/ Doubleday, NY, 1978.

Lindsay, Jack. *Helen of Troy, Woman and Goddess*. Constable, 1974.

Lings, Martin. *Muhammad, His Life Based On the Earliest Sources*. George Allen and Unwin, 1983.

Lurker, Manfred. *A Dictionary of Gods and Goddesses, Devils and Demons*. Routledge and Kegan Paul,, 1987.

Lyttleton, Margaret and Forman, Werner. *The Romans, their Gods and their Beliefs*. Orbis, 1984.

Maccoby, Hyam. *The Mythmaker; Paul and the Invention of Christianity*. Weidenfeld and Nicholson, 1986.

Mackenzie, Donald A. *Scottish Folk-Lore and Folk Life*. Blackie and Son, 1935.

Mallory, J.P. *In Search of the Indo-Europeans*. Thames & Hudson, 1989.

Maraini, Fosco. *Meeting With Japan*. Hutchinson, 1959.

Marian-Macneill, F. *The Silver Bough*. 4 Vols. William McLennan, Glasgow, 1959.

Markale, Jean. *Women of the Celts*. Gordon Cremonesi Ltd., 1980 (1975).

Marliave, Olivier De. *Tresor de la Mythologie Pyreneenne*, Annales Pyreneennes, *ESPER*, Toulouse, 1987, 2nd edn., 1989.

Marwick, Ernest W. *The Folklore of Orkney and Shetland*. batsford, 1975.

Metford, J.C.J. *Dictionary of Christian Lore and Legend*. Thames and Hudson, 1983.

Messerschmidt, L. *The Hittites*. London, 1903.

Miles, Rosalind. *The Women's History of the World*. Paladin, 1989.

Monaghan, Patricia.* (1) *Women in Myth and Legend*. Junction Books, 1981.

Monaghan, Patricia.(2) "She Want It All—The Sun Goddess in Contemporary Women's Poetry," *Frontiers Magazine*, Autumn, 1990.

Monaghan, Patricia.(3) *The Book of Goddesses and Heroines*. Llewellyn, U.S.A., 1990.

Monaghan, Patricia.(4) *The Sun Goddess*. (in preparation)

*Information about books and lectures by Patricia Monaghan can be obtained by writing to The Definite Article, 1625 West 101st Street, Chicago, Ill. 60643, U.S.A.

Mookerjee, Ajit and Khanna, M. *The Tantric Way*. Thames & Hudson, 1977.

Mooney. "Myths of the Cherokee," *Annual Report of the American Bureau of Ethnology*, No. 19, 1900.

Morris, M.C.F. *Yorkshire Folk Talk; with Characteristics of Those Who Speak it in the North and East Ridings*. John Sampson, York, 1892.

Mueller, F. Max. (1) *Introduction to the Science of Religion*. Longmans, Green and Co., 1873.

Mueller, F. Max. (2) *Contributions to the Science of Mythology*. 2 Vols., Longmans, Green and Co., 1897.

Murphy, Wendy B. *Tradition and Revolt: Islands of the Rising Sun*. Cassell, 1980.

Musil, Alois. *The Manners and Customs of the Ruala Bedouins*. American Geographical Society, NY, 1928.

Nansen, Fridtjof. *Eskimo Life*. Longmans, Green and Co., London, 1893.

Neumann, E. *The Great Mother*. Routledge and Kegan Paul, 1970 (1963, 1955).

Newall, Venetia. *An Egg at Easter*. Routledge and Kegan Paul, 1971.

Newman, Bernard. *Baltic Background*. Robert Hale, 1948.

Nicholson, Shirley, ed. *The Goddess Re-Awakening—The Feminine Principle Today.* Quest Books, 1989.

North, Gerald. *Mastering Astronomy.* Macmillan Educational, 1988.

Oda, Mayumi. *Goddesses.* Volcano/ Kazan, 1988.

Oesterley, W.O.E. and Robinson, T.H. *Hebrew Religion, Its Origin and Development.* SPCK, 1930.

Olcott, William Tyler. *Sun Lore of All Ages.* G.B. Putnam's Sons, 1914.

Ono, Sokyo. *Shinto, the Kami Way.* Prentice-Hall, 1962.

Osman, T. and McCorry, V. *All About Science.* Orbis Books, 1973.

Parker, K. Langloh. *The Euahlayi Tribe.* Archibald Constable and Co., 1905.

Parrinder, Geoffrey. (1) *A Dictionary of Non-Christian Religions.* Hulton Educational, 1971.

Parrinder, Geoffrey. (2) *Sex in the World's Religions.* Sheldon, 1980.

Paterson, Adrian. *Old Lithuanian Songs.* Kaunas, 1939.

Perera, Sylvia Brinton. *Descent to the Goddess: A Way of Initiation for Women.* Inner City Books, Toronto, 1981 (Studies in Jungian Psychology Series).

Piercy, Marge in *The Woman in the Moon,* Karen Lindsey. New Women's Times Feminist Review No. 15, April/May 1981.

Piggott, Stuart. *The Druids.* Thames and Hudson, 1968.

Potter, G.F. *The Story of Religion.* Harrap, 1930.

Ralston, W.R.S. (1) *Russian Folk Tales.* Smith, Elder and Co., 1872.

Ralston, W.R.S. (2) *[Folk] Songs of the Russian People.* Smith, Elder and Co., 1873.

Randi, James. *Flim Flam! Psychics, ESP, Unicorns and Other Delusions.* Prometheus, NY, 1982.

Rasmussen, Knud. (1) *Eskimo Folk Tales.* Glyldendal, London, 1921.

Rasmussen, Knud. (2) *The People of the Polar North.* Kegan Paul, Trench and Co., 1908.

Ray, Dorothy Jean. *Eskimo Masks.* University of Washington Press, London, 1967.

Rees, Alwyn and Brinley. *Celtic Heritage: Ancient Tradition in Ireland and Wales.* Thames and Hudson, 1961.

Reinach, Salomon. *Orpheus, A General History of Religions.* Heinemann, 1909.

Renate, Rolle. *The World of the Scythians.* Batsford, 1989.

Rice, Patty. *Amber, Golden Gem of the Ages.* New York, 1974.

Rice, Tamara Talbot. *The Scythians.* Thames and Hudson, 1957.

Richards, Janet Radcliffe. *The Sceptical Feminist—A Philosphical Enquiry.* Penguin, 1984.

Ross, Anne. (1) *Everyday Life of the Pagan Celts.* Batsford, 1970.

Ross, Anne. (2) *Folklore of the Scottish Highlands.* Batsford, 1976.

Ross, Anne. (3) *Pagan Celtic Britain.* Sphere Books, 1974.

Rothery, Guy Cadogan. *The Amazons in Antiquity and Modern Times.* Griffiths, London, 1910.

Rubulis, Aleksis. *Latvian Folktales.* AKA Publishing, Michigan, 1982.

Rush, Anne Kent. *Moon, Moon.* Random House, 1976.

Rustaveli, Shota. *The Knight in the Panther's Skin.* Trans. by Venera Urushadze. Sabchota Sakartvelo, Tblisi, 1979.

Rydberg, Viktor. *Teutonic Mythology.* Swann Sonnenschein, London, 1889.

Sagan, Carl. (1) *Cosmos.* Macdonald, London, 1981.

Sagan, Carl. (2) *The Dragons of Eden.* Random House, 1977.

Saggs, H.W.F. *Civilization Before Greece and Rome.* Batsford, 1989.

Sandys, John, ed. and trans. *The Odes of Pindar.* Heinemann, 1961 (1915).

Savill, Sheila. *Pears Encyclopaedia of Myths and Legends: Oceania and Australia, the Americas.* Pelham Books, 1978.

Saward, Jeffrey. "Geranos, Ancient Origins of the Labyrinth," *Caerdroia*, No. 12, April 1983, p. 23-37.

Sayce, A.H. (1) *Assyria, Its Princes, Priests and People.* Williams & Norgate, London, 1885.

Sayce, A.H. (2) *Lectures on the Origin and Growth of Religion as illustrated by the Religion of the Ancient Babylonians.* London, Williams & Norgate, 1887.

Sayce, A.H. and Pinches, T.G. *The Tablet from Yuzgat in the Liverpool Institute of Archaeology.* Asiatic Society Monographs, Vol. XI, London, 1907.

Schuon, Frithjof. (1) *Esoterism as Principle and as Way.* Perennial Books, 1981.

Schuon, Frithjof. (2) *Gnosis, Divine Wisdom.* Perennial Books, 1959.

Schwarz, B. *A Hittite Ritual Text.* NY, 1947.

Seklemian, A.G. *The Golden Maiden, and other Folk Tales and Fairy Stories as told in Armenia.* Helmen Taylor, NY, 1898.

Shapiro, J.L. et al. "The Moon and Mental Illness: A failure to confirm the Transylvania Effect," *Perceptual and Motor Skills*, No. 30, 1930, p. 827-830.

Shuttle, P. and Redgrove, P. *The Wise Wound, Menstruation and Everywoman.* Revised edn., Paladin/Grafton, 1989 (Gollancz, 1978).

Simpkins, J. and Williams, J.I. *Advanced Biology.* Bell and Hyman, 1986.

Sjöö, Monica and Mor, Barbara. *The Great Cosmic Mother—Rediscovering the Religion of the Earth.* Harper and Row, 1987.

Smith, George H. *Atheism, The Case Against God.* Prometheus, NY, 1979.

Smith, W.R. *The Religion of the Semites.* A&C Black, London, 1927.

Smith, W. Ramsay. *Myths and Legends of the Australian Aboriginals.* Harrap, 1930.

Smyth, Daragh. *A Guide to Irish Mythology.* Irish Academic Press, 1988.

Speck, Frank G. *Ethnology of the Yuchi Indians.* University of Pennsylvania Museum, Anthropological Publications, Vol. I, No. 1, Philadelphia, 1909.

Spencer, Arthur. *The Lapps.* David and Cahrles, 1978.

Spencer, B. and Gillen, F.J. (1) *The Arunta.* 2 Vols. Macmillan, 1927.

Spencer, B. and Gillen, F.J. (2) *The Native Tribes of Central Australia.* Macmillan, 1899.

Spencer, B. and Gillen, F.J. (3) *The Northern Tribes of Central Australia.* Macmillan, 1904.

Starhawk (Miriam Simos). *Dreaming the Dark; Magic, Sex and Politics.* 2nd edn., 1988 (Beacon Press, Boston, 1982).

Stein, Diane. *The Women's Spirituality Book.* Llewellyn Publishing, Minnesota, 1987.

Sterne, Carus. "The Northern Origin of the Story of Troy," *The Open Court* No. 8, August 1918, pp. 449-546.

Stevens, Anthony. *Archetype—A Natural History of the Self.* Routledge and Kegan Paul, 1982.

Stewart, Bob. *The Waters of the Gap.* Bath City Council, 1981.

Stirling, M.W. "Concepts of the Sun Among American Indians," *Smithsonian Report*, 1945, p. 387-400.

Stone, Merlin. (1) *Ancient Mirrors of Womanhood.* 2 Vols. New Sibylline Books, 1979.

Stone, Merlin. (2) *The Paradise Papers.* Virago, 1979.

Strong, Roy. *The Cult of Elizabeth.* Thames and Hudson, 1977.

Sulimirski, T. *The Sarmatians.* Thames and Hudson, 1970.

Surmelian, Leon. *Apples of Immortality—Folktales of Armenia.* George Allen and Unwin, 1968.

Sykes, Egerton. *Dictionary of Non-Classical Mythology.* J.M. Dent, 1952.

Thompson, Stith. *Motif-Index of Folk Literature.* 6 Vols. Bloomington, Indiana, 1955-1958.

Thompson, Stith and Balys, J. *Motif and Type Index of the Oral Tales of India.* Bloomington, Indiana, n.d.

Thoules, Robert H. *Straight and Crooked Thinking.* Hodder and Stoughton, 1930 (and numerous reprints).

Todd, Ian A. *Catal Huyuk in Perspective.* Cummings, 1976.

Tolkien, J.R.R., ed. Tolkien, Christopher. *The History of Middle Earth.* Vol I, *The Book of Lost Tales.* George Allen and Unwin, 1983.

Tolkien, J.R.R. *The Lord of the Rings.* (Single Volume Edition). George Allen and Unwin, 1968.

Tyler, J.E.A. The Tolkien Companion. Picador, 1977.

UNESCO. *The Scythians.* Unesco Courier, December 1976.

Vana, Zdenek. *The World of the Ancient Slavs.* Orbis, 1983.

Vorren, Ørnulv and Manker, Ernst. *Lapp Life and Culture.* London, 1962.

Wagner, Günter. "Yuchi Tales." *Publications of the American Ethnological Society*, Vol. XIII. Stechert and Co., 1931.

Walker, Barbara G. (1) *The Women's Encyclopedia of Myths and Secrets.* Harper and Row, 1983.

Walker, Barbara G. (2) *The Women's Dictionary of Symbols and Sacred Objects.* Harper and Row, 1989.

Ward, Donald. (1) *Solar Mythology and Baltic Folksongs. Folklore International.* ed. D.K. Wilgus and C. Sommer, Folklore Associates, Hatboro, PA. 1967.

Ward, Donald. (2) *The Divine Twins: An Indo-European Myth in German Tradition.* University of California Press, Berkeley, 1968.

Warner, Elizabeth. *Heroes, Monsters and Other Worlds from Russian Mythology.* Peter Lowe/Eurobook, 1985.

Warner, Marina. *Alone of All Her Sex, The Myth and Cult of the Virgin Mary.* Quartet Books, 1978.

Waterman, Patricia Panyity. *A Tale-Type Index of Australian Aboriginal Oral Narratives.* Suomalainen Tiedeakatemia Academia Scientarum Fennica, Helsinki, 1987.

Watts, Alan. (1) *The Watercourse Way.* Jonathon Cape, 1976.

Watts, Alan. (2) *Myth and Ritual in Christianity.* Thames and Hudson, 1954.

Weideger, Paula. *History's Mistress.* Penguin, 1986.

Westermarck, Edward A. *Pagan Survivals in Mohammedan Civilization.* Macmillan and Co., London, 1933.

Weyer, Edward Moffat. *The Eskimos, Their Environment and Folkways.* Archon Books, Hamden, U.S.A., 1962.

Whitehead, Henry. *The Village Gods of South India.* Oxford University Press, 1916.

Wheeler, Sir Morimer. *Early India and Pakistan.* Thames and Hudson, 1959.

Wilkins, Eithne. *The Rose Garden Game—The Symbolic Background to the European Prayer Beads.* Gollancz, 1969.

Winnet, F.V. "The Daughters of Allah," *The Moslem World*, Vol. XXX, 1940, p. 113-130.

Wolkstein, Diane and Kramer, Samuel Noah. *Inanna, Queen of Heaven—Her Stories and Hymns from Sumer.* Rider, London, 1984.

Yenne, Bill. *The Encyclopaedia of North American Indian Tribes—from the Abitibi to the Zuni.* Brompton, 1988.

Young, Gordon H., ed. *Ugarit in Retrospect.* Eisenbrauns, 1981.

Young, Jean I., trans. *The Prose Edda of Snorri Sturluson—Tales from Norse Mythology.* Bowes and Bowes, 1954.

Yusuf Ali, A. *The Holy Qur'an; Text, Translation and Commentary.* Aman Corporation, Brentwood, U.S.A., 1983.

Zaehner, R.C., ed. *The Concise Encyclopaedia of Living Faiths.* Hutchinson, 1971.
Zoete, Beryl de, and Spies, Walter. *Dance and Drama in Bali.* Oxford University Press reprint, 1973 (Faber 1938).

Eclipse of the Sun

Index

A

aborigines, Australian 182, 186, 196
Abraham 2
Alchemy 7, 22
Amazon 189
Amazons 27, 189, 196, 234, 253
amber 77, 87, 217
anima 22, 23
animus 22, 23
apples 77, 90, 217
Arabs 2, 7, 183, 188
archetypes 21, 23, 24, 30
arms 154, 180
Arya Samaj 178
Australian myth 218
Australian aborigines. *See* aborigines,
    Australian
authority 224

B

Bachofen, Johann Jacob 27, 28
baetyl 162, 166, 170
Beltane 82, 97, 101
birch 89, 122
birds 87, 89, 91, 97, 125, 141, 151
Blessed Virgin 5, 7, 106, 115, 185, 218
boat 78, 118
bonfire 68, 81, 82, 101
brain, left/right hemispheres 256
bread 90, 202, 203
breast 131
Briffault, Robert 11, 12
Buddhism 61, 62, 63, 65
bull 182, 198, 210, 218, 249, 253
bull-faced Men 218

C

cake 90, 92, 122, 200, 242
calendar, lunar. *See* lunar calendars
candle 108, 215
cannibalism 135, 172
caste system 178
cat 192, 196
cat's cradle 129
cave 17, 67, 71, 82, 101, 175, 183, 187,
    225, 233
chariot 77, 113, 181, 242
Cherokee 63
Chicago, Judy 211
cobra 193, 196
cockerel 90, 113, 174
colours 75, 77, 142, 172, 185, 195, 196,
    210
Confucianism 61, 62
cow 172, 181, 182, 198
creativity 229
crown 90, 175
crystal 87, 98, 100, 155
cup-and-ball 129

D

dance, ritual 68, 89, 90, 92, 142, 192
dawn 181
defloration 37, 42, 148
Dendera 196
Dinner Party, The 211
dolmens 101
Druidism 96, 242

E

Earth-energies 58, 237
Earth-goddess 255
Earth-mother 38, 78, 89, 106, 127, 129,
    148, 169, 173, 185, 217, 219, 235,
    242
Easter 90, 91, 97, 102
eclipse 131
eclipse, lunar 128, 148, 152
eclipse, solar 128, 131, 143, 146, 163, 165,
    202
Edda 233
eggs 90, 242
Eliade, Mircea 15
eros 22, 26
Eskimo 186
exposure, ritual 68, 192, 239
eye 65, 99, 123, 150, 164, 170, 192, 193,
    196, 214
eye-well 243

F

fairy-queen 100
faith 224, 233, 256
Farnham, Eliza 26
Father Earth 193
feminism 27
feminist spirituality xix, 28, 223
fever 97, 117, 140, 154, 164, 170
fiery-haired 185
fire 78, 82, 88, 97, 98, 107, 129, 130, 138,
    143, 146, 148, 155, 173, 243, 245,
    246, 247, 250, 252
fire, sacred 186
fire-birds 243
fire-god 195, 213
fire-goddess 124, 213
firebirds 90
flowers 67, 69, 76, 81, 90, 108, 175, 246
Frazer, Sir James 10
frog 137
fundamentalism 227

G

Gage, Matilda Joslyn 10
games 129
garlands 123
Gayatri mantra 180
germination 52, 58, 237
gold 75, 77, 113, 115, 217, 239
Golden Age 28, 227
grape-vines 188
Great Mother 24, 30

H

Hamadcha 162
Hammurabi, Law Code of 206
Harding, Esther 22, 23
hares 245
healing 80, 88, 96, 99, 123, 126
Hebrew 69
Hebrews 2, 54
herbs 57, 67, 108, 246
holy wells 98, 106, 118, 167
homeostasis 46
horses 66, 77, 80, 81, 89, 92, 112, 113, 124,
    181, 186, 218, 255
house-snake 83, 241
Hurrian 185
Hyperborean tradition 11

I

imprisonment 82
incest 88, 128, 131, 139, 145, 148, 151,
    170, 174, 186, 214, 225
intuition 28, 223, 227, 228, 256
Inuit. See Eskimo
Islam 5, 28, 165
island 77, 217
island, western 86, 87

J

Jewish tradition 242
Judaism 3, 28, 165, 231, 254
Jung, Carl Gustav 21, 24, 25, 233

K

Kraft, John 219
Krause, Ernest 219
Kurgan culture 62

L

labyrinth-games 82, 92, 115, 179, 219
ladder 65, 240
lamps 130, 131, 170
leopards 210
lioness 192, 194, 196, 208
loaf 90
logos 2, 3, 6, 22, 25, 26, 231
Loon 125
lunar calendars 36, 37, 167
lunar eclipse. See eclipse, lunar
lunar energy 44, 56, 58
lunar gravity 44, 45, 56, 59
lunar month 47, 48
lunar year 101
lunisolar calendar 37

M

Mahabharata, the 178, 180
maiden 114. See also Sun-maidens
Manichaeism 232
mare 77, 101, 181
masks 130
matriarchy 24, 173, 178, 189, 210
May 54, 97, 116, 243
maze-games. See labyrinth-games
megaliths 38, 173
menstruation 24, 37, 41, 42, 47, 48, 49, 65,
    80, 126, 132, 135, 142, 148, 152, 158,
    181, 182, 235, 236, 252
Midsummer 249. See also solstice, summer
Midsummer Eve 81, 91, 92, 101, 106
Midwinter. See solstice, winter
Milky Way, the 77, 153
mirror 64, 65, 67, 69, 91, 97, 102, 122, 124,
    125, 126, 170, 194, 210, 214, 225,
    242, 251
mole 137
monotheism 165
monstrance 105, 108

Moon, ring around the 237
moonbathing 227
moonlight 44
moons, multiple 164
Mother Sky 193
mountain 77, 82, 100, 106, 136, 186, 187,
    196
Mueller, Max 10

N

necklace 77
neopaganism xix, 2, 8
Neoplatonism 7, 232, 256
New Grange 38

O

oaths 117, 124
objectivity 256

P

parhelion 128, 131, 136
patriarchy 24, 207, 225, 228, 234, 236, 256
photosynthesis 52, 53, 54
Phrygians 185, 218
pillar 65, 247
Pindar 216
pluralism 229
Poem of the Gracious Gods, the 203
post, sacred 240
priestess 173, 178, 195, 203, 207
psychic realm 229
pysanky eggs 90

Q

Queen of Heaven 200

R

rabbits 245
rainbow 81, 131, 156, 243
rape 128, 131, 132, 145
rationality 227, 228, 229, 234, 256
reason 223, 224, 227, 256
reincarnation 126, 132, 156, 158, 182
reindeer 121, 122
respiration 53

Rig Veda 178
ring 77, 121, 122, 124, 128
ring and pin 129
roof-tree 65, 240
rope 68, 136, 146, 194, 253
rose 77, 90, 108, 115
Rustaveli, Shota 188

S

Samhain 101
sap 56
Sarmatians 189
satanic verses, the 167
science 227, 228, 234, 256
Scythians 62, 177, 189
sea-god 101
seasons 34, 37, 44, 54, 151, 202
semen 42, 164, 181, 252
shamanism 61, 63, 65, 66, 67, 121, 124,
    134, 156, 238
Shekinah 64
silver 75, 77, 170, 239
sky-arch 139, 140
sky-father 77, 79, 256
sky-plain 64, 135, 136
smith 82
smoke-hole 137, 247
snake 141, 241
solar eclipse 128, 137
solar energy 52, 53, 54, 55, 56
solar principle xx
solar year 101
solstice, summer 76, 91, 92, 123
Solstice, winter 35, 38
solstice, winter 82, 92, 123, 130, 147, 214
solstices 35
spear 65
spindle 123, 187, 210
spinning 87, 111, 115, 123, 210
spirituality 229
spirituality, feminist xix
spring 118, 186, 237
springs, holy 99. *See also* holy wells
springs, hot 99
Statue of Liberty 216
stone 87, 112
storm god/goddess 65

storm-god 79, 80, 181, 201, 210, 214, 225
storm-goddess 88, 106
Sun dance 71, 81, 91, 97, 106, 118
Sun-chariots 85
Sun-disc 155, 195, 196
Sun-discs 205
sun-eyed 185
Sun-flower 108
sun-flower 67
Sun-maiden 78, 79, 114, 141, 178, 179,
    217, 218, 225
Sun-room 100
Sun-vigil 70, 81, 97, 101, 117
Suns, multiple 157
supernatural 229
Surya 74
Suryasakta, the 178
swallow 82, 97, 243
swan 87, 89, 166, 242
swastika 106
swift 97, 243
sympathetic magic 52

T

Taoism 61, 62
Tarot 227
throne 116, 162, 167
thunder-god 74, 92, 93, 148
thunder-goddess 91
toads 137, 143
Tolkien, J.R.R. 118
torch 88, 131, 150, 152, 154, 155, 156
tower 82
transpiration 56
Transylvania effect 42
trees 63, 64, 67, 70, 77, 89, 108, 174, 175,
    217, 255
trinity motif 38, 87, 160
twins 101, 115, 136, 137, 161, 178, 179,
    183, 218, 242, 245, 254, 255

U

Unconquered Sun, the 105
underworld 66, 138, 202, 233
Upanishads 180, 182
Ur 2

V

Vedas 182
Venus, planet 6, 130, 207, 231
Vepkhistqaosani 188
vine 203
Virgin Mary 214. *See also* Blessed Virgin

W

walking-sticks 131, 154
warrior, female 194
weather-god 65, 66, 91, 96
weather-goddess 216
weaving 67, 76
wells 200, 237, 243
wells, holy. *See* holy wells

wheel 92, 108, 111, 114, 115, 116, 123
Wisdom 3
withdrawal (of the Sun) 82, 116, 137, 141, 175, 225
women priests 222
wreaths 76, 81, 202
wren 97

Y

yang xx, 13, 221, 231
yin xx, 13, 221, 231
Yuzgat Tablet, the 206

Z

Zaltys. *See* house-snake

GOTHIC IMAGE
P U B L I C A T I O N S

Gothic Image Publications is a Glastonbury-based imprint dedicated to publishing books and pamphlets that offer a new and radical approach to our perception of the world in which we live.

As ideas about the nature of life change, we aim to make available those new perspectives which clarify our understanding of ourselves and the Earth we share.

Devas, Fairies & Angels: A Modern Approach
William Bloom   £3.50

Dragons—Their History & Symbolism
Janet Hoult   £4.95

Glastonbury—Maker of Myths
Frances Howard-Gordon   £4.95

The Glastonbury Tor Maze
Geoffrey Ashe   £2.25

The Green Lady & the King of Shadows—A Glastonbury Legend
Moyra Caldecott   £4.95

Hargreaves' New Illustrated Bestiary
Joyce Hargreaves   £10.95

Meditation in a Changing World
William Bloom   £6.95

Needles of Stone Revisited
Tom Graves   £6.95

New Light on the Ancient Mystery of Glastonbury
John Michell   £9.95

Spiritual Dowsing
Sig Lonegren   £5.50